Preserving

PRESERVING

ODED SCHWARTZ

Photography by
IAN O'LEARY

Food styling by
ODED SCHWARTZ

DORLING KINDERSLEY
London • New York
Sydney • Moscow

A Dorling Kindersley Book

Project Editors: Jane Middleton, Kate Scott
Senior Editors: Carolyn Ryden, Nicky Graimes
Art Editor: Jane Bull
DTP Designer: Karen Ruane
Managing Editor: Susannah Marriott
Managing Art Editor: Toni Kay
Production Manager: Maryann Rogers
Assistant Food Stylist: Alison Austin

*This book is dedicated
to my mother, Pnina Schwartz,
the ultimate pickler:
her culinary creativeness
is the inspiration
for my work*

First published in Great Britain in 1996
Reprinted 1997
by Dorling Kindersley Limited,
9 Henrietta Street, London WC2E 8PS
Visit us on the World Wide Web at
http://www.dk.com

Copyright © 1996 Dorling Kindersley Limited,
London
Text copyright © 1996 Oded Schwartz

A CIP catalogue record for this book is available
from the British Library.

ISBN 0 7513 0345 3

Reproduced in Italy by GRB Editrice, Verona
Printed and bound in Great Britain
by Butler & Tanner Ltd

CONTENTS

INTRODUCTION

BEING AN ISRAELI, I feel that pickling is in my blood. In the Middle East, the love of preserved food crosses all cultural and religious boundaries and is shared by Jews and Arabs, Muslims and Christians alike. Walk into any Middle Eastern food market and you will be amazed by the variety of pickles and preserves available: in the cool, dark interiors you will find a gastronomic Aladdin's cave, stuffed to the brim with exotic spices, oils, fish and meats.

When I moved to England in the 1970s, I was disappointed by the lack of variety and availability of preserves that I had grown up to believe were everywhere. But the raw ingredients were all there – wonderful fresh fruit and vegetables, and different types of meat and fish. Armed with an extensive knowledge gleaned from my youth, I set out to develop and modify ancient recipes that would work better in the modern, international market and appeal to a Western palate. The culmination of my endeavours can be seen in this book, which covers a variety of preserving techniques, both sweet and savoury. My aim has been to give these recipes a truly contemporary feel so that preserving can become as much a part of your life as it is of mine. They are easy to follow and practical, and take into account the constraints and pressures that exist in today's society.

There is a natural and continuous rhythm to the preserving year. Winter is a quiet period when fresh ingredients are often expensive and less readily available. It is the best time to make marmalades, tidy cupboards and plan the year ahead. The onset of spring brings young shoots and tender vegetables, and when summer finally arrives the pace quickens as soft fruit come into season and market stalls are laden with ripened fruit and berries. Now is the time to make clear, fragrant jellies, jams and sweet preserves. During late summer and autumn, your kitchen should exude the delicious, sweet aroma of luscious fruit, spices and drying herbs. It is also the traditional and most suitable time to cure meats and sausages, smoke fish and make pâtés.

I sincerely hope that *Preserving* will encourage you to experience the pleasure and immense satisfaction of preserving your own food. Believe me, there are few things in life more enjoyable than producing your own pickles, relishes and sauces, and consuming the fruit of your labour together with family and friends. Try it for yourself!

Oded.

PRESERVED GOODS in the author's pantry.

THE HISTORY OF PRESERVING

Today you can walk into any supermarket or delicatessen and be faced with a profusion of foods preserved in exciting and exotic ways. Even with the advent of modern preserving methods such as freezing and canning, many people still yearn for traditionally preserved goods. Ancient techniques, including pickling, smoking and curing, add a distinctive and delicious flavour to fresh produce.

Moreover, preserves offer a comforting alternative to our usual ephemeral foods. In this age of microwave cookery and instant fast food, the art of preserving reminds us to observe the seasons and the changes that occur throughout the year. It also helps to revive our jaded senses and, especially for those of us living in an urban environment, can bring us closer to nature. In order to master this wonderful culinary art, we need to know something of its history and the evolution of the technical processes that are used today.

Why Food Spoils

Spoilage is caused by the natural deterioration of organic matter as a result of enzyme activity and the growth of yeasts, moulds and bacteria. These processes need certain conditions: a warm, moist, balanced pH environment and a supply of oxygen. Eliminate one or more of these factors and deterioration will be greatly slowed down or will cease. Throughout history, people have discovered many ingenious and inventive ways to prevent spoilage, thus the art of preserving has become of fundamental and lasting importance.

Sun, Wind and Fire

It is safe to assume that drying was the first method of preservation to be discovered – a piece of meat left out and dried by the sun was found to have an appetizing smell, lasted longer than fresh meat, and was lighter and easier to transport. This discovery meant that there was no need to consume the meat at the site of a kill. It could be dried and transported to a safe, permanent settlement, and stored. This enabled our ancestors to begin to settle down; to organize their food supplies for the community; and start to plan their lives. They were able to travel further and explore more congenial environments, where food could be grown and animals reared. Slowly, the first primitive settlements gave way to more permanent hamlets and villages, laying down roots from which grew our present-day towns and cities.

Sun- and wind-drying were fine in hot, dry climates but not very practical in cold, damp environments. In areas where wood was abundant, fire and smoke were used to hasten the drying process. Smoked fish and meat were found to have a more savoury smell and to last even longer, partly because the smoky coating deterred insects.

PREPARED FISH hanging on poles in a nineteenth-century smokehouse.

SALT HAS ALWAYS been a valuable commodity: this illustration from a French manuscript, dated 1528, shows the measuring of salt according to royal regulation.

Salt of the Earth

Ancient man discovered the preserving qualities of salt. They found it to be a strong dehydrator, extracting moisture from tissues, drying them and creating an environment that inhibited the growth of harmful bacteria.

For our ancestors, salt became an essential commodity, highly prized and fiercely guarded: the first biblically recorded war was fought over the rights to control salt pans (Genesis: 14:10). In Ancient Egypt, large quantities of salt, together with vinegar and honey, were used in the process of mummifying. Salted meat and fish played an essential role in the medieval European diet – especially during Lent when salted fish was the only available source of protein. Salt reached a price that was sometimes higher than the value of the flesh preserved – "not worth its salt" indeed! Salted meat and fish were also convenient foodstuffs to take on board ship for long voyages, allowing sixteenth-century Europeans to explore and colonize, and change the course of world history.

Sweet and Deadly

Like salt, sugar is one of nature's most powerful poisons – in high concentrations it creates an environment that cannot support any living organism. In a historical context, sugar is a rather late arrival. It was unknown to the Ancient Egyptians and Hebrews and is not mentioned in early Greek or Roman writings – their sweetener was honey from bees or fruit (concentrated nectar).

Originally, most sugar was refined from the sweet sap of the sugar cane, which is indigenous to the Indus Valley. A variety of wild grass, sugar cane was considered to be a gift from the gods and symbolized everything that was good on earth. The complicated technique of sugar refining was perfected at the courts of the emerging Arab Empire, which at one stage ruled almost all the known world. While Europe was in the depths of the "medieval winter", the conquering Arab tribes

THE ROMANS used honey in the preservation of meat.

SUGAR being extracted and made into cones, illustrated in the fifteenth century.

VINEGAR IS PRODUCED from different types of alcohol, each one having its own distinctive colour and flavour.

were establishing a creative, indulgent and luxurious way of life. Trading caravans from all corners of the ancient world brought rare and mysterious new culinary ingredients, spices and cooking techniques. In the kitchen, sugar was combined with fruit and spices and turned into fragrant syrups, halvas, marzipan and sweetmeats.

In the twelfth century, Arab merchants and returning Crusaders brought sugar into Europe. Refined sugar soon became an essential ingredient in the laboratories of alchemists and apothecaries where it was used, literally, to sweeten bitter pills and potions. Sugar-craft reached its peak in the wealthy kitchens of Renaissance Italy, where it was used to produce elaborate centrepieces made of sugar paste and lifelike candied fruit. But it was not until the sixteenth century, when sugar was introduced to Europe from the West Indies, that it became an indispensable ingredient, included in everything from sweets and cakes to savoury dishes. It was later discovered that sugar played an important role in curing meat, as it counteracts the toughening effect of salt. The Europeans' insatiable appetite for sugar had a devastating and everlasting effect on history, changing our palate and health for ever, and encouraging the rise of colonialism and the slave trade.

Vinegar – the Acidic Element

Vinegar, the third essential preserving ingredient, works by creating an acidic environment in which contaminating bacteria cannot thrive. In vine-growing countries, vinegar is made from grapes; in brewing countries, from wheat and other grains. In the East, vinegar is made from rice and fruit. Vinegar is formed by an organic process: when wine or any other fruit-based or grain-based alcoholic brew is exposed to air, a bacterial reaction turns the alcohol into acetic acid.

Vinegar was the most important flavouring agent in the diets of our ancestors. It was used as a dip to add flavour and moisture to otherwise bland or strong-tasting ingredients – bread and bitter vegetables were always dipped in vinegar before eating – a habit which probably led to the development of our modern-day salads and salad dressings.

Oils and Fats

Our ancestors also discovered that food can be preserved by the exclusion of air. This technique is mentioned in the works of Apicius, who wrote the only surviving Roman cookery book. Honey and oil, ingredients that air cannot pass through, were routinely used in meat preservation. In the colder north, where oil was not available, animal fat was used in the same way. This technique is applied when making pâtés,

PRESERVING the summer's bounty.
Photograph from 1920.

HOMEMADE PRESERVES make a
colourful display in the kitchen.

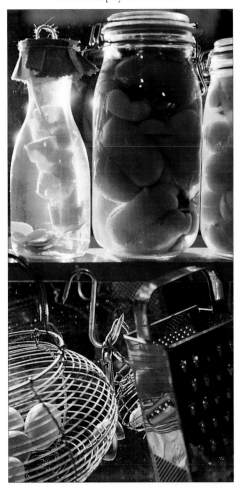

pies, rillettes and confits. The same principle of preserving (preventing food coming into contact with air) is behind modern practices such as vacuum-packing, bottling and canning.

The Global Larder

The most interesting chapter in food preservation started with the European discovery of the "New World" and the sea route to India. This brought a flood of new and exciting ingredients and recipes. Eventually exotic pickles, cured meats, and jams and marmalades started to appear in many European cookery books and began to influence our palates. By the end of the nineteenth century, the availability of cheap sugar, salt and spices meant that preserves were no longer the privilege of the rich. The art of preserving food blossomed, and homemade jams, chutneys and sauces appeared on even the humblest table.

For European colonists abroad, food preservation was essential — it meant survival. Living in isolation, surrounded by different cultures, they saw preserving as a way of keeping in touch with home. Yet the food these settlers cooked was often adapted, a combination of local ingredients and traditional know-how. Recipes from this time make fascinating reading — specialities from all parts of the world are amalgamated with indigenous ingredients and techniques, creating unique and delicious dishes. This is particularly evident in North America: where else can one find pastrami and salt herring, ketchup and piccalilli living in harmony with salsa, jerky and chilli sauce?

With the advantage of hindsight, we can see how ancient techniques have evolved to suit our hectic lifestyle, and how the art of preserving has had a fundamental impact on our development and survival. Food preservation not only makes sense economically, utilizing gluts of fresh fruit and vegetables and prolonging shelf life, it also provides an opportunity to improve the flavour of bland ingredients and create a *fond de cuisine* of ready-made sauces, relishes and condiments upon which all creative cooking is based.

SAFETY PRECAUTIONS FOR PRESERVING

• Care should be taken at all times when making preserves. Many factors affect the end result: correct standards of hygiene, temperature control, timing, acidity and sugar levels, storage conditions and shelf life are all vital.
• Study the information on safety and hygiene, potting and heat processing (see pages 42–45) and the relevant technique before starting a recipe.

• Follow the instructions given in each recipe and do not consume anything that seems unsafe (see page 186).
• Extra care should always be taken with foods for vulnerable groups, such as pregnant women, young children and the elderly. Government health guidelines recommend that they do not consume unpasteurized foods and therefore should not eat home-preserved products.

A GALLERY *of* PRESERVES

THIS INSPIRATIONAL gallery of fresh produce shows how diverse preserving can be. It illustrates the remarkable range of fresh ingredients – both familiar and exotic – that can be made into an array of visually exciting and delicious preserves. Creative serving suggestions enable you to turn these mouthwatering recipes into original and appetizing accompaniments and dishes.

TOMATOES

FOR MANY COOKS the tomato is indispensable, yet its popularity is relatively recent. It was introduced to Europe from South America in the sixteenth century, but it was only when the Italians embraced it with enthusiasm in the nineteenth century that the tomato became widely known. In preserving, tomatoes can be used at all stages of maturity. Choose firm, vine-ripened, unblemished specimens with a fine flavour, but avoid "forced" tomatoes as they contain too much moisture. Tomatoes are a very good source of vitamin C, which prevents oxidation and so helps to maintain a good colour.

TYPES OF TOMATO

There are many varieties of tomato to choose from: familiar red ones, like the flavoursome plum tomato and enormous beef tomato; green tomatoes, which are unripe red varieties rather than a separate strain; and more novel kinds such as tiny, sweet-fleshed yellow and red cherry tomatoes.

Yellow cherry tomatoes

Plum tomato

Red cherry tomatoes

Green tomato

Vine-ripened tomatoes

Round tomato

Beef tomato

SERVING SUGGESTIONS

PEAR AND TOMATO CHEESE *is delicious on its own or with roast poultry. (See page 174 for recipe.)*

COOKED TOMATO AND PEPPER SALSA, *a Mexican-style relish, complements grilled foods. (See page 115 for recipe.)*

OVEN-DRIED TOMATOES PRESERVED IN OIL, *tasty with crème fraîche and basil. (See page 108 for recipe.)*

YELLOW TOMATO PRESERVE, essentially a sweet mixture, is enlivened with lemon zest. (See page 163 for recipe.)

SPICED CHERRY TOMATOES provide an evocative taste of summer. (See page 93 for recipe.)

PICKLED GREEN TOMATOES, an excellent way to use up a glut of unripe produce. (See page 92 for recipe.)

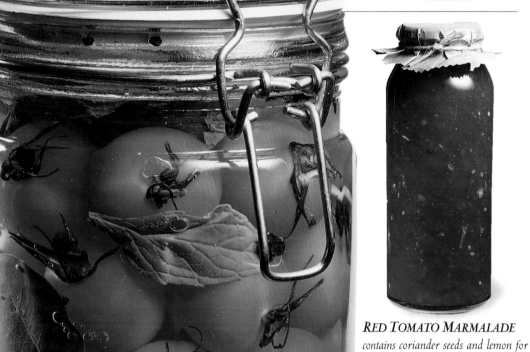

FERMENTED TOMATOES, a spicy variation of Brined Cucumbers. (See page 93 for recipe.)

RED TOMATO MARMALADE contains coriander seeds and lemon for a tangy taste. (See page 164 for recipe.)

TOMATO SAUCE, the indispensable topping for pizzas and pasta. (See page 112 for recipe.)

GREEN TOMATO CHUTNEY, a mild, fruity relish, good with curries. (See page 120 for recipe.)

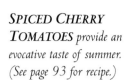

THE PEPPER FAMILY

LIKE TOMATOES, peppers were introduced to Europe from the New World, where they used to grow wild. The chilli pepper quickly replaced peppercorns as the world's favourite hot seasoning, while its larger, milder cousins became important ingredients in Mediterranean cooking. Large sweet peppers can be preserved in oil or vinegar, and are often included in mixed vegetable pickles for their bright colour. Fresh and dried chillies are an essential ingredient in savoury preserves, from judiciously spiced traditional British chutneys to searingly hot chilli pastes from Africa and the Middle East.

TYPES OF PEPPER

The *Capsicum* family includes dozens of chilli peppers as well as mild peppers, ranging in colour from the common red and green to purple and black. All are rich in vitamin C. Chillies tend to be smaller and slimmer than sweet peppers and, usually, elongated in shape.

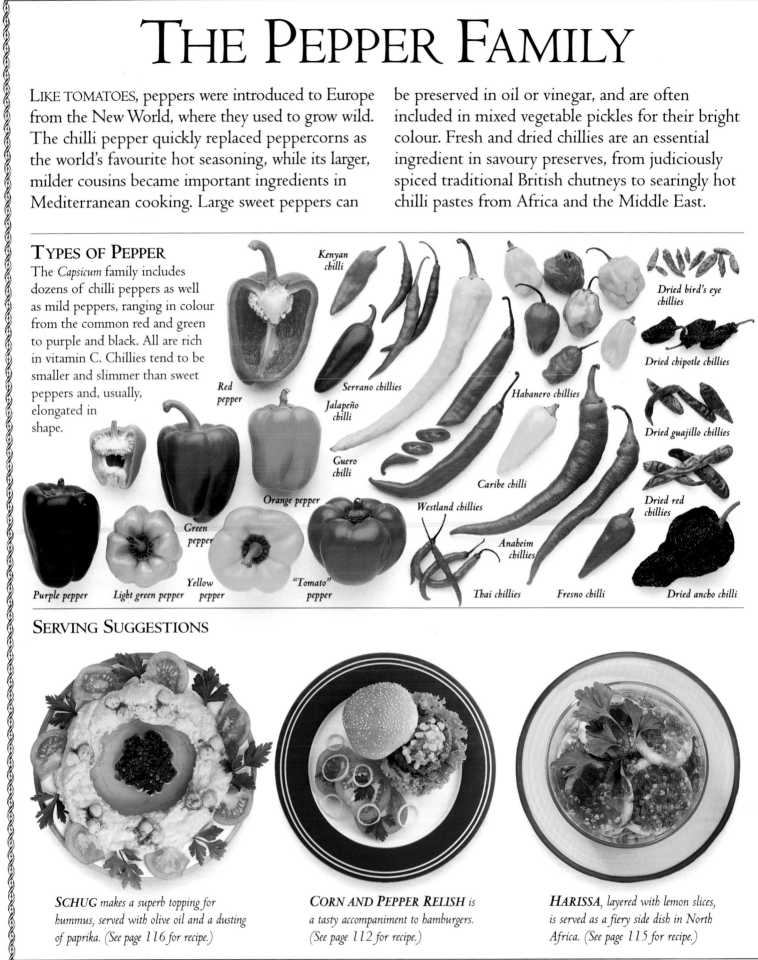

Kenyan chilli

Dried bird's eye chillies

Dried chipotle chillies

Red pepper

Serrano chillies

Jalapeño chilli

Habanero chillies

Dried guajillo chillies

Guero chilli

Orange pepper

Caribe chilli

Dried red chillies

Westland chillies

Anaheim chillies

Dried ancho chilli

Green pepper

Dried red chillies

Purple pepper

Light green pepper

Yellow pepper

"Tomato" pepper

Thai chillies

Fresno chilli

SERVING SUGGESTIONS

SCHUG makes a superb topping for hummus, served with olive oil and a dusting of paprika. (See page 116 for recipe.)

CORN AND PEPPER RELISH is a tasty accompaniment to hamburgers. (See page 112 for recipe.)

HARISSA, layered with lemon slices, is served as a fiery side dish in North Africa. (See page 115 for recipe.)

SCHUG, a Yemenite spice paste made with coriander and green chillies. (See page 116 for recipe.)

HOT CRAB APPLE JELLY is spiced with fresh red chillies. (See page 166 for recipe.)

HARISSA, a ferociously hot paste, is strictly for chilli fans. (See page 115 for recipe.)

HUNGARIAN PICKLED PEPPERS are especially good made with fleshy "tomato" peppers. (See page 99 for recipe.)

CORN AND PEPPER RELISH is an all-American classic. (See page 112 for recipe.)

PEPPERS IN OIL, a variation of Chargrilled Vegetables in Oil, make an instant snack. (See page 106 for recipe.)

THE ONION FAMILY

SINCE ANTIQUITY, onions, shallots and garlic have been almost essential items in every kitchen. They play an invaluable role in preserving – on their own they make delicious crunchy pickles and chutneys and when combined with other ingredients, they add texture, flavour and sweetness. If used raw in preserves, they should be salted, brined or blanched. Onions and garlic do not keep well as they have a tendency to ferment easily, or sprout and become bitter. It is best to buy them in small quantities and store by hanging in cloth sacks or nets, in a cool, dry, dark place.

TYPES OF ONION

Onions vary in size, flavour and colour and range from the mild, sweet Spanish variety to strong cooking onions. Shallots are interchangeable with onions, though they have a milder, more distinct flavour. Garlic can have a white or purple skin, but both types taste the same.

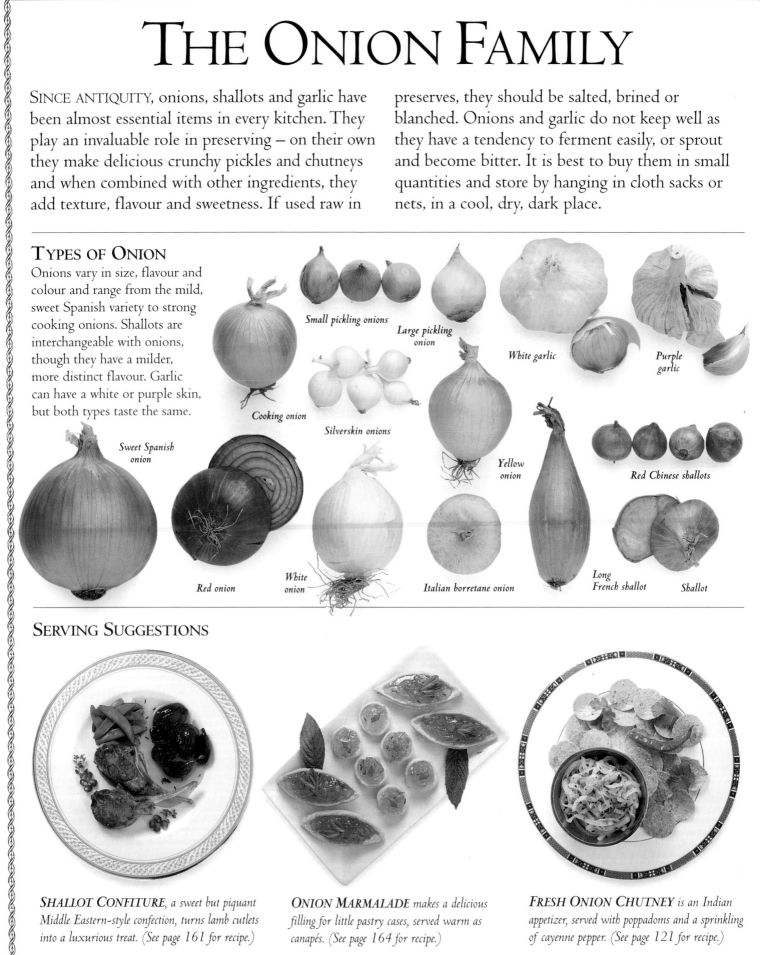

Small pickling onions

Large pickling onion

White garlic

Purple garlic

Cooking onion

Silverskin onions

Sweet Spanish onion

Yellow onion

Red Chinese shallots

Red onion

White onion

Italian borretane onion

Long French shallot

Shallot

SERVING SUGGESTIONS

SHALLOT CONFITURE, *a sweet but piquant Middle Eastern-style confection, turns lamb cutlets into a luxurious treat. (See page 161 for recipe.)*

ONION MARMALADE *makes a delicious filling for little pastry cases, served warm as canapés. (See page 164 for recipe.)*

FRESH ONION CHUTNEY *is an Indian appetizer, served with poppadoms and a sprinkling of cayenne pepper. (See page 121 for recipe.)*

PICKLED SHALLOTS *are prepared in exactly the same way as Pickled Onions. (See page 92 for recipe.)*

PICKLED GARLIC, *an ancient Persian recipe, has a mild, mellow flavour. (See page 92 for recipe.)*

SHALLOT CONFITURE *owes its rich, succulent texture to long, slow cooking over several days. (See page 161 for recipe.)*

ONION MARMALADE *has an affinity with sour-sweet flavours. (See page 164 for recipe.)*

SHALLOT VINEGAR, *a fragrant variation of Salad Vinegar. (See page 127 for recipe.)*

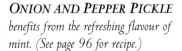

ONION AND PEPPER PICKLE *benefits from the refreshing flavour of mint. (See page 96 for recipe.)*

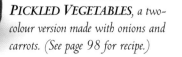

PICKLED VEGETABLES, *a two-colour version made with onions and carrots. (See page 98 for recipe.)*

THE SQUASH FAMILY

THIS DIVERSE FAMILY — made up of cucumbers, pumpkins, squashes, gourds and melons — includes some of the first plants ever to be cultivated. They come in a staggering variety of shapes, sizes and colours, ranging from the giant Cinderella's carriage-type pumpkin to the dainty and petite cornichon. The group is divided into short-life, perishable summer squash, now imported year-round, and long-lasting winter squash, in season from late summer to winter. All squash are very versatile — since they have a delicate flavour they can be used in both sweet and savoury preserves.

TYPES OF SQUASH

Cucumbers, gherkins (a variety of cucumber especially suited to preserving), courgettes, pattypan squash, Galia and Charentais melons are all types of summer squash. Winter varieties include "onion" squash, butternut squash and pumpkins.

Mini cucumber

Crook

Gherkin

Pattypan squash

Kabocha pumpkin

Butternut squash

Galia melon

English cucumber

Custard squash

Green courgette

Marrow

"Onion" squash

Piel di sapo melon

Honeydew melon

Charentais melon

Yellow courgettes

Pumpkin

SERVING SUGGESTIONS

BREAD AND BUTTER PICKLE *turns a simple ham sandwich into a feast. (See page 97 for recipe.)*

MELON PICKLED AS MANGO *is a spectacular centrepiece for a cold buffet. (See page 101 for recipe.)*

PUMPKIN MARMALADE *makes a deliciously tangy filling for a sweet flan. (See page 164 for recipe.)*

TOBY'S PICKLED CUCUMBERS are a zesty, sweet and sour relish. (See page 98 for recipe.)

MELON BUTTER has a subtle fruity taste, enlivened by lemongrass. (See page 172 for recipe.)

BRINED CUCUMBERS (GHERKINS) contain dill and chillies for a flavourful pickle. (See page 93 for recipe.)

PUMPKIN MARMALADE, an unusual addition to the breakfast table. (See page 164 for recipe.)

MELON KONFYT is a variation on Fig Konfyt, a South African speciality. (See page 160 for recipe.)

OLIVE OIL PICKLE has a mild and refreshing flavour. (See page 97 for recipe.)

BREAD AND BUTTER PICKLE goes well with mature cheese. (See page 97 for recipe.)

ROOT VEGETABLES

FOR CENTURIES, root vegetables have formed the basis of winter fare; being hardy and long-lasting, they supplied nourishment when little else was available. Traditionally, root vegetables are cooked before pickling, but I like to use mine raw to maintain their crunchiness and vitamin content.

Many vitamins and trace elements are found in the skin and, other than for aesthetic reasons (the peel tends to discolour during preservation), there is no need to peel these vegetables unless they are old and thick-skinned. Root vegetables also make good jams as they have a high sugar content.

TYPES OF ROOT VEGETABLE

All root vegetables add texture to preserves, while some, such as beetroot and carrot, add colour as well. The odd one out is kohlrabi – strictly speaking it is not a root but a swollen stem, as it grows above ground.

Beetroot

Baby beetroot

Daikon radish (mooli)

Kohlrabi

Radishes

European radish

Turnips

Celeriac

Jerusalem artichoke

Parsnips

Carrots

SERVING SUGGESTIONS

CARROT AND ALMOND CHUTNEY *has a sour-sweet flavour that adds zest to a simple meat pie and salad. (See page 121 for recipe.)*

PICKLED TURNIPS *are served with Pickled Aubergines and Beetroot as an appetizer in the Middle East. (See pages 94 and 91 for recipes.)*

FERMENTED BEETROOT *juice doubles as a light, refreshing borscht. Serve hot or cold, with soured cream and dill. (See Brined Cucumbers, page 93.)*

CARROT JAM, a Middle Eastern-style preserve, contains sultanas and ginger. (See page 159 for recipe.)

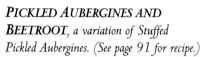

PICKLED AUBERGINES AND BEETROOT, a variation of Stuffed Pickled Aubergines. (See page 91 for recipe.)

PICKLED CELERIAC AND CARROT SALAD is flavoured with dill seeds and orange. (See page 94 for recipe.)

TURNIP PRESERVE is an unusual variation on Marrow and Ginger Preserve. (See page 162 for recipe.)

PICKLED TURNIPS are given a vivid purple tint by the addition of a little beetroot. (See page 94 for recipe.)

CARROT AND ALMOND CHUTNEY has a delicate texture and bright colour. (See page 121 for recipe.)

PICKLED BEETROOT, a popular variation of Pickled Onions. (See page 92 for recipe.)

MEAT

WHEN MAN DISCOVERED how to preserve meat, a new chapter in human development opened. The ability to transport long-lasting, protein-rich food over great distances enabled humans to create permanent settlements. Meat is now preserved to improve flavour and add variety. For the recipes in this book, find a reliable butcher who can supply you with good-quality meat that has been properly hung. Organically reared, free-range animals, which have matured naturally, give the best flavour. When preserving meat, always adhere to a very high standard of hygiene (see page 42).

TYPES OF MEAT

Lean cuts, such as beef and venison leg meat, are excellent for drying and curing. Fattier meat portions, including duck, goose and pork, can be made into pâté. The latter also provide good quantities of fat, which is essential for potted goods.

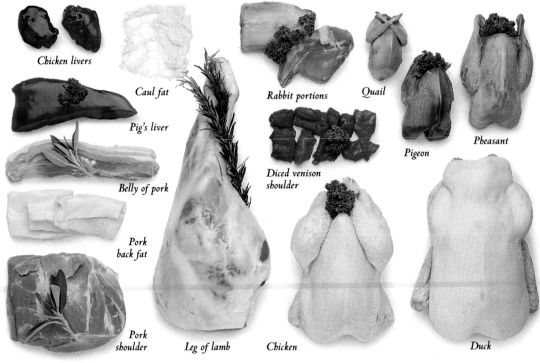

Chicken livers

Caul fat

Pig's liver

Belly of pork

Rabbit portions

Quail

Diced venison shoulder

Pigeon

Pheasant

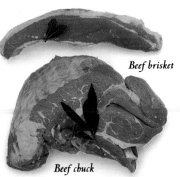

Beef brisket

Pork back fat

Beef chuck

Pork shoulder

Leg of lamb

Chicken

Duck

SERVING SUGGESTIONS

SMOOTH LIVER PATE *tastes delicious baked en croûte in puff pastry. (See page 144 for recipe.)*

SMOKED CHICKEN *makes a perfect lunch dish with salad and a creamy yogurt dressing. (See page 135 for recipe.)*

CHILLI SALAMI *added to a Spanish-style bean stew creates a hearty winter meal. (See page 138 for recipe.)*

Chilli salami

Landjäger

Dried lamb sausages

Rillettes

Garlic and herb salami

Preserved Toulouse sausages

Wind-dried duck sausages

CHILLI SALAMI, *similar to Spanish chorizo, is spiced with red chillies. (See page 138 for recipe.)*

LANDJÄGER *are well-flavoured dried sausages, made from beef and bacon. (See page 137 for recipe.)*

RILLETTES *is a coarse-textured, potted pork dish that makes excellent picnic fare. (See page 146 for recipe.)*

RABBIT PATE *(above), a low-fat version of a traditional French recipe, includes carrots, shallots and fresh herbs to keep it moist. Serve as a light lunch or appetizer. (See page 142 for recipe.)*

QUAIL AND PHEASANT TERRINE *(below) contains quail stuffed with spinach and parsley. (See page 143 for recipe.)*

DRIED LAMB SAUSAGES *are aromatic with fennel, paprika and mint. (See page 136 for recipe.)*

GARLIC AND HERB SALAMI *can be thinly sliced and served with an aperitif. (See page 138 for recipe.)*

PRESERVED TOULOUSE SAUSAGES, *a versatile stand-by. (See page 136 for recipe.)*

WIND-DRIED DUCK SAUSAGES *taste sweet and spicy. (See page 137 for recipe.)*

FISH & SEAFOOD

FISH AND SHELLFISH are a good source of essential fatty acids, vitamins, minerals and trace elements, and for past generations, preserved fish – salted, cured or smoked – was a staple food. Today it is considered more of a delicacy. Preserved seafood develops a strong, distinctive aroma and flavour and, as in the case of anchovy or oyster sauce, can be used as a condiment to add instant savour to many dishes. Use only the freshest seafood that smells pleasantly of the sea. Whole fish should be bright, shiny and firm to the touch; live mussels and clams should have tightly shut shells.

TYPES OF SEAFOOD

Use mussels, scallops and oily fish – herring, salmon, mackerel and tuna – for curing and smoking as they retain their moisture; white fish, such as cod, are more suited to drying and salting.

Scallops

Sardine

Baby squid

Squid rings

Clams

Mussels

Rainbow trout

Raw king prawn

Sprat

Cooked king prawn   Prawn

Shrimp

Octopus

Salmon

Tuna steak

Monkfish tail

Herring

SERVING SUGGESTIONS

ANCHOVIES IN OIL *form a savoury topping and a quick decoration for pizza. (See Salt-cured Sprats, page 153.)*

HERRINGS IN MUSTARD SAUCE & HERRINGS IN CREAM SAUCE *make a tasty lunch. (See page 151 for recipes.)*

GRAVAD LAX *is best eaten with a simple accompaniment such as dill and mustard sauce. (See page 153 for recipe.)*

ROLLMOPS are a German delicacy that are traditionally served as a starter. (See page 150 for recipe.)

ANCHOVIES IN OIL, a tasty variation of Salt-cured Sprats. (See page 153 for recipe.)

SEAFOOD IN OIL is prepared with a variety of ingredients to make an attractive preserve. (See page 109 for recipe.)

SMOKED TROUT can be served like salmon. (See page 152 for recipe.)

SALT-CURED SPRATS just need soaking in water before using. (See page 153 for recipe.)

PICKLED SALMON (left) is a delicious preserve based on an old Canadian recipe. (See page 150 for recipe.)

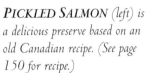

HERRINGS IN SPICED OIL (above) are flavoured with dried red chillies to make a piquant appetizer. (See page 109 for recipe.)

CITRUS FRUIT

CITRUS FRUIT make delicious conserves and marmalades, yet they also play an essential role in preserving other types of fruit. Being rich in pectin and acid, they are added to jams and jellies to help achieve a good set. Do not discard the pips as they contain the highest amount of pectin: tie them in a piece of muslin and add to the boiling fruit. Citrus fruit are also a good source of vitamin C, a natural anti-oxidant that prevents the discoloration of fruit and vegetables. Most of the citrus fruit available have been waxed to prevent deterioration; remove the wax by scrubbing the fruit in warm, soapy water.

TYPES OF CITRUS FRUIT

Ranging from the small and sweet kumquat to the large, green pomelo, citrus fruit are very versatile and can be used to make pickles as well as the traditional marmalade. They can also be candied, dried or preserved in alcohol.

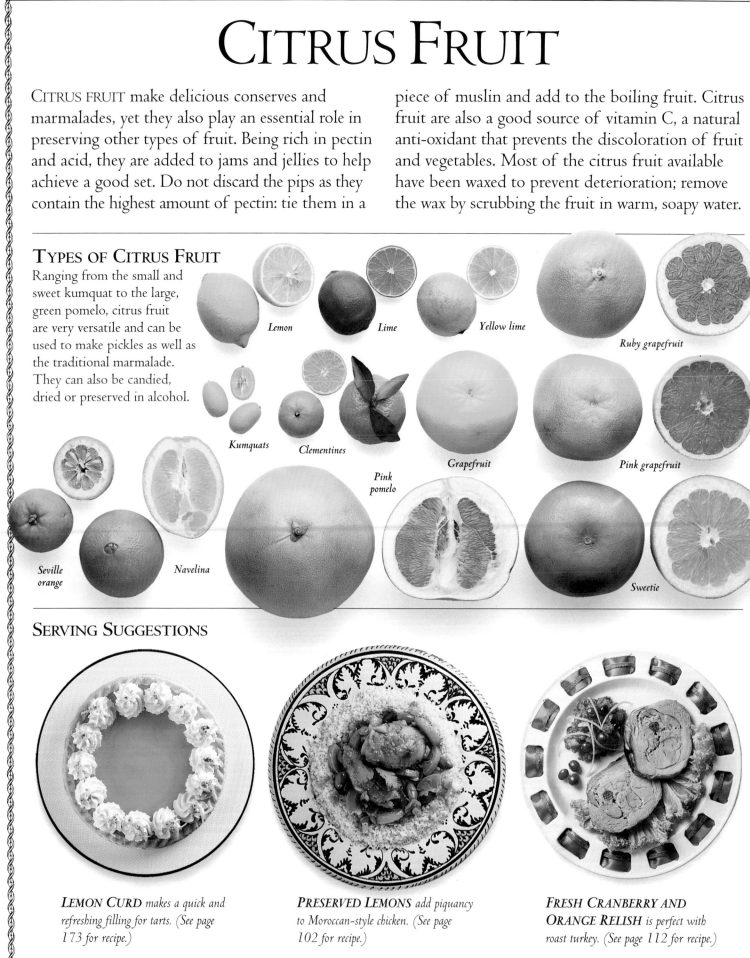

Lemon

Lime

Yellow lime

Ruby grapefruit

Kumquats

Clementines

Pink pomelo

Grapefruit

Pink grapefruit

Seville orange

Navelina

Sweetie

SERVING SUGGESTIONS

LEMON CURD *makes a quick and refreshing filling for tarts. (See page 173 for recipe.)*

PRESERVED LEMONS *add piquancy to Moroccan-style chicken. (See page 102 for recipe.)*

FRESH CRANBERRY AND ORANGE RELISH *is perfect with roast turkey. (See page 112 for recipe.)*

DRIED ORANGE PEEL *gives stewed fruit and pies an instant citrus note. (See Oven-drying Chart, page 185.)*

PICKLED LIMES *add zest to hot and spicy foods. (See page 100 for recipe.)*

CITRUS VINEGAR *is Salad Vinegar with a skewer of orange peel added to impart an intense flavour. (See page 127 for recipe.)*

LEMON CURD *has a rich and creamy taste — delicious on scones. (See page 173 for recipe.)*

SPICED WHOLE ORANGES *are studded with cloves to make a Christmas delicacy. (See page 100 for recipe.)*

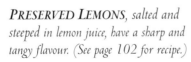

PRESERVED LEMONS, *salted and steeped in lemon juice, have a sharp and tangy flavour. (See page 102 for recipe.)*

ORANGE MARMALADE WITH CORIANDER *is enhanced with an orange-based liqueur. (See page 163 for recipe.)*

ORCHARD FRUIT

IN ART AND LITERATURE, orchard fruit have long been used to symbolize everything that is good and luscious. Most orchard fruit, especially apples, are high in pectin and therefore play an important role in jam- and jelly-making. Although you can use apples on their own, they lose their flavour in cooking and are mainly added to boost the pectin content of other fruit. The peel and cores can be made into a pectin "stock" (see page 47), as the highest level of pectin is found in the skin and seeds or stones of fruit. Today, different varieties of most orchard fruit are readily available all year round.

TYPES OF ORCHARD FRUIT

Orchard fruit can be divided into sweet dessert varieties and tart cooking ones. Usually the cooking varieties have a more solid, compact flesh that will withstand the lengthy cooking process.

Packham pear

Williams pear

Greengage

Burbank plum

Stanley plum

Victoria plum

Bramley apple

Crab apples

Montmorency cherries

Black cherries

Damsons

Sungold plum

Switzen plum

Apricot

Yellow-flesh peach

Granny Smith apple

Quince

White-flesh peach

SERVING SUGGESTIONS

DAMSON JAM and **STRIPED SPICED PEARS** complement roast pigeon. (See pages 156 and 103 for recipes.)

CANDIED FRUIT make a colourful decoration for a traditional Christmas cake. (See pages 181–183 for recipes.)

APRICOT JAM, warmed to use as a glaze, adds the finishing touch to an apple tart. (See page 158 for recipe.)

GREENGAGE JAM, a variation of Plum Jam, is a traditional French country preserve. (See page 156 for recipe.)

PEARS IN EAU DE VIE (right) are subtly spiced with a vanilla pod. (See page 179 for recipe.)

PLUM JAM (left) can be made with any variety of plum; here, mirabelle plums give an orange hue. (See page 156 for recipe.)

DAMSON JAM (right), based on Plum Jam, has a sharp flavour that goes well with savoury and sweet dishes. (See page 156 for recipe.)

MINTED APPLE JELLY is an ideal way to use up windfall apples and fresh garden mint. (See page 167 for recipe.)

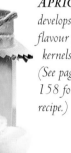

APRICOT JAM develops a mild almond flavour if the apricot kernels are added. (See page 158 for recipe.)

PEACH CHUTNEY, a light and fragrant preserve, is good for cooling down hot curries. (See page 125 for recipe.)

SOFT FRUIT

IN MIDSUMMER, fresh berries flood the markets; high in pectin and acid, they make wonderful jams, jellies and sweet preserves. Choose punnets of firm, unblemished fruit with no bruises or mould, and check the bottom of each container for any leakage of juice – a sign of squashed fruit. As soft fruit contain large amounts of water, they do not keep well and should be used as soon as possible. For jellies and jams, the fruit should be slightly under-ripe, so the pectin content is at its highest; fully ripe fruit are best suited to drying or for making brightly coloured, crystal-clear vinegars.

TYPES OF SOFT FRUIT

Fresh, soft summer fruit appear in a wide spectrum of colours, from the jewel-like ruby redcurrants, through the cool and elegant green of gooseberries to dark blue, almost purple, blueberries. Pretty and full of flavour, they make excellent preserves.

Redcurrants

White currants

Blackcurrants

Raspberries

Blackberries

Strawberries

Wild strawberries

Blueberries

Gooseberries

SERVING SUGGESTIONS

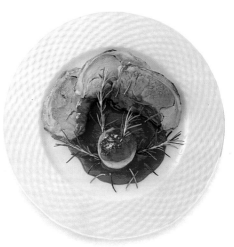

DRIED STRAWBERRIES add a touch of luxury to homemade muesli. (See Oven-drying Chart, page 185.)

PICCALILLI is a classic accompaniment to bread and cheese; this tangy version includes gooseberries. (See page 96 for recipe.)

REDCURRANT JELLY with roast lamb, artichokes and rosemary, makes a simple but elegant serving. (See Raspberry Jelly, page 166.)

STRAWBERRY VINEGAR (right) with a skewer of strawberries and basil added to the bottle for a particularly intense flavour. (See page 128 for recipe.)

RASPBERRY JELLY, a translucent preserve with a delicate flavour. (See page 166 for recipe.)

REDCURRANT JELLY, a variation of Raspberry Jelly, used in sweet and savoury dishes. (See page 166 for recipe.)

Gooseberry vinegar

Blackcurrant vinegar

FRUIT VINEGARS (left) subtly enhance sauces, marinades and salad dressings, and many of them can be diluted to make a refreshing drink. (See page 128 for recipes.)

PICCALILLI contains bite-sized chunks of crisp vegetables and refreshing summer fruit. (See page 96 for recipe.)

BLUEBERRY JAM, the perfect accompaniment to pancakes and waffles. (See page 157 for recipe.)

RASPBERRY JAM is densely packed with juicy berries for a year-round taste of summer. (See page 157 for recipe.)

EXOTIC FRUIT

THERE IS NO ULTIMATE definition of an exotic fruit – what is unusual and foreign in one part of the world may be considered commonplace and humble in another. Most exotic fruit have evocative aromas and vibrant colours that enhance and flavour other foods; they also make the most wonderful preserves. Buy fruit from a store that has a fast turnover so you get the freshest produce possible. Look for specimens without any bruising and, where applicable, a good fragrance. Store the fruit in a cool, dark place and use quickly while they are still at their best.

TYPES OF EXOTIC FRUIT

The variety of exotic fruit available in the market is ever increasing, and this gallery includes a taster of some of the fruit from around the world, as well as those grown in the sub-tropics and tropics.

Prickly pears

Lychees

Kiwi fruit

Fresh dates

Passion fruit

Guava

Persimmon

Sharon fruit

Mangoes

Dessert banana

Fresh figs

Finger bananas

Red bananas

Pomegranate

Baby pineapple

Pineapple

SERVING SUGGESTIONS

PINEAPPLE CHUTNEY *perfectly complements the flavour of fried chicken. (See Pumpkin Chutney, page 120.)*

MANGO BUTTER *served in a tartlet case with a crème anglaise sauce makes an appealing dessert. (See page 172 for recipe.)*

KIWI FRUIT BUTTER *can be used as an unusual filling for pancakes. (See page 172 for recipe.)*

FIG CHUTNEY *makes an unusual accompaniment to cheese dishes, and is excellent with a ploughman's lunch. (See page 125 for recipe.)*

PINEAPPLE IN KIRSCH, *delicious served with cream for an indulgent dessert. (See page 179 for recipe.)*

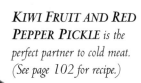

KIWI FRUIT AND RED PEPPER PICKLE *is the perfect partner to cold meat. (See page 102 for recipe.)*

SPICY PRICKLY PEAR JELLY *made with purple fruit has the brightest colour. (See page 169 for recipe.)*

POMEGRANATE SYRUP *can be diluted as a drink or used as a sauce for ice cream. (See page 181 for recipe.)*

HOT MANGO CHUTNEY *adds heat and a tangy, fruity flavour to curries. (See page 123 for recipe.)*

DATE BLATJANG (DATE SAUCE) *is a favourite in South Africa. (See page 116 for recipe.)*

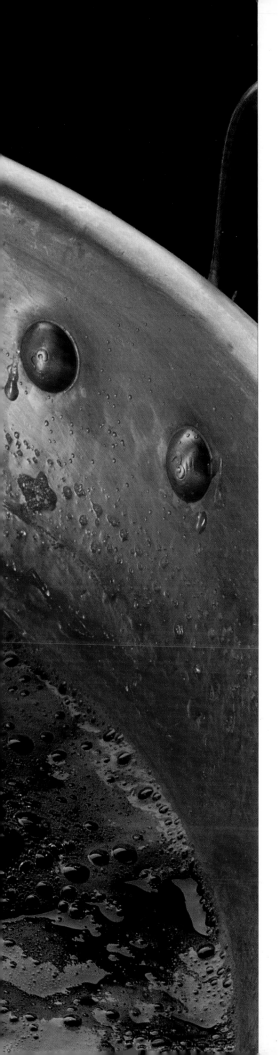

PRESERVING EQUIPMENT & TECHNIQUES

LEARN THE BASIC SKILLS of preserving
with this step-by-step guide. Besides the
well-known techniques of pickling and
jam-making, the easy-to-follow recipes
feature the less familiar practices
of salting, curing and sausage-making. In
addition, a visual guide to the most useful
equipment and the basic ingredients,
together with practical advice on safety
and hygiene, provides you with all the
essentials necessary for
successful preserving.

EQUIPMENT

YOU DO NEED to have good-quality kitchen equipment for successful and efficient preserving. Most of the equipment shown below can be found in any well-established kitchen, but a few items, such as the mechanical shredders and grinders, preserving pans and other specialist utensils, are required to make preserving easier: you can find most of these in a good kitchen shop. Top-quality utensils might be expensive but they will last a long time. Some equipment, such as the dehydrator and smoker, is best obtained from specialist suppliers. See page 192 for some addresses of stockists.

Large cook's knife

Filleting knife

Boning knife

Kitchen scissors

KNIVES: sharp knives are essential. Select the best quality you can afford, with solid, well-balanced handles. Sharpen your knives frequently to maintain them.

Hand grater

Mandolin

Paring knife

Hardwood chopping board

Food mill

GRATERS AND MANDOLINS: these ease the task of slicing and shredding vegetables into neat, even slices. Choose a good-quality mandolin with an adjustable blade.

FOOD MILLS: useful for puréeing fruit and vegetable mixtures.

MINCERS: good for chopping fruit for butters and curds as well as for mincing meat.

Canelle knife

Zester

Corer

Floating blade peeler

Pestle and mortar

Coffee grinder

Hand mincer

PEELERS, CORERS AND ZESTERS: all make light work of preparing fruit and vegetables.

GRINDERS: the traditional pestle and mortar is ideal for coarsely grinding small quantities of spices. For fine powders use an electric coffee grinder or spice mill.

Mincing plates

Mincer attachment

Sausage-making nozzle

ELECTRIC MINCERS: essential if you frequently make sausages. They are available as an attachment to many food mixers. Many also have a sausage-making device.

HAND-HELD SAUSAGE MAKERS: these are available from specialist suppliers (see page 192).

Sausage maker

Wooden spoons

Measuring spoons

Measuring jug

Meat thermometer

Sugar thermometer

Palette knives

MEASURING EQUIPMENT: use glass, china or stainless steel, and avoid corrosive metals such as aluminium.

WOODEN SPOONS: keep a separate set for sweet and savoury products.

PALETTE KNIVES: useful for smoothing surfaces.

FUNNELS AND SIEVES: funnels make potting much simpler; metal sieves should not be used with acid fruit as metal can affect colours and flavours.

Funnel

Jam funnel

Calico

Muslin

Jelly bag

Coffee filter paper

JELLY BAGS AND FILTERS: unbleached muslin, cheesecloth or calico are ideal for filtering and straining. Always sterilize before use (see page 42). For filtering small quantities of liquid, use coffee filter papers.

SKIMMING SPOONS: skimming is important to give a crystal-clear jam or jelly. Use slotted or perforated spoons or special skimmers. Always dip them in cold water before use.

Nylon sieve

Meat hooks for hanging

Kitchen string

Ladle

Slotted spoon

Skimmer

Colander

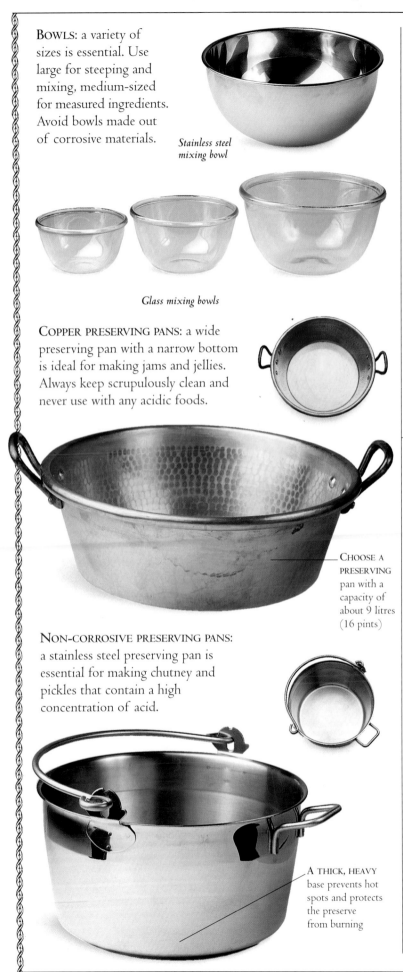

BOWLS: a variety of sizes is essential. Use large for steeping and mixing, medium-sized for measured ingredients. Avoid bowls made out of corrosive materials.

Stainless steel mixing bowl

Glass mixing bowls

COPPER PRESERVING PANS: a wide preserving pan with a narrow bottom is ideal for making jams and jellies. Always keep scrupulously clean and never use with any acidic foods.

CHOOSE A PRESERVING pan with a capacity of about 9 litres (16 pints)

NON-CORROSIVE PRESERVING PANS: a stainless steel preserving pan is essential for making chutney and pickles that contain a high concentration of acid.

A THICK, HEAVY base prevents hot spots and protects the preserve from burning

DEHYDRATORS

Drying can be carried out in a domestic oven, but if you intend to dry large quantities of produce, it is advisable to buy a special dryer. Although relatively expensive, domestic dehydrators are flexible, efficient, consume very little energy and are easy to use. Always follow the manufacturer's instructions.

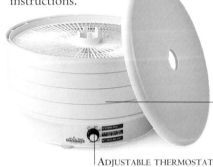

THE DESIGN of these trays allows fast, even drying with no need for rotation and no tainting of flavours

STACKABLE TRAYS enable you to dry different quantities of fruit and vegetables. Drying pressure increases automatically

ADJUSTABLE THERMOSTAT for temperature settings

SMOKERS

A domestic smoker is a wonderful luxury. Choose a model that is easy to operate and clean, and has an automatic temperature and time control. Make sure that your smoker allows you smoke at low temperatures – in many models this is an optional extra. Always follow the manufacturer's instructions.

THE SMOKE BOX controls and directs the flow of smoke. Hardwood chips provide the smoke

VARIABLE TEMPERATURE CONTROL and timer settings allow food to be smoked at just the right temperature and for the correct length of time

THE STEEL DOOR is airtight and should be left ajar when the oven is not in use

CONTAINERS

A SELECTION of containers is required for both visual and practical reasons. For storing moist foods and liquids, always select non-absorbent materials such as glazed earthenware, enamel, glass, porcelain or stainless steel. Avoid vessels made of corrosive material, such as aluminium, or plastic, which tends to stain and absorb flavours. Before using a container, check to make sure it has no chips or cracks, then wash it well. Sterilize all storage containers thoroughly before use (see page 42).

HEATPROOF CONTAINERS

Pâtés, potted goods, and other preserves that are baked in the oven, require glass, earthenware, porcelain or enamelled heatproof containers. Select dishes that complement the colour of the finished product. Glass is the ideal material to show bottled preserves at their best, and is also non-corrosive. Re-used glass jars are only suitable for short-term storage. For long-term preservation, it is advisable to use new specialist preserving jars that are suited to high temperatures and have non-corrosive seals.

Enamelled rectangular terrine

Porcelain ramekins

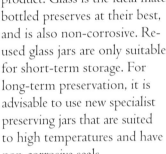

Earthenware ramekin

Earthenware bowl

Earthenware oval terrine

Earthenware crock

WIDE-NECKED JARS are essential for recipes using whole fruit or vegetables

DECORATIVE BOTTLES can be used for flavoured oils and vinegars

MAKE SURE stoppers or lids provide an airtight seal

HYGIENE & SAFETY

IT IS CRUCIAL to follow strict hygiene and safety practices. I find that common sense and diligence about timing, temperature and cleanliness are essential for preventing food contamination. Take care that all the ingredients you use are in prime condition and keep them at the recommended temperatures at all times. Kitchen surfaces and utensils must be kept thoroughly clean. Wipe down surfaces with a sterilizing solution before you start and as you work. Ensure that all preserves are properly sealed (see opposite) before storing, then check them regularly and discard any that show signs of deterioration, have an unpleasant smell, uneven discoloration or broken seals (see page 186).

Hygiene and Safety with Meat

Extra care must be taken when preserving meat. If the following hygiene precautions are observed, you should have no difficulty in enjoying any of the preserved meat products in this book.

• The kitchen must be scrupulously clean. Use a separate set of sterilized utensils for meat and keep them in pristine condition.
• Sterilize equipment in boiling water. Plastic utensils can be cleaned with sterilizing tablets or in a specialist sterilizing unit used for babies' bottles.
• Warm, moist hands encourage bacterial growth. Wash them frequently with anti-bacterial soap and always dry them well on a clean towel or kitchen paper. Keep your nails short and well scrubbed.
• Always work in a cool, well ventilated kitchen, ideally between 10–12°C (50–54°F).

• Always buy the best quality meat you can afford from a reliable butcher and tell him the purpose of your purchase.
• Never allow meat to become warm: keep it refrigerated at 4°C (40°F). Check the temperature of your refrigerator to ensure it is working efficiently.
• Follow the recipes accurately and always use the recommended quantities of saltpetre, salt and sugar. Never guess amounts.
• Check your stored products at regular intervals and discard any that develop an unpleasant smell, or show any signs of mould or deterioration (see page 186).

SALTPETRE WARNING

There is some controversy about saltpetre (sodium nitrate). Saltpetre is a naturally occurring substance that, when used in very small quantities, ensures the safety of preserved meats by inhibiting the growth of harmful bacteria. Sodium nitrate (and a similar substance, sodium nitrite) is added to commercially cured meats and I would not recommend drying or curing meat without it.

• Saltpetre is only available from pharmacists. You will probably have to order it.
• Store it very safely: keep it clearly labelled and out of the reach of all children.
• When using saltpetre, measure it accurately and make sure it is evenly mixed with the other ingredients.
• All the recipes in this book that use saltpetre are marked with the following warning symbol *.

Sterilizing Methods

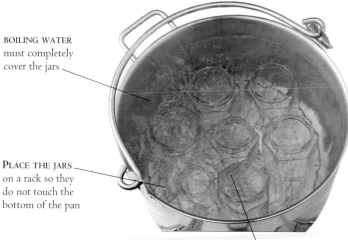

BOILING WATER must completely cover the jars

PLACE THE JARS on a rack so they do not touch the bottom of the pan

MAKE SURE THE JARS do not touch each other or the sides of the pan

BOILING WATER METHOD

Sterilize jars (and bottles) before use. Place the washed jars in a deep pan and cover with boiling water. Bring to the boil and boil rapidly for 10 minutes. Lift the jars out and drain upside down on a clean kitchen towel. Place the jars on a covered tray and dry in a cool oven. All lids, rubber seals and corks must be immersed for a few seconds in boiling water.
Sterilize muslin, calico, cheesecloth and **jelly bags** by pouring boiling water through them.

OVEN METHOD

Place jars on a paper towel-lined tray and place in an oven preheated to 160°C/325°F/gas 3 for 10 minutes. Allow to cool slightly then fill with the hot product.

JARS MUST BE without chips or cracks; wash them in hot, soapy water before sterilizing

LINE THE TRAY with paper towels to diffuse the heat

FILLING & SEALING

TYPES OF CONTAINER

Always use sterilized containers with the appropriate lids or seals. For ordinary jars, use vinegar-proof lids to seal pickles and chutneys, and waxed paper discs and cellophane seals for sweet preserves. Special preserving jars are essential if a product is to be heat processed (see pages 44–45).

Jam jars

Cellophane seals

Waxed paper discs

Elastic bands

Corks

Candle wax

Sealing wax

Glass bottle

Filling and Sealing Jars Without Lids

1 Use a ladle and a jam funnel to fill the hot sterilized jar. Fill the jar to within 1cm (½ in) of the top.

2 Wipe the rim clean with a damp cloth and carefully smooth a waxed paper disc on to the jam (waxed side down).

DAMPEN THE CELLOPHANE disc before use

3 Wipe the cellophane disc with a wet cloth, place over the top, moist side up, and secure with an elastic band. When dry it will shrink and create a tight seal.

Filling and Sealing Bottles

1 Use a ladle and non-corrosive funnel to fill the hot sterilized bottle to within 3.5cm (1½ in) of the top. Wipe the rim clean.

2 Soak the cork in hot water for a few minutes. Push it into the bottle as far as it will go, then tap in with a wooden mallet to within 5mm (¼ in) of the top.

THE WAX MUST cover part of the neck of the bottle as well as the cork

3 When the bottle is cold, tap the cork down level with the top using a wooden mallet. Dip the top of the bottle several times into melted candle or sealing wax, allowing the wax to set between applications.

HEAT PROCESSING

BOTTLED PRESERVES WITH low acidity, or a low sugar or salt content, are at risk of contamination by moulds and bacteria. If you want to keep them for longer than three or four months, it is essential that they are heat processed. The high temperature and exclusion of oxygen produce an environment in which most spoilants cannot survive. The technique is simple: the preserve is packed into

sterilized jars or bottles, sealed and immersed in water. It is then heated to boiling point and boiled for a specific length of time (see box, opposite). On cooling, the contents contract and create a vacuum. Store in a cool, dry, dark place for no more than two years, checking for any signs of deterioration. Discard a preserve with a swollen or damaged seal (see page 186).

TYPES OF CONTAINER

Specialized preserving jars come in many shapes and sizes. Select the type that is readily available, for which spare new lids or rubber rings can be found easily. It is always advisable to use new containers that have acid-resistant seals. With one-piece lidded jars you can see when a vacuum has formed and also if the seal is broken. Bottles without lids require corks to seal them. Always use new lids and corks.

Clamp-top preserving jars

Vacuum one-piece lidded preserving jar

Vacuum lid and screw-band preserving jar

Bottles must have a ridge so corks can be secured

Clamp-top bottles must have new rubber seals

Kitchen string

One-piece lid

Corks

Lid and screw-band seal

Rubber seal must be new

Heatproof bottle   *Clamp-top bottle*

Clamp-top Jar

1 Place the new, sterilized rubber ring (see page 42) on the edge of the lid. Grip the lid tightly with one hand and fit the ring over it.

2 Fill the hot sterilized jar to within 1cm (½in) of the top or to the manufacturer's mark. Clamp the lid shut, using a cloth to hold it steady.

Lid and Screw-band Jar

1 Fill the hot sterilized jar (see page 42) to within 1cm (½in) of the top. Wipe the rim and cover with the sterilized rubber-coated lid.

2 Hold the jar steady with a cloth. Screw the band down until it is tight, then release it by a quarter turn, or as directed in the manufacturer's instructions.

Sealing Bottles

1 Cork the bottle (see page 43), then make a shallow cut in the top of the cork. Cut a piece of string 50cm (20in) long and, keeping one end 10 cm (4in) longer than the other, secure it in the cut, as shown right.

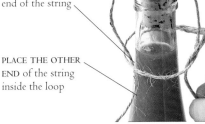

FORM A LOOP with the long end of the string

PLACE THE OTHER END of the string inside the loop

2 Loop the long end of the string around the neck of the bottle, then insert the end of it through the front of the loop.

3 Pull both ends of the string down, to tighten the loop, and tie the loose ends over the cork in a double knot, as shown right.

MAKE SURE the cork is tied securely: it must stand up to the pressure inside the bottle when it is heat processed

Heat Processing

1 Wrap each jar or bottle in a few layers of cloth or folded newspaper to prevent them from knocking against each other. Stand them on a metal rack placed in the bottom of a large lidded pan.

3 Remove from the heat and lift out the jars with tongs. Place on a rack or cloth-covered surface, tighten screw-bands immediately, then leave to cool completely. As the jars cool a partial vacuum is formed.

—— TIP ——

If a vacuum seal has not formed properly on any preserving jar, refrigerate the product and use within 1 week.

2 Pour in enough hot water to cover the lids or corks by at least 2.5cm (1in). Cover, bring to the boil and boil for the stated time (see below). Check the water level occasionally and top up, if necessary.

4 To check the seal, gently undo the clamp or screw-band and grip the rim of the lid with your fingertips. Carefully lift the jar; if sealed it will support the weight. One-piece lidded jars will dip in the centre if a vacuum has formed. If using corked bottles, rest them on their sides to check for any leaks, then seal with melted wax before storing (see Filling and Sealing Bottles, step 3, page 43).

HEAT PROCESSING TIMES

All times are counted from the moment the water comes back to the boil.

Cold-packed Preserves	Hot-packed Preserves
500g (1lb) jars – heat process for 25 minutes	500g (1lb) jars – heat process for 20 minutes
500ml (1 pint) bottles – heat process for 25 minutes	500ml (1 pint) bottles – heat process for 20 minutes
1kg (2lb) jars – heat process for 30 minutes	1kg (2lb) jars – heat process for 25 minutes
1 litre (1¾–2 pint) bottles – heat process for 30 minutes	1 litre (1¾–2 pint) bottles – heat process for 25 minutes

BASIC SKILLS

THE VARIOUS SKILLS described on these pages are designed to help ensure that all your preserves, from jams and jellies to cured meats and pickles, are successful and trouble-free. They are simple yet essential techniques, some of which you may be familiar with already. Each one is referred to frequently in the extensive range of preserving recipes that follow on pages 52–182.

Blanching

Blanching plays an important role in preserving as it destroys the enzymes in fruit and vegetables that cause their deterioration and discoloration on exposure to the air (known as oxidation). **Green vegetables** are usually blanched in salted water (1 tablespoon salt to every 1 litre/1¾ pints water), while **fruit** are blanched in acidulated water (3 tablespoons vinegar or lemon juice or 2 teaspoons citric acid to every 1 litre/1¾ pints water).

1 Place the ingredients in a wire basket and immerse in a large pan of boiling water. Return to the boil as quickly as possible and blanch for the time specified in the recipe.

2 Tip the contents of the basket into a bowl of iced water, ensuring that they are submerged. This arrests the cooking process and refreshes them. Drain well before use.

Skinning Tomatoes

The simplest way to peel tomatoes is to immerse them in boiling water: this loosens the skin, making it easy to remove. Peaches can be prepared in exactly the same way, while onions are left unscored and steeped in the water until cool enough to handle.

1 Remove any stems and score each base lightly. Place in a bowl and cover with boiling water for a few seconds.

2 Drain off the boiling water and cover with cold water. Peel off the loosened skin with the help of a knife.

Weighting Down

Weighting down keeps the ingredients immersed under liquid, protecting them from the deteriorating effects of oxidation. Use non-porous objects that can be sterilized easily, such as a water-filled glass bottle or jar, or glazed plate. When using a wide-necked jar, a mesh made of wooden skewers can be added to the top of the container to keep the contents submerged. After weighting down, check that the liquid covers the ingredients by at least 1cm (½ in), and add more if necessary.

A BOTTLE OR JAR filled with water makes a useful weight

FOR PATES AND MEAT use smooth, clean pebbles (or cans of food) to weight down a foil-covered piece of card or board.

STERILIZED PEBBLES can be added to jars to keep the ingredients submerged. Do not use with delicate foods that can be squashed

A PLATE PLACED in the top of a bowl will keep soaking fruit and vegetables immersed in the liquid

Pectin

A jam or jelly requires pectin to set. You can test its content in fruit, as shown below, and increase it by adding a third to a half the total volume of fruit pulp in pectin stock. Test it again and increase the sugar content in the recipe if necessary (see page 76).

TESTING FOR PECTIN CONTENT

Place 1 tablespoon each of the cooked, unsweetened fruit juice and methylated spirits in a bowl. Stir together for a few minutes, until it starts to clot. A large lump indicates a high pectin level, while small clots indicate a low pectin level.

PECTIN STOCK
(makes about 1 litre/1¾ pints)

Core 1kg (2lb) apples, reserving the cores, and chop in a food processor. Place the chopped fruit and the cores in a preserving pan with enough water to cover. (Alternatively, use 1kg/2lb of apple cores and peel.) Bring slowly to the boil, then reduce the heat and simmer for 25–30 minutes or until soft. Strain through a sterilized jelly bag (see step 4, page 80) and reserve the juice. Return the pulp to the pan, with water to cover. Bring to the boil, then reduce the heat and simmer for 30 minutes. Strain again. Combine both quantities of juice in the pan. Boil rapidly for 10–15 minutes, or until reduced by a quarter. Pour into sterilized bottles, then seal (see pages 42–43). Refrigerate and use within 1 week. To keep for up to 1 year, heat process (see pages 44–45).

Testing for Set

When a jam, or similar preserve with a high sugar content, is heated to 105°C (220°F) the sugar reacts with the pectin and starts to gel. Check with a sugar thermometer for accuracy or carry out the "spoon" or "plate" test (see page 76 for technique).

Filtering

Sometimes, even carefully prepared liquids can become cloudy and need filtering. Pour the liquid through a sterilized jelly bag, or a double layer of sterilized muslin, thin layer of calico, or paper filter (such as a coffee filter or filter for a home-brewing kit).

Filtering through muslin

Filtering through a paper filter

Use a sieve to hold a small piece of sterilized muslin or calico, or tie a large piece to the legs of an upturned stool. Support a paper filter with a funnel.

Making Brine

Brine is used when curing and drying meat (see Cured Ham, page 134 for recipe). The meat is steeped in a strong salt solution that extracts the moisture. Always use a non-corrosive container when making a brine.

1 Put the spices in a muslin bag, then place all the ingredients in a large pan. Bring slowly to the boil, stirring until the salt has dissolved. Skim well, then reduce the heat and simmer for 5 minutes.

2 Remove the pan from the heat and leave the brine until completely cold. Lift out the spices and herbs, then strain the brine through a muslin-lined sieve to remove any froth and impurities. Use as specified in the recipe.

Spice Bags and Herb Bundles

Putting spices in muslin bags and tying herbs in bundles is a convenient way to add flavour. They are easy to remove after cooking.

PLACE THE FLAVOURINGS in the centre of a small square of muslin, then draw up the corners to enclose the spices and secure with kitchen string

TIE TOGETHER the bundle of herbs with kitchen string

PRESERVING INGREDIENTS

SOME SPECIAL INGREDIENTS are essential to preserving. Buy the best quality available and do not be afraid to experiment with the basics, such as different vinegars, oils and sugars. Many ingredients are affected by oxygen and direct sunlight, so store them in airtight containers in a cool, dark place. Whenever possible, use unrefined ingredients: although they can affect the clarity of preserves, the flavour is better.

SUGARS

Many types of sugar are now available – most of them are interchangeable. White refined sugars produce a clear, sparkling and hard-set preserve, while honey and raw sugars, syrups and molasses give a softer product with a more pronounced flavour.

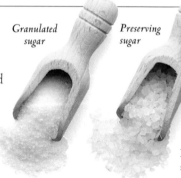
Granulated sugar
Preserving sugar

GRANULATED and PRESERVING SUGARS: refined and interchangeable. For clearest results, use preserving sugar.

MOLASSES: a moist, soft, dark sugar with a strong flavour.

BLACK TREACLE: a rich blend of refined syrup and raw molasses.

HONEY: the natural sweetener, use single flower honey for extra flavour.

LIQUID GLUCOSE: a complex sugar that helps to prevent crystallization.

DEMERARA: mild-flavoured, refined or unrefined sugar.

LIGHT BROWN MUSCOVADO: raw, fragrant, all-round sugar.

DARK MUSCOVADO: moist with a pronounced flavour.

PALM SUGAR: from the sap of palms; fragrant and tasty.

JAGGERY: a raw Indian sugar with a distinct taste.

OILS

Mild oils are best for preserving as they do not mask the flavour of the ingredients. For a more robust end-result use unrefined cold-pressed oils to add flavour. Oils should be kept in a cool, dark place.

MUSTARD OIL: made from mustard seeds, strongly flavoured and used extensively in Indian pickles.

GROUNDNUT OIL: an excellent, refined, mild, all-purpose oil.

REFINED OLIVE OIL: light in flavour and colour, excellent for delicate preserves.

OLIVE OIL: a mixture of refined and virgin; a good all-purpose oil.

EXTRA-VIRGIN OLIVE OIL: strongly flavoured and fragrant.

Mustard oil   *Groundnut oil*   *Refined olive oil*   *Olive oil*   *Extra-virgin olive oil*

FATS

Fats are used extensively to seal and add moisture. They should be a good colour and smell sweet. As they are easily affected by changes in temperature, keep them at the bottom of your refrigerator.

CLARIFIED BUTTER: mild and flavoursome butter-oil, for sealing potted goods.

GOOSE FAT: has a distinctive taste, use in confits and rillettes.

LARD: rendered, clarified pork fat, widely used as a sealant.

BUTTER: adds flavour and enriches meat and sweet preserves alike.

SALTS

Do not use ordinary table salt for preserving. Most brands contain anti-caking agents that will cloud brines and distort flavours. For curing, always use medium crystal, pure salt, sometimes known as Koshering salt.

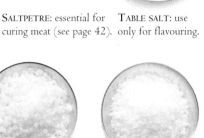

SALTPETRE: essential for curing meat (see page 42). **TABLE SALT:** use only for flavouring.

MALDEN SALT: large crystal salt, perfect for dry-curing fish.

ROCK SALT: crush and use for curing if preserving salt is unobtainable.

PRESERVING SALT: medium crystal salt, used widely in curing.

ACIDS

Acids are very important as they help jams and jellies to set, and prevent discoloration. To retain freshness, buy in small quantities and keep in airtight containers.

CITRIC ACID: sometimes sold as lemon salt; use in place of lemon juice.

LEMON: a natural anti-oxidant; adds pectin and enhances colour.

VITAMIN C: an anti-oxidant; helps to preserve a good colour.

TAMARIND: the sweet-sour pulp of the tamarind pod.

VINEGARS

Select clear vinegars with a good colour and aroma. Dark vinegars are suitable for chutneys and flavouring, while pale and distilled vinegars are used for pickling.

CIDER VINEGAR: a flavoursome and fruity, all-round vinegar, ideal for chutneys.

WHITE WINE VINEGAR: mild and mellow, ideal for delicate preserves.

RED WINE VINEGAR: adds a delicate red colour, ideal for spiced fruits.

MALT VINEGAR: an all-purpose vinegar; use in chutneys and dark pickles.

RICE VINEGAR: a delicate and mild, all-round clear vinegar.

DISTILLED MALT VINEGAR: a clear, all-purpose pickling vinegar.

Cider vinegar   *White wine vinegar*   *Red wine vinegar*   *Malt vinegar*   *Rice vinegar*   *Distilled malt vinegar*

FLAVOURINGS

THE HISTORY OF GOOD COOKING began when people discovered that adding fresh herbs and spices to food turned it into a fragrant delicacy. Since then, achieving the correct balance of flavours has been at the heart of all cuisines. Herbs and spices are valued not only for their flavour and aroma but also because many of them have antiseptic qualities and aid digestion – and they actively help the preserving process. Remember that flavourings are the cook's equivalent of the artist's palette; it is worth experimenting to find your own favourite combinations and so develop a personal touch.

SPICES

Whenever possible, grind spices just before use. Whole spices will keep for up to two years in an airtight container, while ground ones quickly lose their aroma.

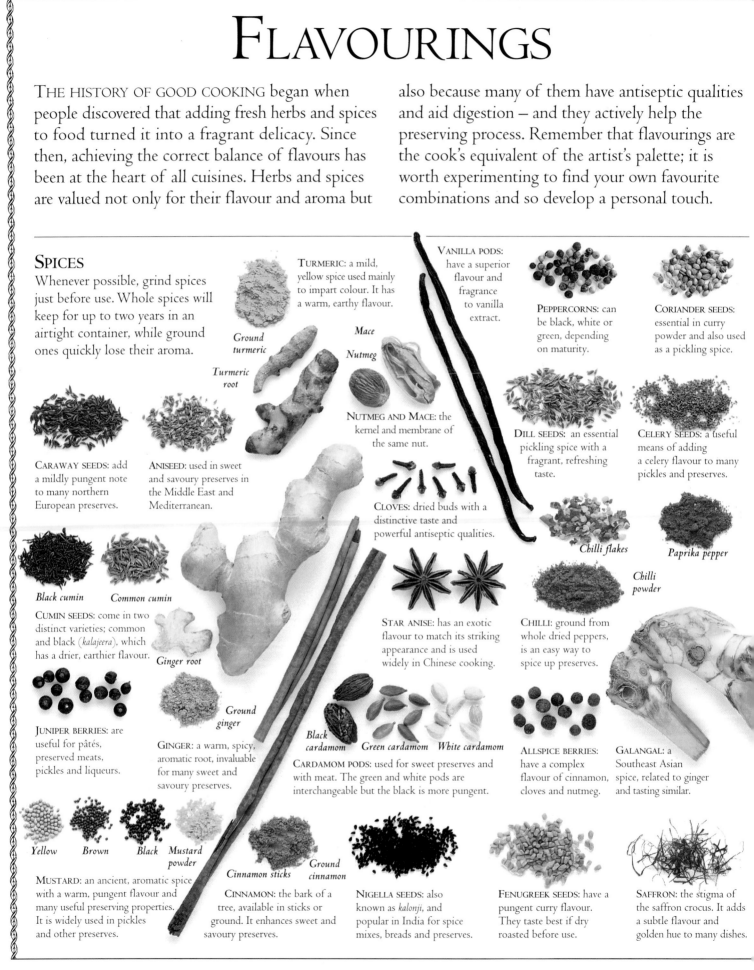

TURMERIC: a mild, yellow spice used mainly to impart colour. It has a warm, earthy flavour.

Ground turmeric

Turmeric root

Mace

Nutmeg

NUTMEG AND MACE: the kernel and membrane of the same nut.

VANILLA PODS: have a superior flavour and fragrance to vanilla extract.

PEPPERCORNS: can be black, white or green, depending on maturity.

CORIANDER SEEDS: essential in curry powder and also used as a pickling spice.

DILL SEEDS: an essential pickling spice with a fragrant, refreshing taste.

CELERY SEEDS: a useful means of adding a celery flavour to many pickles and preserves.

CARAWAY SEEDS: add a mildly pungent note to many northern European preserves.

ANISEED: used in sweet and savoury preserves in the Middle East and Mediterranean.

CLOVES: dried buds with a distinctive taste and powerful antiseptic qualities.

Chilli flakes

Paprika pepper

Chilli powder

Black cumin

Common cumin

CUMIN SEEDS: come in two distinct varieties; common and black (*kalajeera*), which has a drier, earthier flavour.

Ginger root

STAR ANISE: has an exotic flavour to match its striking appearance and is used widely in Chinese cooking.

CHILLI: ground from whole dried peppers, is an easy way to spice up preserves.

JUNIPER BERRIES: are useful for pâtés, preserved meats, pickles and liqueurs.

Ground ginger

GINGER: a warm, spicy, aromatic root, invaluable for many sweet and savoury preserves.

Black cardamom

Green cardamom

White cardamom

CARDAMOM PODS: used for sweet preserves and with meat. The green and white pods are interchangeable but the black is more pungent.

ALLSPICE BERRIES: have a complex flavour of cinnamon, cloves and nutmeg.

GALANGAL: a Southeast Asian spice, related to ginger and tasting similar.

Yellow

Brown

Black

Mustard powder

MUSTARD: an ancient, aromatic spice with a warm, pungent flavour and many useful preserving properties. It is widely used in pickles and other preserves.

Cinnamon sticks

Ground cinnamon

CINNAMON: the bark of a tree, available in sticks or ground. It enhances sweet and savoury preserves.

NIGELLA SEEDS: also known as *kalonji*, and popular in India for spice mixes, breads and preserves.

FENUGREEK SEEDS: have a pungent curry flavour. They taste best if dry roasted before use.

SAFFRON: the stigma of the saffron crocus. It adds a subtle flavour and golden hue to many dishes.

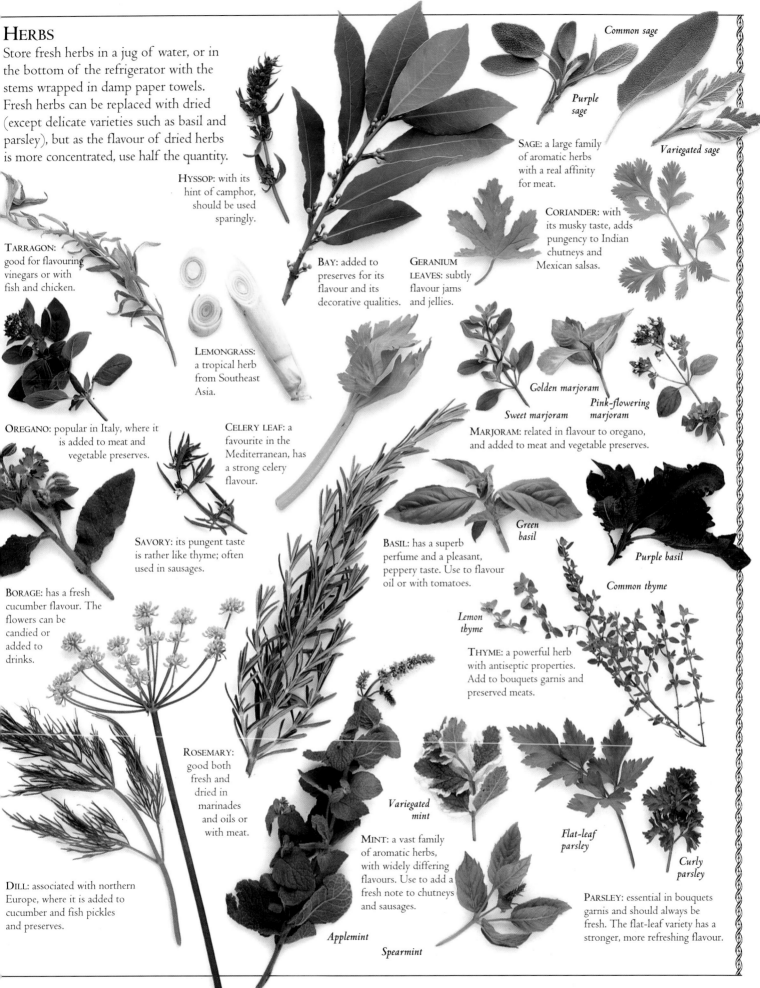

HERBS

Store fresh herbs in a jug of water, or in the bottom of the refrigerator with the stems wrapped in damp paper towels. Fresh herbs can be replaced with dried (except delicate varieties such as basil and parsley), but as the flavour of dried herbs is more concentrated, use half the quantity.

Common sage

Purple sage

SAGE: a large family of aromatic herbs with a real affinity for meat.

Variegated sage

CORIANDER: with its musky taste, adds pungency to Indian chutneys and Mexican salsas.

HYSSOP: with its hint of camphor, should be used sparingly.

TARRAGON: good for flavouring vinegars or with fish and chicken.

BAY: added to preserves for its flavour and its decorative qualities.

GERANIUM LEAVES: subtly flavour jams and jellies.

LEMONGRASS: a tropical herb from Southeast Asia.

Golden marjoram

Pink-flowering marjoram

Sweet marjoram

MARJORAM: related in flavour to oregano, and added to meat and vegetable preserves.

OREGANO: popular in Italy, where it is added to meat and vegetable preserves.

CELERY LEAF: a favourite in the Mediterranean, has a strong celery flavour.

SAVORY: its pungent taste is rather like thyme; often used in sausages.

Green basil

Purple basil

BASIL: has a superb perfume and a pleasant, peppery taste. Use to flavour oil or with tomatoes.

Common thyme

BORAGE: has a fresh cucumber flavour. The flowers can be candied or added to drinks.

Lemon thyme

THYME: a powerful herb with antiseptic properties. Add to bouquets garnis and preserved meats.

ROSEMARY: good both fresh and dried in marinades and oils or with meat.

Variegated mint

Flat-leaf parsley

Curly parsley

MINT: a vast family of aromatic herbs, with widely differing flavours. Use to add a fresh note to chutneys and sausages.

DILL: associated with northern Europe, where it is added to cucumber and fish pickles and preserves.

Applemint

Spearmint

PARSLEY: essential in bouquets garnis and should always be fresh. The flat-leaf variety has a stronger, more refreshing flavour.

PICKLING IN VINEGAR

THERE ARE TWO STAGES to pickling in vinegar. First the ingredients are salted to draw out excess moisture that would otherwise dilute the vinegar. This is done either by dry-salting or by steeping in a strong saline solution. Vegetables should be soaked for 12–48 hours, depending on size, and kept in a cool place. In hot climates it is advisable to change the salt solution daily as it tends to ferment. The second stage is to cover the vegetables with vinegar, which can be plain, spiced or sweet (see pages 129 and 130). Flavourings, such as dried chillies, peppercorns and mustard seeds, are usually added. If you like crunchy pickles, leave the vinegar to cool before pouring it in; for a softer pickle, use boiling vinegar. Pickled green vegetables tend to lose their colour with keeping but blanching them briefly will combat this to some extent. A little bicarbonate of soda can be added to the water to preserve their colour (1 teaspoon for every 500ml/17fl oz water) but it does destroy vitamins in the vegetables so is not ideal. Pickled Onions are shown below, but other vegetables can be prepared in the same way.

Pickled Onions
(See page 92 for recipe.)

1 For easy peeling, pour boiling water over the onions and leave until cool enough to handle. Peel off the skins and place the onions in a glass bowl.

2 Make enough strong brine to cover the onions, using 75g (2½ oz) salt for each litre (1¾ pints) water. Pour this over the onions, weight down (see page 46) and leave in a cool place for 24 hours.

3 The next day, rinse the onions well to remove the salt and arrange in hot sterilized jars with the mustard seeds, bay leaves and chillies, if desired.

4 To make a flavoured vinegar, prepare a spice bag (see page 47) and place in a non-corrosive pan with the vinegar of your choice. Bring to the boil and boil for about 5 minutes. For a fuller flavour, leave to cool, then discard the spice bag and bring the vinegar to the boil once more.

TIE THE SPICE BAG to the side of the pan for easy removal

5 Pour the boiling vinegar over the onions, making sure they are completely submerged in the pickling liquid. Weight down (see page 46) and seal the jars with vinegar-proof lids (see page 43). Store in a cool, dark place. The onions will be ready to eat in 3–4 weeks.

POUR ENOUGH boiling vinegar over the onions to cover them. For crunchier pickles, allow the vinegar to cool first

Shelf life
2 years

SERVING

SUGGESTION

Traditionally, Pickled Onions are eaten with bread and cheese, but they can also be used to garnish a cheese flan.

53

PRESERVING IN OIL

ALTHOUGH OIL IS NOT technically a preservative it does act as a good sealant, protecting the steeped ingredients from exposure to the air and therefore deterioration. Because the food is not fully preserved, it is best to process it first — by salting, cooking, marinating in vinegar or, as in the recipe below, making it into cheese. Use a good-quality mild oil as a strong-tasting one can be overwhelming. I prefer a light olive oil combined with a milder type, such as groundnut or grapeseed. Herbs and whole spices are frequently added to the jar for extra flavour. Any oil left over after the preserved contents have been eaten can be used in salads, stews or soups, or drizzled over grilled food.

Labna (Soft Cheese) — *(See page 108 for recipe.)*

1 Put the yogurt in a large bowl with the olive oil, lemon rind and juice and the dried mint and thyme, if desired. Beat well with a wooden spoon until everything is amalgamated.

2 Line a large bowl with a double layer of muslin or cheesecloth, leaving plenty of material overlapping the sides. Pour in the yogurt mixture.

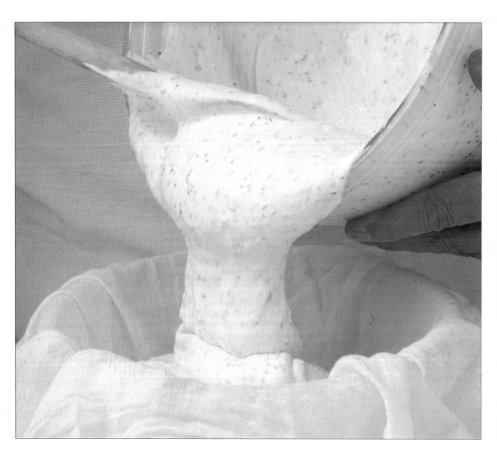

3 Tie the ends of the muslin together and hang it over the bowl. Leave to drain in a cool place, such as a larder or an unheated room (between 6–8°C/42–46°F), for 2–3 days in winter or 2 days in summer. On hot days, you may need to refrigerate the mixture.

LIGHTLY ROLL the cheese into a ball on the palm of your hand

4 Chill the mixture until firm; this makes it easier to handle. Using your fingers, shape the resulting cheese into 4cm (1½in) balls.

5 Chill the cheese balls again if necessary, so they retain their shape, then arrange them in the sterilized, wide-necked jar.

6 Top up with olive oil, making sure that there are no air pockets and the cheese is completely covered. The cheese is ready to eat immediately but improves with keeping, soaking up the flavour of the oil.

SERVING SUGGESTION

Serve the Labna drizzled with oil as an appetizer, with raw vegetables and pitta bread.

 Shelf life 6 months

MAKING KETCHUP

KETCHUP ORIGINALLY came from China, where, many centuries ago, it was the liquid in which fish had been pickled and was popular among seafarers for pepping up their boring diet of rice gruel. It was brought to Europe at the beginning of the eighteenth century by merchants returning from the Orient. Ketchup, or rather tomato ketchup in particular, quickly became the most popular condiment in the world. Homemade ketchup is an altogether superior product compared with the bland, sweet commercial varieties. It can be made from many other fruit and vegetables besides tomatoes; especially good are red peppers (as shown here) mushrooms, peaches, apples, pears and plums.

Red Pepper Ketchup
(See page 113 for recipe.)

1 Either roast the peppers over an open flame or grill them for 5–7 minutes, until evenly charred. Put in a plastic bag for 5 minutes (this makes peeling easier).

2 Remove the peppers from the bag and rub off the skin with your fingers under cold running water. Remove the core and seeds and wash the peppers well.

3 Finely chop the pepper flesh, using a knife or a food processor, along with the shallots or onions, apples and chillies, if desired.

4 Make a herb bundle and spice bag (see page 47). Place in a non-corrosive preserving pan with the vegetables and enough water to cover. Bring to the boil, then simmer for 25 minutes, or until soft.

5 Leave to cool, then discard the herbs and spice bag. Pass the mixture through a food mill or sieve.

SERVING SUGGESTION

Serve Red Pepper Ketchup with grilled red mullet. It also makes an excellent pasta sauce.

6 Place the resulting purée in the cleaned preserving pan and add the vinegar, sugar and salt. Bring to the boil, stirring until the sugar has dissolved, then simmer for 1–1½ hours, until it is reduced by half.

BOTTLES WITH CORKS need to be sealed with wax to keep them airtight

A FUNNEL is the easiest way to fill bottles

7 Mix the arrowroot or cornflour to a paste with a little vinegar and stir into the sauce. Boil for 1–2 minutes, until slightly thickened.

Shelf life
4–5 months, refrigerated; 1 year, heat processed

8 Pour the ketchup into hot sterilized bottles and seal. Heat process (see pages 44–45), then leave to cool. Check the seals and dip corks in wax (see page 43).

MAKING CHUTNEY

IN INDIA the word "chutney" refers to a wide range of products, from slow-cooked preserves that are matured for several weeks before use to simple relishes made from finely chopped raw ingredients that are ready to eat after a few hours' marinating. What they all have in common is the inclusion of acid, spices and a sweetener. Shown below is the method for making a traditional cooked chutney. It is a very straightforward recipe and can be based on almost any combination of fruit and vegetables; here, pumpkins are used. Although any type of vinegar is suitable, I prefer to use cider vinegar, as its fruity flavour seems particularly appropriate for chutney.

Pumpkin Chutney (See page 120 for recipe.)

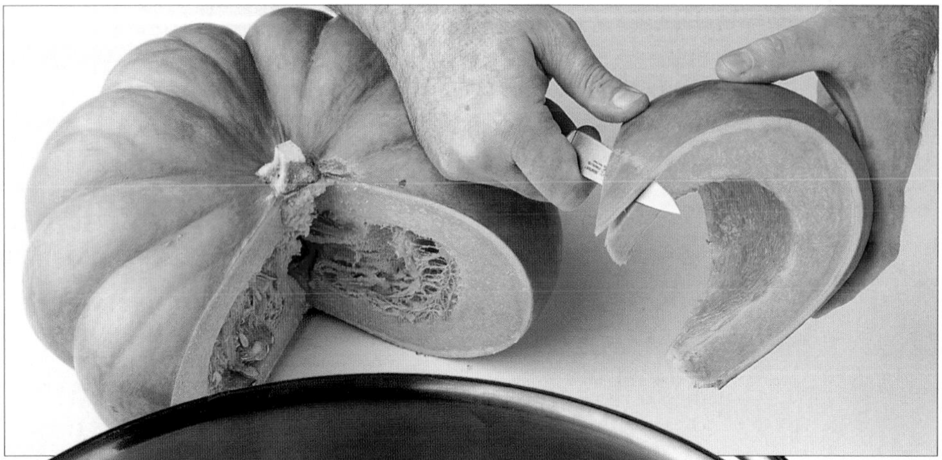

1 Cut the pumpkin into quarters, then peel and remove the seeds and fibres. Cut the flesh into 2.5cm (1in) cubes. (Do not throw away the seeds – they make a delicious and healthy snack. Wash them well to remove any fibres, then dry them in the sun or a cool oven.)

2 Put the pumpkin in a non-corrosive preserving pan with the chopped apples, fresh ginger, chillies, mustard seeds, vinegar and salt and mix well. If you prefer a hotter chutney, do not deseed the chillies.

3 Bring to the boil, then reduce the heat and simmer gently for 20–25 minutes, or until the pumpkin is just soft but not mushy. Stir occasionally to prevent it sticking. If the mixture seems dry, add a little more vinegar or water.

4 Add the soft brown sugar, stirring until it has dissolved, then bring the mixture back to the boil. The sugar prevents the pumpkin from softening any further, so if you prefer a softer product cook the pumpkin for a little longer before adding the sugar.

5 Cook for 50–60 minutes, until the mixture is thick and most of the liquid has evaporated. Stir frequently to prevent it sticking.

Shelf life
2 years

6 Ladle through a funnel into hot sterilized jars, then seal immediately. The chutney will be ready to eat in about 3 weeks, but improves with longer keeping. Store in a cool, dark place.

SERVING SUGGESTION

Serve Pumpkin Chutney with lamb curry and steamed basmati rice.

DRYING FRUIT & VEGETABLES

DRIED FRUIT AND VEGETABLES make convenient storecupboard stand-bys: they have a prolonged shelf life and are easy to use as they simply require steeping in hot water to rehydrate. Vegetables can be added to casseroles and soups, while fruit are ideal for desserts and baking – and as the drying process concentrates flavours, dried fruit also make a delicious snack on their own. In hot, sunny weather produce can be dried outside in the full sun, over a period of 2–3 days. Lay it out on trays and cover with muslin, bringing the trays inside at night to protect against dew. Alternatively, hang produce up to dry in an airy room (see opposite). If you dry fruit and vegetables completely, until brittle, they will keep indefinitely; however, I prefer to dry fruit until most of the moisture has evaporated but they are still pliable. In this state they will keep for up to 2 months. In unsuitable weather, drying can be carried out in an oven, as shown below using peaches (for oven-drying other fruit, see page 185). For drying large quantities of produce on a regular basis, it is best to use a dehydrator (see page 40).

Oven-drying Peaches

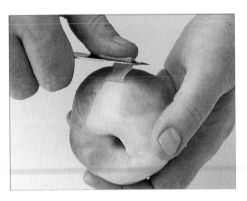

1 Blanch some peaches in boiling water for a few seconds (see page 46). Refresh in cold water, then peel off the skin.

2 Halve the peaches, remove the stones and either leave as they are, or slice into quarters or even smaller pieces.

3 As the fruit are prepared, put them in a bowl of acidulated water (see Dips, opposite), then lift out and drain well.

4 Arrange the peaches flat-side down on a wire rack set over a foil-lined baking tray. Put in an oven preheated to 110°C/225°F/gas ¼, leaving the door slightly ajar.

5 Peach halves will take 24–36 hours to dry, quarters about 12–16 hours and smaller pieces 8–12 hours. Turn the peaches over when they are half-way through drying.

6 To store the peaches, arrange them in layers, between pieces of waxed paper, in an airtight container. Store in a cool place and keep in the dark if the container is transparent.

Air-drying Vegetables

String mushrooms and chillies on cotton thread and hang up in the sun or in an airy room for 2 weeks, until shrivelled and dry.

STORE DRIED VEGETABLES in cloth or paper bags to allow any remaining moisture to evaporate

ACIDULATED AND HONEY DIPS

Some fruit discolour during drying (see Drying Chart, page 185). To prevent this, coat with an acidulated dip or a honey dip first.
• For an acidulated dip, add 6 tablespoons lemon juice or 2 tablespoons ascorbic acid crystals or powder to 1 litre (1¾ pints) warm water and mix thoroughly.
• For a honey dip, blend 250g (8oz) honey and 250g (8oz) sugar with 250ml (8fl oz) water in a heavy-based saucepan. Stir over a low heat to dissolve the sugar, then bring to the boil. Boil for a second or two, then remove from the heat and leave until cold.

TIPS

• Use good-quality fresh fruit that are just ripe and unblemished.
• For oven-drying, remember to turn produce over half-way through the drying process, and to swap tray positions around.
• Make sure dried produce is completely cold before storing.
• Regularly check stored dried fruit and vegetables to make sure that no moisture has entered the container. If there is any sign of mould, the produce must be thrown away.

SERVING SUGGESTION

Dried Mushrooms can be rehydrated and used to make a sauce for pasta.

Shelf life
2 years, fully dried; 2 months, semi-dried

DRYING MEAT

IN THE DAYS BEFORE refrigeration, dried meat was more convenient than fresh; it kept for much longer and did not need cooking. Now that fresh meat is so readily available, the technique of drying meat is used more to add flavour. In hot, dry climates, meat can be dried outside, although this is not recommended in urban areas – it needs the fresh, clean breeze of country air. But ideally, for hygiene reasons, the meat should be dried indoors, in the oven if necessary. There are two main types of dried meat: Biltong, a South African speciality; and Jerky from North America. The drying technique is the same for both, but Jerky, unlike Biltong, is not cured before drying and originally was not flavoured either.

Ask your butcher to keep the meat in one piece, then freeze it for a few hours until it is just firm. This will make slicing a lot easier. Select only lean meat for drying – leg and back are the most suitable. Remove all traces of sinew and loose fat from the meat; they tend to go rancid with long keeping.

IMPORTANT INFORMATION

• The rules of proper hygiene should be followed strictly at all stages of preparation and storage (see page 42).
• The meat should be marinated in a cool place, preferably the bottom of the refrigerator.

• Discard the meat if it starts to smell "off" during the drying process.
• Check the stored meat regularly; if it goes mouldy or starts to smell "off", discard it immediately.

Biltong
(See page 139 for recipe.)

1 Using a sharp cook's knife, slice the meat along the grain into long strips about 5cm (2in) thick. If the meat was partially frozen, leave the slices to defrost.

2 For the marinade, put the salt, sugar, saltpetre, lightly toasted coriander seeds and crushed black pepper into a glass bowl and mix until evenly blended.

3 Sprinkle an earthenware baking dish with a layer of the salt mix. Add the meat and cover it with the remaining mix, rubbing it in well.

4 Spoon the vinegar evenly over the meat and rub the salt mix into both sides of the meat again. Cover the dish and leave to marinate in the bottom of the refrigerator for 6–8 hours. To ensure even curing, rub the meat again with the marinade after 3–4 hours.

5 After the meat has marinated in the cure it will become paler and stiffer. Lift the meat out of the cure and brush off any excess salt.

6 Press a meat hook through one end of the meat or make a hole in each piece and tie a loop of string through it. Hang it up in a cool, dry, dark, airy place (between 6–8°C/42–46°F) for 1½ weeks. After this time the Biltong will only be semi-dry, so its shelf life will be limited. Wrap in waxed paper, refrigerate and eat within 3 weeks.

THE MEAT will be a lot paler when it has finished marinating

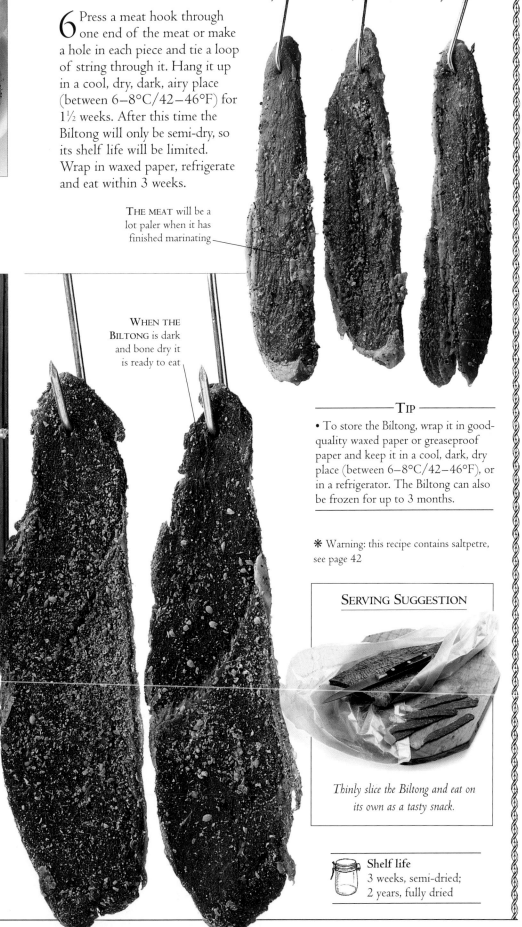

WHEN THE BILTONG is dark and bone dry it is ready to eat

7 For a longer lasting product, dry the meat further. To speed up the drying process, the Biltong can be dried in an oven instead. First line the bottom of the oven with aluminium foil to catch the drips. Place one of the oven shelves on the highest position and hang the meat from the bars. Dry the Biltong at the lowest possible oven setting, for 8–16 hours, until it is fully dry and dark, and splinters when bent in two.

—— TIP ——

• Do not cut off the "rind" of fat on the edge of the meat, as this acts as a protective layer while the Biltong is drying.

—— TIP ——

• To store the Biltong, wrap it in good-quality waxed paper or greaseproof paper and keep it in a cool, dark, dry place (between 6–8°C/42–46°F), or in a refrigerator. The Biltong can also be frozen for up to 3 months.

✷ Warning: this recipe contains saltpetre, see page 42

SERVING SUGGESTION

Thinly slice the Biltong and eat on its own as a tasty snack.

Shelf life
3 weeks, semi-dried;
2 years, fully dried

CURING HAM

ORIGINALLY, MEAT was salted to preserve it for the lean winter months – today, curing is used to give additional flavour to meat. There are two basic methods of curing meat (and fish): dry-curing, which preserves the flesh by burying it in salt (see Salt-cured Sprats, page 74); and wet- or brine-curing, when the meat is totally immersed in a saline solution. A softening agent, usually sugar, is added to the meat as the salt makes it tough, and aromatic herbs and spices are also included to impart their own special flavours. An important ingredient in any cure is saltpetre (see page 42), which inhibits the growth of bacteria and helps to maintain the appetizing pink colour of cured meats such as ham and pastrami. The recipe below produces a mild-flavoured ham and is also suitable for using with mutton.

IMPORTANT INFORMATION

• Buy the best quality and freshest meat you can from a reliable supplier.
• Do not attempt to cure meat in the summer, or if you do not have the proper facilities: all preparation and storage must be carried out at low temperatures, below 8°C (46°F).
• Always follow the preparation and storage procedures laid out in the recipes, and carefully observe the proper hygiene rules at all times (see page 42).
• The meat should have a pleasant smell at each stage of preparation; if it starts to smell "off", do not eat it.
• If the brine starts to smell "off", changes consistency or becomes "ropy", lift the ham out and rinse it well. Discard the brine and cover the meat with a fresh, cold brine.

Cured Ham

(See page 134 for recipe.)

1 Rub the pork with salt, making sure it is pushed into all the crevices. Place on a thin layer of salt in a dish and cover with the remaining salt. Refrigerate for 24 hours.

2 For the brine cure, put the water in a large pan, add the salt and the rest of the ingredients. Boil steadily for 10 minutes, then switch off the heat and allow the mixture to cool completely.

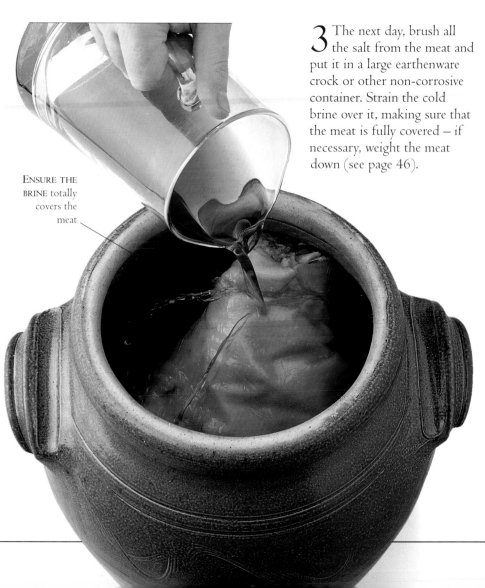

ENSURE THE BRINE totally covers the meat

3 The next day, brush all the salt from the meat and put it in a large earthenware crock or other non-corrosive container. Strain the cold brine over it, making sure that the meat is fully covered – if necessary, weight the meat down (see page 46).

4 Cover with a lid or clingfilm and leave in a cool place, between 6–8°C (42–46°F), for 2–2½ weeks. Check the meat every day to ensure the brine has not deteriorated (see Important Information, opposite).

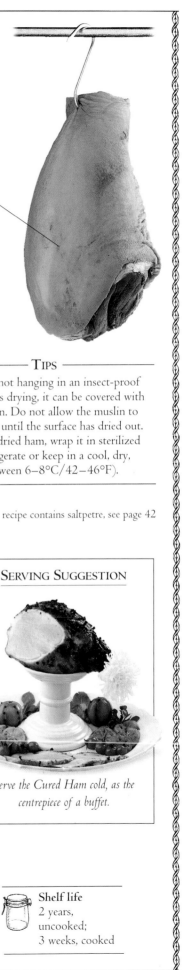

AFTER HANGING for 2–3 days, the surface of the ham will dry out

5 Remove the meat from the brine, rinse it well, then dry. Insert a meat hook into the knuckle end of the leg and hang it up in a cool, dry, dark, airy place (between 6–8°C/42–46°F) for 2–3 days.

TIPS

• If the ham is not hanging in an insect-proof larder while it is drying, it can be covered with sterilized muslin. Do not allow the muslin to touch the meat until the surface has dried out.
• To store the dried ham, wrap it in sterilized calico and refrigerate or keep in a cool, dry, dark place (between 6–8°C/42–46°F).

✱ Warning: this recipe contains saltpetre, see page 42

6 After the ham has hung for 2–3 days it can be cooked (see page 134 for recipe). To give the ham a stronger flavour, continue the hanging process, following step 7, below.

THE COLOUR of the skin will darken during drying

7 Mix the flour, salt and water together to make a paste. Spread it over all the exposed meat, to seal, then hang the ham for a further 2–2½ weeks. If wished, the ham can be smoked before cooking.

SERVING SUGGESTION

Serve the Cured Ham cold, as the centrepiece of a buffet.

Shelf life
2 years, uncooked;
3 weeks, cooked

SMOKING FISH

SMOKING IS ONE of the most ancient preserving techniques: its anti-bacterial and anti-fungal properties help to inhibit the growth of moulds, and it adds its own distinctive flavour to all types of fish (and meat). As smoking does not fully preserve foods, the produce needs to be cured first. There are two methods of smoking: cold-smoking, when the smoke does not exceed a temperature of 28°C (82°F), and the final product's texture is not altered as the flesh remains raw; and hot-smoking, carried out at a temperature no lower than 55°C (130°F), when the flesh is semi- or fully cooked. Most types of wood can be used for smoking, but resinous ones, such as pine, should be avoided or used sparingly as they impart a strong, bitter taste. Hard fruit woods, like apple, pear and cherry, as well as oak and hickory and the exotic mesquite, are especially good. Aromatic herbs and spices can be added to the wood to give extra flavour. After mastering the basic technique, experiment to create your own flavour combinations. Smokers are available in several shapes and sizes. Always follow the manufacturer's instructions.

Smoked Salmon

(See page 152 for recipe.)

1 To fillet the salmon, cut around the head on one side, using a sharp filleting knife. Slide the knife between the flesh and the backbone, keeping it as close to the bone as possible, and slice off the fillet in one piece.

2 Turn the salmon over and repeat the filleting procedure on the other side. Run your fingers along each fillet to locate all the remaining bones, then remove them with tweezers. Rinse the fillets and dry well.

3 Sprinkle some of the sea salt and sugar into a non-corrosive container to form a 5mm (¼ in) layer. Lay one fillet skin-side down on top, then sprinkle with another layer, about 1cm (½ in) thick, thinning the mixture towards the tail end.

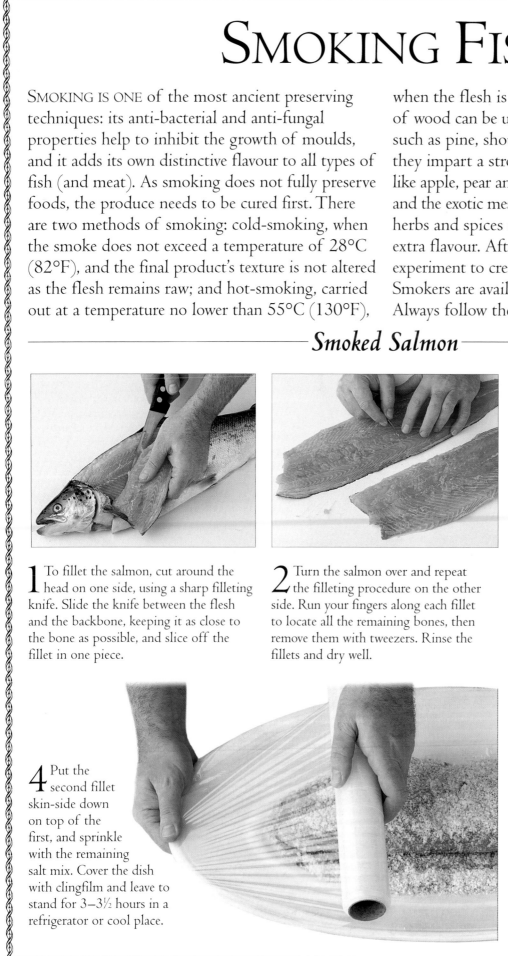

4 Put the second fillet skin-side down on top of the first, and sprinkle with the remaining salt mix. Cover the dish with clingfilm and leave to stand for 3–3½ hours in a refrigerator or cool place.

5 Remove the salmon from the salt mix and rinse under cold running water, to remove the excess salt. Dry well with paper towels. Push a wooden skewer through the back of each fillet at the head end.

6 Brush both sides of each fillet with the whisky and hang up to dry in a cool, dry place for about 24 hours, or until the sides of the fish are almost dry to the touch and have developed a shiny salt glaze.

THE SALMON will have a glaze by the time it is ready to be smoked

7 Put the fillets on a rack in the smoker and either cold-smoke at 28°C (82°F) for 3–4 hours, or hot-smoke at 55°C (130°F) for 2–3 hours. Remove the salmon from the smoker and allow to cool completely.

LOOP A PIECE of string around the skewer to hang the fish up

WRAP THE SALMON in waxed paper to store

TIPS

• To store the salmon, slide each fillet on to a piece of foil-wrapped card for support, then wrap well in good-quality waxed paper or more foil. Refrigerate the salmon for 24 hours before serving, to allow it to mature.

• To serve cold-smoked salmon, cut it into very thin slices using a long serrated knife at a 45° angle. For hot-smoked salmon, cut the fillets into vertical slices about 5mm (¼in) thick.

Shelf life
3 weeks, refrigerated

SERVING SUGGESTION

Cold-smoked Salmon and cream cheese make a delicious filling for bagels.

PLACE THE SALMON on a piece of foil-covered card to make it easier to lift

CURING SAUSAGES

DRIED SAUSAGES are probably one of the most ingenious inventions of the charcutier – a tasty way of using up scraps of meat left over after jointing a carcass. Making dried sausages at home is relatively easy, but should be attempted only if you have the right environment to work in. Your kitchen must be cool, between 10–12°C (50–54°F), scrupulously clean, and all equipment must be sterilized before use (see page 42). A cool, dry and dark area (between 6–8°C/42–46°F) should be available for drying the sausages – I use a cool larder but a clean, dry cellar or unheated room would also be suitable.

Always use the freshest possible ingredients and keep the meat chilled at all times – temperature affects the keeping quality of the sausages and also plays an important part in their final texture (see page 64). Organic, free-range meat gives the best flavour and is drier and firmer to work with. Sausage-making requires some specialist equipment – a strong mincer and a sausage maker, or mincer and sausage funnel attachments for a food mixer (see Equipment, page 39) for grinding the meat and filling the casings. Sausage casings are available in different lengths from some butchers or specialist suppliers (see page 192).

Garlic and Herb Salami *(See page 138 for recipe.)*

 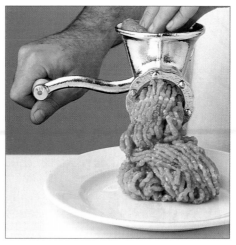 

1 Put the meat in a large bowl, sprinkle with the salt, saltpetre and vodka and mix together well with your hands. Cover and refrigerate for 12 hours.

2 Put the meat through the fine plate of a mincer, and the fat through the coarse plate. Mix together well, adding any liquid left in the bowl.

3 Add the garlic, thyme, whole and ground black peppercorns, coriander seeds and allspice. Mix thoroughly but lightly, then chill for at least 2 hours.

4 Meanwhile, prepare the casing. Rinse it to remove the excess salt, then soak in cold water for 30 minutes. Next, rinse the inside of the casing by fitting it over a slow-running cold tap and allowing the water to run through it for a few seconds.

5 Put the casing in a bowl of water, add the vinegar and leave to soak until needed.

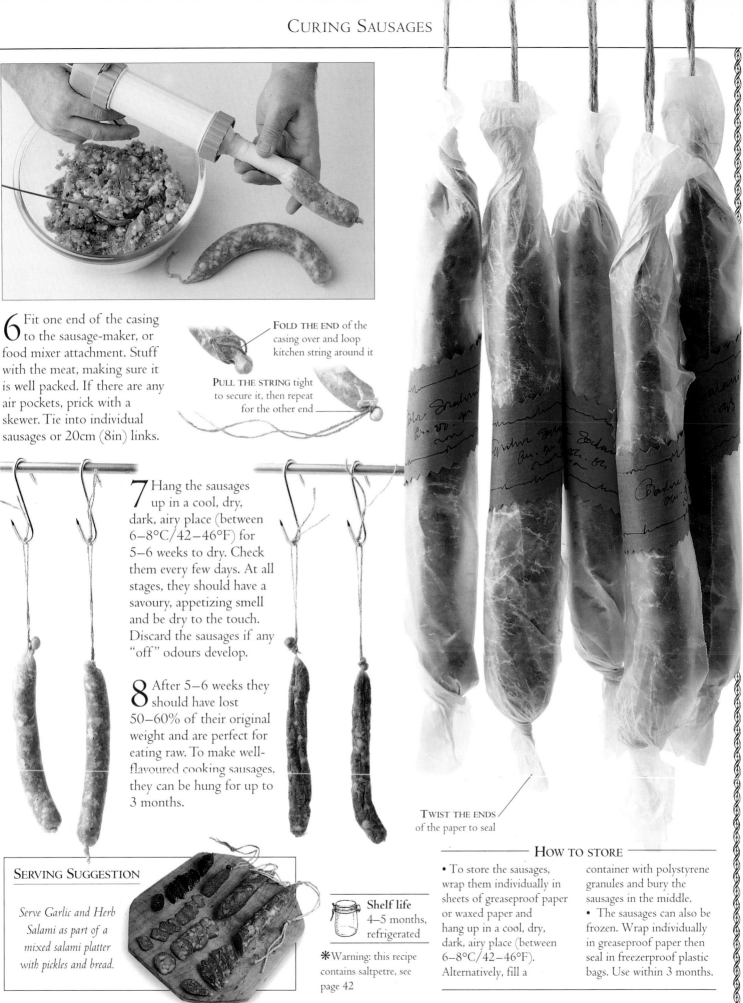

6 Fit one end of the casing to the sausage-maker, or food mixer attachment. Stuff with the meat, making sure it is well packed. If there are any air pockets, prick with a skewer. Tie into individual sausages or 20cm (8in) links.

FOLD THE END of the casing over and loop kitchen string around it

PULL THE STRING tight to secure it, then repeat for the other end

7 Hang the sausages up in a cool, dry, dark, airy place (between 6–8°C/42–46°F) for 5–6 weeks to dry. Check them every few days. At all stages, they should have a savoury, appetizing smell and be dry to the touch. Discard the sausages if any "off" odours develop.

8 After 5–6 weeks they should have lost 50–60% of their original weight and are perfect for eating raw. To make well-flavoured cooking sausages, they can be hung for up to 3 months.

TWIST THE ENDS of the paper to seal

SERVING SUGGESTION

Serve Garlic and Herb Salami as part of a mixed salami platter with pickles and bread.

Shelf life
4–5 months, refrigerated

✽Warning: this recipe contains saltpetre, see page 42

HOW TO STORE

• To store the sausages, wrap them individually in sheets of greaseproof paper or waxed paper and hang up in a cool, dry, dark, airy place (between 6–8°C/42–46°F). Alternatively, fill a container with polystyrene granules and bury the sausages in the middle.
• The sausages can also be frozen. Wrap individually in greaseproof paper then seal in freezerproof plastic bags. Use within 3 months.

MAKING PATE

THERE ARE FEW THINGS more delicious than a slice of homemade pâté, a chunk of fresh bread and a glass of wine. Simple pâtés are a great stand-by, as well as being inexpensive and easy to make. They are preserved by sealing the surface with fat, which excludes air and moisture and therefore slows down the activity of bacteria. Before the days of refrigeration, pâtés were stored in cold cellars for up to 3 months, but now it is recommended that they are refrigerated and used within 4 weeks. Many pâtés, especially highly flavoured ones, should not be kept for more than 3 weeks, as their flavour quickly deteriorates. Always make sure pâtés are visually pleasing, since cooked meat can turn an unattractive shade of grey. The pink colour of commercially produced pâté is usually due to the inclusion of sodium nitrate (saltpetre – see page 42). The recipe below uses bacon to lend a pinkish hue.

Pâté de Campagne

(See page 144 for recipe.)

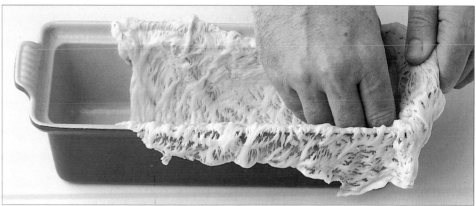

1 Mix together the pork, liver and bacon and put through the fine plate of a mincer. Add the garlic, herbs, spices, seasoning, prunes, white wine and brandy and mix well. Cover and refrigerate for 3–4 hours to allow the flavours to develop.

2 Line the terrine with caul fat, leaving an overhang of at least 2.5cm (1in) so it can be folded over to cover the pâté. Alternatively, line it with bacon: remove the rinds then stretch the rashers with the back of a knife blade. Overlap the bacon in the dish and leave the ends to overhang.

LINING WITH BACON

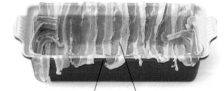

ALLOW THE ENDS of the bacon to hang over the edge of the terrine

OVERLAP THE BACON rashers to form a seal

3 Fill the dish with the meat, pushing it well into the corners, then rap it on a work surface to release any air pockets. Fold over the flaps of caul or bacon and place the lemon or orange slices and bay leaves on top. Cover with the lid or foil.

4 Put the terrine in a roasting tin filled with enough warm water to come half-way up the sides of the dish. Cook in an oven preheated to 160°C/ 325°F/gas 3 for 1½–2 hours, until the pâté has shrunk from the sides of the dish and is surrounded by liquid fat.

5 Leave the pâté to cool, then cover with a piece of card wrapped in foil and weight down (see page 46), to make it easier to slice. Refrigerate overnight.

6 The next day, remove the lemon or orange slices and bay leaves, run a hot knife blade around the edge of the terrine and carefully unmould the pâté. Wipe off all traces of the jelly surrounding the meat with paper towels.

7 Pour melted lard over the base of the terrine in a layer about 1cm (½ in) thick. Leave to set, then place the pâté on top and pour over enough melted lard to cover the pâté by about 1cm (½ in). Cover with the lid or foil and refrigerate. Leave to mature for 2–3 days before serving.

Shelf life
1 month,
refrigerated

GARNISH WITH
juniper berries,
bay leaves and
cranberries

SERVING SUGGESTION

Serve Pâté de Campagne with fresh country bread, salad and pickle.

POTTING

THE VICTORIANS used potting as a convenient means of preserving any leftover meat, adding flavourings such as pepper, cayenne, nutmeg or anchovy paste. Potting preserves food by insulating it from the air with a layer of solid fat. In the past this tended to be lard or mutton fat, but now clarified butter is more common. The ingredients to be potted are cooked first and are then usually pounded to a smooth paste with some butter or other fat. If you are potting meat, use only the best cuts and make sure you trim away any sinew and connective tissue. Illustrated below is Potted Venison. Other game, poultry, fish and cheese can all be preserved in the same way.

Potted Venison

(See page 146 for recipe.)

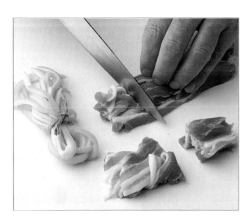

1 Trim the rinds from the bacon rashers, tie them together with string and set aside. Coarsely chop the bacon. Make a herb bundle with the thyme, sage, bay leaf and lemon rind (see page 47).

2 Put the bacon and rinds in the casserole with the venison, butter, garlic, juniper berries, pepper, mace, herbs and red wine. Cover and bake in an oven preheated to 160°C/325°F/gas 3 for 2½–3 hours, until the meat is very tender.

3 Remove the herbs, mace and the bacon rinds and process the meat to a smooth paste in a food processor.

4 Pack the paste into an earthenware dish or individual ramekins and leave to cool completely. Refrigerate for 2–3 hours.

5 Pour clarified butter over the potted venison until it forms a layer about 1cm (½in) thick. Refrigerate until the butter has set. Garnish with bay leaves and cranberries, if liked.

SERVING SUGGESTION

Serve Potted Venison with watercress and melba toast.

A DECORATIVE GARNISH gives the meat paste an attractive appearance

HOW TO CLARIFY BUTTER

To clarify the butter for sealing potted goods and pâtés, melt it in a small saucepan over a very low heat, then let it foam for a few seconds. Skim the froth from the surface and leave the butter to cool slightly. Pour the cooled butter through a muslin-lined sieve, leaving the milky sediment in the bottom of the pan. If you rinse the muslin in cold water before use and wring it out well, this helps to catch any remaining froth.

TO ENSURE A good seal, the butter should cover the meat by about 1cm (½in)

Shelf life
1 month, refrigerated

SALTING

SALT IS a natural dehydrator. It preserves by drawing moisture out of food, thus inhibiting the growth of bacteria. The technique of salting has played an essential role in the history of how and what we eat. For centuries salted fish, mainly herring, was the staple food of Europe. Demand for this humble, silvery fish started wars and made the fortunes of many nations. A good source of protein and vitamins A, B and D, salt-cured fish can still make a useful contribution to our diet. The recipe below uses sprats, but works well with herrings and anchovies, too. Choose perfectly fresh fish with a good shiny skin. Leaving the heads on results in a stronger flavour, since they contain a lot of oil.

Salt-cured Sprats — *(See page 153 for recipe.)*

1 Using a small, sharp pair of scissors, make a little cut in each fish just below the gills.

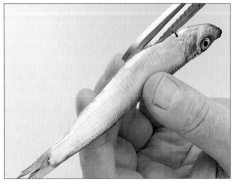

2 Next, carefully snip right down the belly of each fish from gills to tail and open out the cut slightly.

3 Pull out the stomach contents with your fingers and discard. Rinse the fish under cold running water.

4 Sprinkle a little fine salt in the cavity of each fish and all over the outside, rubbing the salt well into the flesh.

5 Arrange the fish in layers in a shallow dish, adding a thin sprinkling of the fine salt between each layer. Cover and refrigerate for 2–3 hours, until some of the moisture has been drawn off.

— TO KEEP THE FISH —

• First remove the oil that will have accumulated on top. If not enough brine has developed to cover the fish, top it up with a strong salt solution made with equal quantities of salt and water. Seal the container tightly and store in a cool, dark place.

• When you want to use the sprats, remove them from the brine and soak for a few hours in water or a mixture of milk and water.

SERVING SUGGESTION

Dress Salt-cured Sprats in oil and Blackcurrant Vinegar (see recipe, page 128) and serve garnished with parsley and finely diced red onion.

6 Lift out the fish and dry thoroughly on paper towels.

Shelf life
2 years

7 Sprinkle a layer of the pickling salt over the base of a large container. Arrange some fish on top with a bay leaf and a few peppercorns. Cover with a 5mm (¼in) layer of pickling salt. Repeat the layers, finishing with a layer of salt.

8 Have ready a plate that just fits the opening of the container. Place it over the fish and weight down – a bottle filled with water is ideal. Cover and refrigerate or leave in a cool, dark place (between 6–8°C/42–46°F) for one week before eating.

MAKING JAM

JAM-MAKING is one of the simplest methods of preserving; almost any fruit can be used, and a surprising number of vegetables. Sugar reacts with pectin and acid to make a jelly, and also works as a preservative as its high concentration in the jam prevents the growth of moulds. The crucial factor is to have a balance of acidity and pectin, which creates a good set. Many fruits naturally have the right balance (see Preserving Chart, page 184), but some need a little help. You can do this by adding lemon juice and pectin-rich fruit, such as apples, or a homemade pectin stock (see recipe, page 47); alternatively, you can buy a commercially prepared liquid pectin. If you have to increase the pectin level by a large amount, it is necessary to raise the sugar content accordingly: for example, if the addition of pectin stock increases the volume of fruit pulp by a third, then a third more sugar must be added. The amount of sugar in the following jam recipes can be reduced by up to 30 per cent, if desired. Generally this results in a fresher-flavoured product, but the jam will be softer and have a much shorter shelf life; it must be kept refrigerated as the proportion of sugar will not be high enough to prevent mould growth.

TESTING FOR THE SET

A jam is ready for potting when it reaches the setting point. This can be tested in any of the following ways:

Sugar thermometer
Warm the sugar thermometer in a bowl of hot water before using it, or it could break. Clip it on to the side of the preserving pan, making sure the bottom end is not touching the base of the pan. Boil the jam at a good rolling boil, until the thermometer registers 105°C (220°F).

Flake test
Dip a metal spoon into the jam, then turn it so that the jam runs off the side. The drops should run together and fall from the spoon in flat flakes or sheets.

Wrinkle test
Pour a little hot jam on to a cold saucer and leave it for a few minutes to cool. Push the jam with a finger; if it wrinkles it has reached the setting point.

Exotic Fruit Jam (See page 159 for recipe.)

1 Finely chop the peeled and cored pineapple and apple in a food processor. Transfer to the preserving pan and add the canned or fresh lychee halves, water, lemon rind and juice.

2 Bring the mixture to the boil, then reduce the heat and simmer for 20–25 minutes, or until the apples have turned to a pulp and the pineapple pieces have softened.

3 Add the preserving sugar to the pan and stir well over a medium heat until it has completely dissolved. Increase the heat and bring the mixture to a rapid, rolling boil.

4 Boil the fruit mixture rapidly for 20–25 minutes, stirring frequently, until the setting point is reached (see Testing for the Set, opposite). Skim off any froth as it rises to the surface of the jam.

THE JAM WILL start to thicken as it reaches the setting point

5 Remove the pan from the heat and leave for a few minutes to allow the jam to settle. Skim again if necessary.

6 Ladle the jam into hot sterilized jars (see page 42), then seal immediately with waxed paper discs and cellophane seals (see page 43).

SERVING SUGGESTION

Serve Exotic Fruit Jam with fresh scones and cream.

Shelf life
2 years

MAKING FRUIT CURD

A CURD IS A CURIOUS mixture, something between a hollandaise sauce and an egg custard. It consists of fruit pulp or juice sweetened with sugar and thickened with eggs and butter. The traditional lemon curd has been popular since Edwardian times, but other citrus fruit and even exotic fruit can be used. An important point to remember when making curd is that patience is needed as you wait for it to thicken, which can take anything up to 45 minutes. Heat it very gently over a pan of barely simmering water and stir frequently so the heat is well distributed. Do not try to hurry the process by increasing the heat: like an egg custard, it will curdle if boiled, and cannot be rescued.

Pink Grapefruit Curd
(See page 173 for recipe.)

1 Grate the rind of one grapefruit on the fine side of a hand grater, then squeeze the juice.

2 Using a sharp knife, cut off all the peel and pith from the other grapefruit, following the curve of the fruit.

3 Carefully cut out all the segments of flesh from between the membranes and chop them coarsely.

ADD THE BUTTER in pieces so that it melts quickly

4 Put all the grapefruit juice, zest and flesh in a saucepan with the lemon juice, sugar and butter. Heat gently until the butter has melted, then transfer the mixture to a double boiler or a bowl placed over a pan of barely simmering water.

5 Strain the beaten eggs into the fruit mixture through a fine mesh sieve, stirring constantly with a wooden spoon to ensure they are evenly incorporated.

SIEVE IN THE beaten eggs to avoid lumps forming in the curd

6 Cook the mixture very gently, stirring frequently, for 25–45 minutes, until it is thick enough to coat the back of the spoon. Do not allow the mixture to boil or it will curdle.

TIP

• Curd does not have a long shelf life: it can be refrigerated for 3 months. To extend its shelf life 6 months, heat process for 5 minutes (see pages 44–45) after potting.

7 Remove the pan from the heat, or take the bowl off the pan of simmering water, and stir in the orange-flower water.

8 Ladle the curd into warm sterilized jars (see page 42), then seal immediately with waxed paper discs and cellophane seals (see page 43).

SERVING SUGGESTION

Use Pink Grapefruit Curd to fill cakes, tarts and pavlovas.

Shelf life
3 months, refrigerated; 6 months, if heat processed

MAKING JELLY

JELLY-MAKING IS a miraculous process – dull and cloudy fruit juice is transformed into a clear, jewel-like substance. Three elements are necessary to achieve this: pectin, which is found in varying degrees in all fruit (see Preserving Chart, page 184), acidity and sugar. Low-pectin fruit such as cherries, peaches and strawberries are usually supplemented with pectin-rich ones such as apples, cranberries, citrus fruit or currants. Raspberries, used below, have a medium pectin content, so apples are included to help achieve a set. Some recipes for jelly recommend leaving the pulp to drip overnight, but this is usually unnecessary. Leave it until it stops dripping, which normally takes a few hours.

— Raspberry Jelly — (See page 166 for recipe.)

1 Pick over the raspberries, washing them only if necessary. Remove the cores from the apples and set aside. Coarsely chop the apples.

2 Put the apples and raspberries in a food processor and process until finely chopped (you will probably need to do this in batches). Chopping the fruit in a food processor means that it requires less cooking, resulting in a jelly with a fresher, fruitier flavour.

3 Put the fruit and cores in a preserving pan with water to cover. Bring to the boil, then simmer for 20–30 minutes, until the fruit is soft and pulpy.

4 Pour the fruit and liquid into a sterilized jelly bag suspended over a large bowl. Leave for 2–3 hours, or until it stops dripping. Do not be tempted to squeeze the bag or the jelly will be cloudy.

5 Measure the juice and allow 500g (1lb) sugar for every 500ml (17fl oz) juice. Return the juice to the cleaned pan and add the sugar and lemon juice.

6 Heat gently, stirring from time to time with a wooden spoon, until the sugar has dissolved, then bring the liquid to a rapid boil.

ONCE THE MIXTURE has come to a rolling boil, froth will start to form on top as impurities rise to the surface

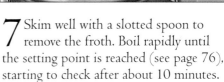

7 Skim well with a slotted spoon to remove the froth. Boil rapidly until the setting point is reached (see page 76), starting to check after about 10 minutes.

TIP

• To extract more liquid from the fruit after it has drained through the jelly bag, return the pulp to the preserving pan and add water to cover. Simmer gently for about 30 minutes, then drain as before. Add the juice to the first batch.

8 Ladle the jelly through a jam funnel into hot sterilized jars. Leave to cool until semi-set, then insert a geranium leaf into the centre of each jar and seal.

SERVING SUGGESTION

Serve Raspberry Jelly in an open sandwich with cold, sliced chicken breast.

 Shelf life
2 years

MAKING FRUIT CHEESE

FRUIT CHEESES and butters are probably the earliest type of sweet preserve, dating back to pre-Roman times when fruit pulp was mixed with honey and dried in the sun. Butters are made in the same way as cheeses but the cooking time is shorter and sometimes the proportion of sugar is lower, resulting in a softer, more spreadable mixture. A set is achieved by boiling out the moisture, which means that any fruit can be used since pectin levels do not matter. Cheeses and butters need long, slow cooking and should be stirred frequently towards the end as they burn easily. Quinces, used below, make the best cheese as they produce a beautifully fragrant dark amber preserve.

Quince Cheese

(See page 174 for recipe.)

1 Wash the quinces well to remove any fluff, then coarsely chop them. There is no need to core them as the mixture will be sieved.

2 Put the quinces in a preserving pan with enough water or dry cider to cover and add the lemon rind and juice. Bring to the boil, then reduce the heat and simmer for 30–45 minutes, until the fruit is very soft and pulpy.

3 Pass the mixture through a sieve or a food mill to purée.

4 To calculate how much sugar to add, spoon the purée into a measuring jug. Allow 400g (13oz) sugar for every 500ml (17fl oz) purée.

5 Return the quince purée to the pan and add the sugar. Slowly bring to the boil, stirring until the sugar has dissolved. Simmer for 2½–3 hours, stirring frequently. Quinces will turn a deep red colour with long cooking. After a while the mixture will become very thick and will start to "plop". It is ready when a wooden spoon drawn across the base of the pan leaves a clear channel. Remove from the heat and leave to cool slightly.

WITH LONG cooking, the fruit pulp will thicken and start to erupt

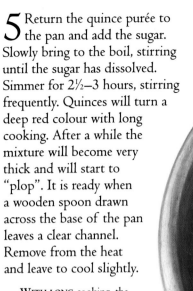

STORE BETWEEN layers of waxed paper in an airtight tin

6 Brush a deep baking tray generously with oil. Pour the cheese into the tray and smooth to an even layer, 2.5–4cm (1–1½ in) thick. Leave to cool completely, then cover with a cloth and keep in a warm, dry place for 24 hours.

7 Loosen the cheese with a palette knife and turn out on to a piece of baking parchment. Cut into squares or diamonds and dust with caster sugar. Arrange on baking trays, cover, and leave to dry.

SERVING SUGGESTION

Serve Quince Cheese as a sweetmeat, decorated with crystallized flowers (see page 183).

Shelf life
2 years

PRESERVING IN ALCOHOL

PURE ALCOHOL is the ideal preservative since nothing can grow in it. It can be used on its own or mixed with a heavy syrup. The combination of fruit and alcohol is sheer indulgence: first you eat the succulent, sweet fruit and then wash it down with the intoxicating perfumed liquor – a marriage made in heaven. This technique originated in the monasteries of medieval Europe. The recipe below uses peaches, although many other fruit, such as plums, apricots, cherries and figs, can be prepared in the same way. You can use almost any kind of spirit for preserving – rum, brandy and eau de vie are particularly good – but make sure that it is no less than 40 per cent proof.

Peaches in Brandy

(See page 178 for recipe.)

1 Blanch the peaches in boiling water for a few seconds. Refresh them in cold water for 1 minute, then peel off the skin with a small paring knife.

2 To remove the stone, run a sharp knife around the middle of each peach. Twist the top half loose and take out the stone with a knife.

3 Put the water and 500g (1lb) sugar in a large pan. Bring to the boil, skim any froth off the top, then reduce the heat and simmer for 5 minutes to make a syrup.

4 Gently slide the peach halves into the syrup. Return to the boil, then reduce the heat and simmer very gently for 4–5 minutes. Lift out the peaches with a slotted spoon and leave to cool. Meanwhile, make a spice bag (see page 47) with the vanilla pod, piece of cinnamon stick, cardamom pods and cloves.

TIE THE SPICES in a piece of muslin for easier removal

5 Put 600ml (1 pint) of the syrup in a pan with the remaining sugar and spice bag. Bring to the boil, skim, then boil rapidly until it reaches 104°C (219°F) on a sugar thermometer. Cool slightly, remove the spice bag, then stir in the brandy.

6 Set a cherry half in the cavity of each peach, if desired, and secure with a wooden cocktail stick. Pack the peaches loosely into the hot sterilized jar.

SERVING SUGGESTION

Serve Peaches in Brandy with crystallized violets (see page 183) for a delicate dessert.

7 Pour the syrup over the peaches, shaking the bottle gently to dispel any air pockets, then seal. The peaches will be ready to eat in 2 weeks, but improve with longer keeping.

Shelf life
2 years

CANDYING & CRYSTALLIZING

CANDYING CAN BE A LONG, slow process but the end result is well worth the effort: a spectacular array of translucent, glistening, jewel-like fruit. The origins of this technique are uncertain. Some maintain that it was developed in Renaissance Italy; a more likely theory is that it was invented in the royal kitchens of the Middle East during the tenth or eleventh century, and was then introduced into Europe by Arab merchants and returning Crusaders. The terms candying and crystallizing are often confused, but there is a distinction: candying refers to the process that replaces most of the fruit's moisture with a saturated sugar solution; while crystallizing (also known as glacéing) describes the sugar coating that is used as a finish for candied fruit or the process of preserving flowers. Fruit is candied by steeping it in an increasingly concentrated syrup, a process that must be carried out slowly, otherwise the fruit will shrink and become tough. Citrus peel and fruit low in moisture, such as pears and green figs, are often soaked first in a strong salt or lime solution, to enable them to absorb enough sugar.

Candied Pineapple Rings

(See page 182 for recipe.)

DAY ONE

1 Put the pineapple rings in a pan with enough water to cover. Bring to the boil, then reduce the heat and simmer for 15–20 minutes, until softened slightly. Drain well and place in a glass bowl.

2 Strain 1 litre (1¾ pints) of the cooking liquid into a pan. Add 250g (8oz) sugar and the lemon juice. Bring to the boil, stirring until dissolved, and boil rapidly for 2–3 minutes. Skim if necessary.

3 Ladle the hot sugar syrup over the pineapple rings, weight them down (see page 46), to ensure they are totally immersed, and leave to stand for 24 hours at room temperature.

DAY TWO

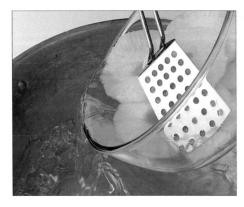

1 The next day, drain the pineapple rings well and return the sugar syrup to the pan.

2 Add 100g (3½oz) sugar to the syrup and bring to the boil, stirring until the sugar has dissolved.

3 Boil for 1–2 minutes, then skim well and ladle over the pineapple rings. Weight down and leave for 24 hours.

DAY THREE

Repeat Day Two.

DAY FOUR

Drain the pineapple rings, place the syrup in the pan and add 150g (5oz) of the sugar. Bring to the boil, stirring until the sugar has dissolved, and boil for 1–2 minutes, then skim and ladle over the pineapple. Weight down and leave for 24 hours.

DAY FIVE

Repeat Day Four.

DAYS SIX & SEVEN

Drain the pineapple rings, place the syrup in the pan and add the remaining sugar. Bring to the boil, stirring until the sugar has dissolved, and boil for 1–2 minutes, then skim and ladle over the pineapple. Weight down and leave for 48 hours.

DAY EIGHT

Put the fruit and syrup in a preserving pan and simmer for about 5 minutes. Lift out the pineapple rings with a slotted spoon. Arrange on a rack placed over a foil-lined baking tray. Allow to drain and cool.

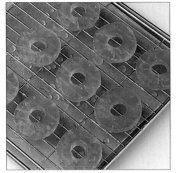 

Put the rack and tray in the oven preheated to 120°C/250°F/gas ½, leaving the door slightly ajar. Leave for 12–24 hours, until the fruit is dry but just sticky to the touch. Leave to cool completely.

Dust the pineapple rings with caster sugar to coat. Store in an airtight container, between sheets of waxed paper.

LAYER THE CANDIED FRUIT and crystallized flowers between waxed paper

SERVING SUGGESTION

Decorate Candied Pineapple with melted chocolate and serve with Crystallized Flowers.

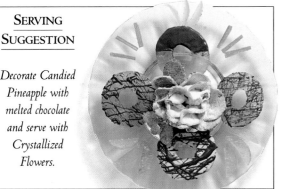

Crystallized Flowers

1 Beat an egg white with a pinch of salt and a few drops of flower water until frothy. Leave to stand for a few minutes. With a small, soft brush, paint the flowers evenly both inside and out with the egg white. Generously sprinkle them with caster sugar, ensuring all surfaces are evenly coated.

2 Fill a baking tray with a layer of caster sugar about 1cm (½in) deep and gently lay the sugared flowers on top. Generously sprinkle with more sugar and leave to dry in a warm, well-ventilated place for 1–2 days. Store the flowers in an airtight container, between layers of waxed paper.

TIPS

• Lemon juice is added to the candying syrup to prevent the sugar from recrystallizing. You could use glucose powder instead, substituting 100g (3½oz) glucose powder for the same amount of sugar in the first syrup.

• Instead of coating the flowers with egg white, you can use a cool gum arabic solution made by dissolving 2 teaspoons gum arabic and 1 tablespoon of sugar in 250ml (8fl oz) water in a bowl placed over a pan of hot water.

 Shelf life
1 year for candied pineapple; 3 months for crystallized flowers

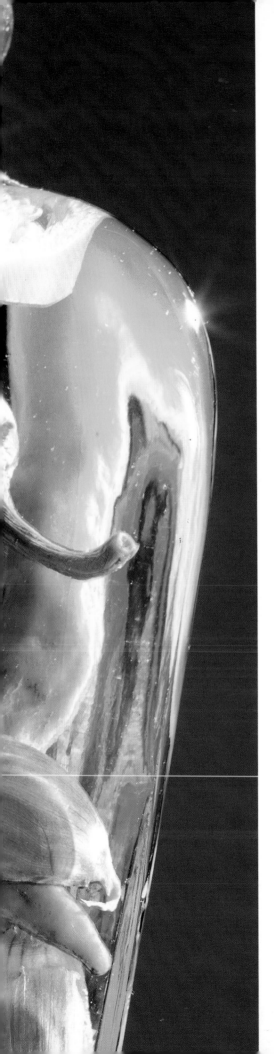

RECIPES

THIS COLLECTION of recipes contains time-honoured classics, such as pickled cucumbers and tomato sauce, as well as more contemporary adaptations, like fruit piccalilli and smoky red pepper ketchup. Enticing ideas are given for both sweet and savoury preserves. Learn how to make exotic, fragrant chutneys; elegant jams and jellies; aromatic spiced meat; and delicately flavoured smoked fish. Serving suggestions offer imaginative ways to use these delicious products.

Enjoy preserving!

PICKLES

IN THE PAST, people made the most of a seasonal glut of vegetables by preserving them in a variety of ingenious ways. This ensured a year-round supply to cheer up what might otherwise have been a monotonous diet. Today, we preserve fruit and vegetables not out of necessity but because they taste so delicious: their pungent flavours enliven even the simplest meal. Some restaurants are in the habit of displaying jars of vividly coloured pickled vegetables, Mediterranean-style, to entice passers-by. In the kitchen, too, rows of homemade preserves make an eye-catching addition to the larder.

Stuffed Pickled Aubergines

Baby purple aubergines

Garlic cloves

Celery stalks and leaves

Carrots

Red chillies

Salt

This deliciously fragrant pickle probably originated in Syria, and is still made in one form or another all over the Middle East. You will need baby aubergines – available from Indian, Oriental and Greek greengrocers – as they are preserved whole. This recipe is my mother's, whose pickled aubergines are the best I've ever tasted.

INGREDIENTS

1kg (2lb) baby purple aubergines
For the stuffing
6 garlic cloves, coarsely chopped
3–4 celery stalks and leaves, coarsely chopped
2–3 large carrots, coarsely grated
1–2 fresh red chillies, thinly sliced
1 tsp salt
For the jar
4–5 garlic cloves, peeled
2–3 fresh red or green chillies
a few vine leaves (optional)
salt
2–3 tbsp cider vinegar

1 Cut a deep slit lengthways in each aubergine to make a pocket. Steam for 5–8 minutes or until just softened. Remove from the heat and weight down (see page 46) to press out any moisture. Leave to stand overnight.

2 The next day, put the stuffing ingredients in a bowl and mix well. Open up the pocket in each aubergine, add 1 teaspoon of stuffing and press together to hold it in place.

3 Pack the aubergines into the sterilized jar with the garlic, chillies and vine leaves, if using. Fill the jar with cold water, then drain it off into a measuring jug. Add 1½ teaspoons salt for every 500ml (17fl oz) water, stirring until the salt has dissolved. Add the vinegar, then pour into the jar and weight down (see page 46).

4 Cover the jar with a clean cloth and leave in a warm, well-ventilated place for 1–3 weeks, until fermentation has finished (see Brined Cucumbers, page 93). Seal the jar and keep refrigerated. The aubergines are ready immediately.

 Degree of difficulty
Moderate

 Cooking time
5–8 minutes

 Special equipment
1.5 litre (2½ pint) wide-necked, sterilized jar with vinegar-proof sealant (see pages 42–43)

 Yield
About 1kg (2lb)

 Shelf life
6 months, refrigerated

TIPS

• Choose firm aubergines with a bright colour and taut, shiny, unblemished skin.
• The cider vinegar and the vine leaves help to speed up the fermentation process in the jar.

STUFFED PICKLED AUBERGINES
can be served as part of a meze, a
wonderfully informal way of eating that
consists of a wide selection of small dishes
accompanied by copious amounts of
bread. You can also eat them as a simple
accompaniment to a plate of cold meats
and a leafy salad.

PURPLE AUBERGINES look
attractive, but you could
also use white or yellow
baby aubergines, or a
mixture of all three

RED CHILLIES spice up the
pickle; adjust the quantity
to suit your own taste

VARIATION

◆ *Pickled Aubergines and Beetroot*
Pickle the aubergines without the stuffing
and add 1 thinly sliced raw beetroot,
6 coarsely chopped cloves of garlic and
2—3 chopped fresh red chillies to the jar.

Pickled Onions

(see page 52 for technique)

It is hard to imagine some dishes being served without pickled onions. I find distilled malt vinegar a little too harsh for pickling but it does help to maintain the whiteness of the onions.

Variation

◆ **Pickled Beetroot**
Use cooked, whole baby or cubed large beetroot. Omit salting, place in the jar and cover with hot vinegar.

INGREDIENTS

1.25kg (2½ lb) silverskin or pickling onions
salt
2 bay leaves
4 tsp mustard seeds
2–4 dried red chillies (optional)
Perfumed Vinegar, to cover (see page 129)

1 For easy peeling, blanch the onions (see page 46). Put in a bowl, cover with water, then drain it off into a measuring jug. Add 75g (2½ oz) salt for every 1 litre (1¾ pints) water. Pour over the onions, weight down (see page 46) and leave for 24 hours.

2 Rinse the onions and put in the sterilized jar with the bay leaves and spices. Pour in the vinegar to cover the onions by 2.5cm (1in), drain into a non-corrosive pan and boil for 2 minutes.

3 Pour the vinegar into the jar. Weight down the onions (see pages 46), then seal. The onions will be ready in 3–4 weeks.

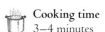 **Degree of difficulty**
Easy

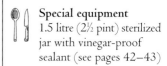 **Cooking time**
3–4 minutes

 **Special equipment**
1.5 litre (2½ pint) sterilized jar with vinegar-proof sealant (see pages 42–43)

 Yield
About 1kg (2lb)

Shelf life
2 years

Pickled Garlic

(see page 19 for illustration)

Pickled garlic originates in Persia, where it is either served on its own or used in cooking instead of fresh garlic. Pickling mellows and changes the flavour of garlic, giving it a delicate, elusive perfume. Use fresh, "green" garlic when it is in season.

INGREDIENTS

500ml (17fl oz) distilled malt vinegar or white wine vinegar
2 tbsp salt
1kg (2lb) fresh garlic

1 Put the vinegar and salt in a non-corrosive pan. Bring to the boil and boil for 2–3 minutes, then remove from the heat and leave to cool.

2 Separate the garlic cloves and blanch to remove the skin (see page 46). If using fresh, "green" garlic, remove the outer skin and slice the bulbs crossways in half.

3 Blanch the garlic in boiling water for 1 minute, then drain and put in the sterilized jars. Pour in the vinegar, weight down the garlic (see page 46), then seal. The garlic will be ready in 1 month.

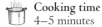 **Degree of difficulty**
Easy

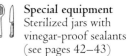 **Cooking time**
4–5 minutes

 **Special equipment**
Sterilized jars with vinegar-proof sealants (see pages 42–43)

 Yield
About 1kg (2lb)

Shelf life
2 years

Pickled Green Tomatoes

(see page 15 for illustration)

An ideal way to utilize a glut of green tomatoes. This crunchy, sour pickle comes from Eastern Europe and is popular in North America, where it is an essential item in any good delicatessen.

Tip

• Try cucumbers and courgettes or fruit like gooseberries and plums. Always blanch green vegetables before pickling (see page 46).

INGREDIENTS

1kg (2lb) green tomatoes
a few sprigs of dill
2–3 bay leaves
2–3 fresh or dried red chillies
1½ tbsp mustard seeds
1 tbsp black peppercorns
4–5 cloves
1 litre (1¾ pints) cider vinegar
125ml (4fl oz) water
4 tbsp honey or sugar
1 tbsp salt

1 Lightly prick each tomato in several places with a wooden cocktail stick. Put in the sterilized jar with the herbs and spices.

2 Put the vinegar, water, honey or sugar and salt in a non-corrosive pan. Bring to the boil and boil rapidly for 5 minutes, then remove from the heat and leave until warm.

3 Pour the warm vinegar into the jar. If there is not enough liquid to cover the tomatoes, top up with cold vinegar. Weight down the tomatoes (see page 46), then seal. The tomatoes will be ready to eat in 1 month, but improve with 2–3 months keeping.

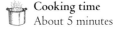 **Degree of difficulty**
Easy

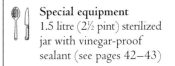 **Cooking time**
About 5 minutes

Special equipment
1.5 litre (2½ pint) sterilized jar with vinegar-proof sealant (see pages 42–43)

Yield
About 1kg (2lb)

Shelf life
1 year

Serving suggestions
Serve with meat, cheese or with drinks

Spiced Cherry Tomatoes

(see page 15 for illustration)

A pickle with a hidden surprise — the tomato flesh softens and bursts in the mouth on biting. This decorative pickle can also be made with small green or yellow tomatoes.

INGREDIENTS

1kg (2lb) firm red or yellow cherry tomatoes, preferably with stalks attached

10–12 mint or basil leaves

Sugar-free Sweet Vinegar, to cover (see page 130)

1 Lightly prick each tomato in several places with a wooden cocktail stick. Arrange in the sterilized jar with the mint or basil.

2 Pour in the Sugar-free Sweet Vinegar, making sure that it covers the tomatoes by at least 2.5cm (1in). Poke the tomatoes with a wooden skewer to ensure there are no air pockets.

3 Weight down the tomatoes (see page 46), then seal. The tomatoes will be ready to eat in 4–6 weeks, but improve with longer keeping.

 Degree of difficulty
Easy

 Special equipment
1 litre (1¾ pint) sterilized jar with vinegar-proof sealant (see pages 42–43)

 Yield
About 1kg (2lb)

 Shelf life
1 year

Brined Cucumbers (Gherkins)

(see page 21 for illustration)

My mother, a superb pickler, maintains that the crunchiness and vivid green colour of pickled cucumbers are achieved by blanching them briefly.

TIPS

• Vine leaves help the fermentation process and add their characteristic flavour to the pickle.
• The brine from this pickle and many others need not be thrown away after the gherkins have been eaten, but can be used as a base for soups, to flavour savoury dishes, or to make a salad dressing.

INGREDIENTS

1kg (2lb) small, firm, pickling cucumbers

5–6 fat garlic cloves, bruised but not peeled

2–3 dill flower heads and stalks

3–4 fresh or dried red chillies

2–3 bay leaves

salt

a few vine leaves (optional)

1 Put the cucumbers into a pan, and blanch in boiling water for 1 minute (see page 46).

2 Arrange the cucumbers, garlic, dill, chillies and bay leaves in the sterilized jar. Fill the jar with water, then drain into a measuring jug. Add 1½ tablespoons salt for every 500ml (17fl oz) water, stirring until dissolved.

3 Pour the brine into the jar, place the vine leaves on top, if using, then weight down (see page 46). Cover with a clean cloth and leave in a warm, well-ventilated place to ferment for 1–2 weeks. When fermentation starts, the brine will turn cloudy.

4 When the liquid starts to clear, indicating that fermentation is over, seal the jar tightly and store. The cucumbers are ready to eat immediately.

VARIATIONS

✦ Fermented Tomatoes
Use 1kg (2lb) small, firm, red tomatoes and prick in several places with a wooden cocktail stick. Arrange in a 2 litre (3½ pint) wide-necked, sterilized jar with 3–4 fresh chillies, slit, 8 garlic cloves, 6–8 celery leaves and 1 tablespoon black peppercorns. Cover with water and proceed as for the main recipe, adding 2 tablespoons salt for every 500ml (17fl oz) water, and 2 tablespoons cider vinegar. Complete as above.

✦ Fermented Beetroot
Use 1.5kg (3lb) small, peeled beetroot, keep whole or cut into large chunks. Arrange in the jar and cover with the brine, as for the main recipe. Weight down, cover and ferment. After several days froth will start to form. Remove it every few days and wipe the top of the jar clean. The beetroot will be ready in about 1 month, then seal the jar tightly. Use the liquid to make borscht; the beetroot can be added to borscht or eaten as a pickle.

 Degree of difficulty
Easy

 Cooking time
1 minute

 Special equipment
1.5 litre (2½ pint) wide-necked, sterilized jar with vinegar-proof sealant (see pages 42–43)

 Yield
About 1kg (2lb)

Shelf life
6 months; 3 months for beetroot

Serving suggestions
Chop the cucumbers and add to sauces or potato salads; use to decorate canapés

Pickled Turnips or Radishes

This vividly coloured pickle is popular all over the Middle East and in the southern part of Russia. In the past, pickled root vegetables were an important source of vitamins B and C during the bleak winter months.

— TIP —

• Any of the turnip family, such as mooli radishes or kohlrabi, can be used instead.

INGREDIENTS

750g (1½lb) white turnips or large radishes, sliced 1cm (½in) thick

250g (8oz) raw beetroot, sliced 1cm (½in) thick

4–5 garlic cloves, sliced

salt

3 tbsp white wine vinegar or distilled malt vinegar

1 Arrange the turnips or radishes in the sterilized jar with the beetroot and garlic.

2 Fill the jar with enough cold water to cover the vegetables, then drain it off into a measuring jug. Add 1½ tablespoons salt for every 500ml (17fl oz) water, stirring until the salt has dissolved. Add the wine vinegar or distilled malt vinegar, then pour into the jar.

3 Weight down the vegetables (see page 46), cover with a clean cloth and leave in a warm, well-ventilated place for about 2 weeks, until fermentation is over (see Brined Cucumbers, page 93). Seal the jar. The pickle will be ready to eat in about 1 month.

 Degree of difficulty
Easy

 Special equipment
1 litre (1¾ pint) wide-necked, sterilized jar with vinegar-proof sealant (see pages 42–43)

 Yield
About 1kg (2lb)

 Shelf life
3–6 months

Serving suggestions
Use in salads or serve as a snack with drinks

Pickled Celeriac and Carrot Salad

Earthy-looking celeriac makes a delicious pickle. Be careful when choosing celeriac: it can become hollow and stringy when too mature. Select solid roots that are heavy for their size and avoid any with green patches.

— TIP —

• I never blanch the orange rind first as I like its full, slightly bitter flavour. If you prefer, blanch the shredded rind in boiling water for 1–2 minutes, then drain and refresh in cold water before use.

INGREDIENTS

1 large celeriac, about 1kg (2lb), peeled and shredded or coarsely grated

5 large carrots, coarsely grated

2 onions, sliced into thin rings

2½ tbsp salt

2 tbsp dill seeds

shredded rind and juice of 1 orange

500ml (17fl oz) white wine vinegar or cider vinegar

150ml (¼ pint) water

1 tbsp sugar (optional)

1 Mix the celeriac, carrots and onions together in a glass bowl and sprinkle with 2 tablespoons of the salt. Mix well and leave to stand for about 2 hours.

2 Rinse the vegetables under cold running water, then drain well. Stir in the dill seeds and orange rind, then pack loosely into the hot sterilized jars.

3 Put the orange juice, vinegar, water, sugar, if using, and the remaining salt in a non-corrosive pan. Bring to the boil and boil for 2–3 minutes, then skim well. Pour into the jars to cover the vegetables. Poke the vegetables with a wooden skewer to ensure there are no air pockets, then seal. The pickle will be ready to eat in 1 week.

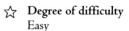 **Degree of difficulty**
Easy

 Cooking time
2–3 minutes

 Special equipment
2 x 1 litre (1¾ pint) sterilized jars with vinegar-proof sealants (see pages 42–43)

 Yield
About 2kg (4lb)

 Shelf life
3–6 months

 Serving suggestion
Especially good with hot or cold chicken

Chow-chow

Recipes for this flavoursome mustard pickle appear in many old cookery books. This is my adaptation of a colonial recipe. The pickle is traditionally made in summer when vegetables are in abundance, and any combination of fresh, colourful ones can be used.

INGREDIENTS

250g (8oz) cornichons or mini cucumbers
1 small cauliflower, divided into florets
250g (8oz) green tomatoes, diced
300g (10oz) carrots, cut into thick matchsticks
250g (8oz) French beans, trimmed
300g (10oz) small pickling onions, peeled
4 red peppers, sliced
1 small head of celery, sliced
100g (3½oz) salt

For the pickling mixture

100g (3½oz) plain or wholemeal flour
75g (2½oz) mustard powder
1½ tbsp celery seeds
1½ tbsp ground turmeric
1 tbsp salt
1.25 litres (2 pints) cider vinegar or malt vinegar
300g (10oz) light soft brown or white sugar

1 If using cornichons, leave them whole; otherwise slice the mini cucumbers into thick rings.

2 Put all the vegetables in a large glass bowl. Cover with cold water and add the salt. Mix well until the salt has dissolved, then weight down (see page 46) and leave to stand overnight.

3 The next day, drain the vegetables well and blanch for 2 minutes (see page 46).

4 To make the pickling mixture, combine the flour, mustard powder, celery seeds, turmeric and salt in a small bowl. Gradually add 250ml (8fl oz) of the vinegar, mixing well to make a smooth, thin paste.

5 Put the remaining vinegar and the sugar in the preserving pan and bring to the boil.

Gradually add the mustard paste, stirring all the time. Add the drained vegetables, return to the boil, then remove from the heat.

6 Pack the pickle into the hot sterilized jars, then seal. It will be ready to eat in 2 weeks, but improves with keeping.

TIPS

• Wholemeal flour makes a darker, more textured pickle.
• For a less crunchy pickle, simmer the vegetables in the vinegar for a further 5 minutes.

☆☆ **Degree of difficulty**
Moderate

Cooking time
About 2 minutes

Special equipment
Non-corrosive preserving pan; sterilized jars with vinegar-proof sealants (see pages 42–43)

Yield
About 3kg (6lb)

Shelf life
1 year

Serving suggestion
Serve as a relish with cold meats or cheese

Piccalilli

(see page 33 for illustration)

At the end of the 17th century this quintessentially British pickle was known as "pickle lila", an Indian pickle. My crunchy version is the exotic forefather of the unpleasantly harsh, bright yellow product found on supermarket shelves. For the vinegar, use any of the Spiced Vinegar recipes (see page 129).

TIPS
• Any combination of crunchy vegetables and fruit can be pickled in the same way.
• For a milder flavour, add the mustard seeds to the vinegar and boil for 3–4 minutes.

INGREDIENTS

250g (8oz) runner beans, cut into bite-sized pieces
250g (8oz) cauliflower, divided into small florets
300g (10oz) carrots, cut into medium-thick slices
250g (8oz) gooseberries, topped and tailed
250g (8oz) honeydew melon, cut into cubes
200g (7oz) seedless grapes
125g (4oz) salt
400g (13oz) yellow mustard seeds
1 litre (1¾ pints) Spiced Vinegar (see page 129)
1 tbsp ground turmeric

1 Put all the vegetables and fruit in a large glass bowl. Cover with cold water and add 100g (3½ oz) of the salt. Mix well until the salt has dissolved, then weight down (see page 46) and leave to stand for 24 hours.

2 The next day, coarsely grind the mustard seeds in the spice mill or coffee grinder; if necessary do this in batches.

3 Drain the vegetables and fruit, rinse under cold running water and drain well. Taste; if too salty, cover with cold water and leave to soak for 10 minutes, then drain, rinse and drain again. Add the ground mustard seeds and mix well.

4 Put the Spiced Vinegar, turmeric and remaining salt in a non-corrosive pan. Bring to the boil, skim well and boil rapidly for 10 minutes.

5 Pour the boiling vinegar over the vegetables and fruit in the bowl and mix well. Pack into the hot sterilized jars, then seal. The pickle is ready to eat immediately, but improves with keeping.

 Degree of difficulty
☆☆ Moderate

 Cooking time
About 12 minutes

 Special equipment
Spice mill or coffee grinder; sterilized jars with vinegar-proof sealants (see pages 42–43)

 Yield
About 3kg (6lb)

 Shelf life
1 year

Serving suggestion
Delicious with cheese

Onion and Pepper Pickle

(see page 19 for illustration)

A colourful pickled salad. Use as many different colours of peppers as you can find, though green peppers lose their colour very quickly. I sometimes add other vegetables such as sliced carrots or celeriac.

INGREDIENTS

1.25kg (2½ lb) onions, sliced into thin rings
2 red peppers, sliced into thin rings
2 yellow peppers, sliced into thin rings
4 tbsp salt
1 litre (1¾ pints) white wine vinegar or cider vinegar
100g (3½ oz) sugar
2 tbsp dried mint
2 tbsp paprika
1 tbsp dill seeds
2 tsp salt

1 Put the sliced onions and red and yellow peppers in a large glass bowl and sprinkle with the 4 tablespoons of salt. Mix well, cover with a clean cloth and leave to stand for 2 hours.

2 Drain off the liquid that has accumulated in the bottom of the bowl, then rinse the vegetables under cold running water and drain again.

3 Put the vinegar, sugar, mint, paprika, dill seeds and the 2 teaspoons of salt in a non-corrosive pan. Bring to the boil, then reduce the heat and simmer for 5 minutes.

4 Pack the vegetables into the hot sterilized jar. Pour in the boiling vinegar mixture, making sure that all the vegetables are completely covered. Poke the contents of the jar with a wooden skewer to ensure there are no air pockets, then seal. The pickle will be ready to eat in about 1 week, but improves with keeping.

 Degree of difficulty
☆ Easy

 Cooking time
About 8 minutes

 Special equipment
2 litre (3½ pint) sterilized jar with vinegar-proof sealant (see pages 42–43)

 Yield
About 2kg (4lb)

 Shelf life
6 months

 Serving suggestion
Drain the vegetables, dress with a little oil and serve as a refreshing salad

Bread and Butter Pickle
(see page 21 for illustration)

This delicious old-fashioned pickle was made to be spread on bread and butter, hence its name. However, some maintain that the name came about because the pickle was as common as bread and butter. This particular recipe is from New England and is one of a large family of pickles of British origin that were developed and perfected in colonial American kitchens.

INGREDIENTS

750g (1½lb) pickling cucumbers

625g (1¼lb) onions, sliced 5mm (¼in) thick

375g (12oz) red or yellow peppers, sliced 5mm (¼in) thick

3 tbsp salt

1 litre (1¾ pints) cider vinegar, white wine vinegar or malt vinegar

500g (1lb) light soft brown or white sugar

2 tsp ground turmeric

1 tbsp mustard seeds

2 tsp dill seeds

1 Put the cucumbers in a bowl and pour boiling water over them. Drain, refresh under cold running water and drain again. Slice the cucumbers into 1cm (½in) thick pieces.

2 Put the cucumbers, sliced onions and peppers in a large glass bowl and sprinkle with the salt. Mix well, then cover the bowl with a clean cloth and leave to stand overnight.

3 The next day, drain off the liquid in the bowl. Rinse the vegetables under cold running water and drain well. Taste a slice of cucumber; if it is too salty, cover the vegetables with more cold water and leave to stand for about 10 minutes, then drain, rinse and drain again.

4 Put the vinegar, sugar, ground turmeric, mustard seeds and dill seeds in the preserving pan. Bring to the boil and boil rapidly for 10 minutes. Add the drained vegetables, return to the boil, then remove from the heat.

5 Pack the pickle into the hot sterilized jars, then seal. The pickle is ready to eat immediately.

 Degree of difficulty
Easy

 Cooking time
About 15 minutes

 Special equipment
Non-corrosive preserving pan; sterilized jars with vinegar-proof sealants (see pages 42–43)

  Yield
About 2kg (4lb)

 Shelf life
1 year

Serving suggestions
Serve with cold meats or spread on bread and butter with cheese

TIP
• The easiest way to slice the vegetables is with a mandolin.

Olive Oil Pickle
(see page 21 for illustration)

A classic from the colonial American kitchen, this pickle is easy to make and is a great standby. It is mildly sour, refreshing, and keeps extremely well. You can replace the cucumbers with thinly sliced, colourful peppers or carrots.

INGREDIENTS

750g (1½lb) pickling cucumbers, sliced 5mm (¼in) thick

625g (1¼lb) onions, finely sliced

75g (2½oz) salt

500ml (17fl oz) cider vinegar

75ml (2½fl oz) water

1 tbsp dill seeds

1 tbsp celery seeds

1 tbsp yellow mustard seeds

75ml (2½fl oz) good fruity virgin olive oil

1 Put the sliced cucumbers and onions in a large glass bowl, cover with cold water and add the salt. Mix well until the salt has dissolved, then weight down (see page 46). Cover the bowl with a clean cloth and leave to stand overnight.

2 The next day, drain the vegetables. Rinse well under cold running water, then drain again, squeezing out as much liquid as possible. Pack into the hot sterilized jars.

3 Put the vinegar, water, herbs and spice in a non-corrosive pan. Bring to the boil and boil for 5 minutes. Remove the pan from the heat and allow the mixture to cool slightly, then whisk in the oil.

4 Pour the vinegar into the jars. Poke the vegetables with a wooden skewer to ensure there are no air pockets. Check that the oil and spices are evenly distributed and the vegetables are covered, then seal. The pickle will be ready to eat in 2 weeks, but improves with keeping.

 Degree of difficulty
Easy

 Cooking time
About 8 minutes

 Special equipment
Sterilized jars with vinegar-proof sealants (see pages 42–43)

 Yield
About 1.5kg (3lb)

 Shelf life
1 year

 Serving suggestion
Delicious with mature hard cheese, such as Cheddar, Red Leicester or white Stilton

Pickled Baby Vegetables

(see page 19 for illustration)

Baby vegetables are now widely available and make a highly decorative and delicious pickle. Any mixture of vegetables can be prepared in the same way. If baby vegetables are not available, use ordinary ones, sliced into bite-sized pieces and salted for 24 hours.

INGREDIENTS

4–5 yellow courgettes, sliced
3 baby white cabbages, quartered
3 baby cauliflowers, left whole
250g (8oz) baby sweetcorn
250g (8oz) shallots, peeled
100g (3½oz) salt
1.5 litres (2½ pints) Spiced Vinegar of your choice, to cover (see page 129)

1 Put the sliced courgettes, quartered white cabbage, whole cauliflower, baby sweetcorn and shallots in a large glass bowl and sprinkle with the salt. Mix well, then cover the bowl with a clean cloth and leave to stand for 24–48 hours, stirring the vegetables from time to time.

2 Drain off the liquid from the bowl. Rinse the vegetables under cold running water and drain well. Cover with more cold water, leave to stand for 1 hour, then drain again.

3 Arrange the vegetables in layers in the sterilized jar, then weight down (see page 46).

4 Pour the chosen vinegar into the jar, making sure that the vegetables are completely covered, then seal. The pickle will be ready to eat in 4–6 weeks.

 Degree of difficulty
Easy

 Special equipment
3 litre (5 pint) wide-necked, sterilized jar with vinegar-proof sealant (see pages 42–43)

 Yield
About 1.5kg (3lb)

 Shelf life
1 year

Serving suggestions
Serve as a winter salad or as the centrepiece of a cold buffet

Toby's Pickled Cucumbers

This is adapted from a recipe given to me by Toby Kay of Johannesburg, but its origins are probably Central European. It is easy to make and ready to eat in just 2 days. Drained and dressed with a little oil and chopped herbs, it makes a colourful salad.

INGREDIENTS

500g (1lb) large cucumbers, sliced 1cm (½in) thick
2 tbsp salt
375g (12oz) onions, sliced into thin rings
275g (9oz) carrots, coarsely grated or sliced into fine julienne
4 garlic cloves, sliced
1 tsp black peppercorns
3–4 bay leaves
750ml (1¼ pints) water
350ml (12fl oz) white wine vinegar or distilled malt vinegar
4 tbsp sugar
1–2 dried red chillies

1 Put the sliced cucumbers in a colander and sprinkle with half the salt. Mix well and leave to stand for about 20 minutes. Rinse the vegetables under cold running water and drain well.

2 Mix the onion rings and carrot julienne together in a bowl, pour over boiling water to cover, then drain well.

3 Arrange a layer of sliced cucumbers in the bottom of the hot sterilized jar. Place a few slices of garlic, a few peppercorns and a bay leaf on top and cover with a layer of the onion and carrot mixture.

4 Repeat the layers until all the vegetables are used up. The jar should be almost full, but loosely packed.

5 Put the water, white wine vinegar, sugar, dried red chillies and remaining salt in a non-corrosive pan. Bring to the boil and boil steadily for a few minutes. Skim well and remove the chillies.

6 Pour the hot vinegar mixture into the jar, filling it right to the top to make sure that the cucumbers are completely covered. Poke the vegetables with a wooden skewer to ensure there are no air pockets, then seal the jar and keep refrigerated. The pickle will be ready to eat in 2 days.

 Degree of difficulty
Easy

Cooking time
About 5 minutes

Special equipment
1.5 litre (2½ pint) sterilized jar with vinegar-proof sealant (see pages 42–43)

Yield
About 1kg (2lb)

Shelf life
3 months, refrigerated

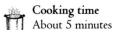 **Serving suggestions**
Serve as a salad or savoury snack with drinks

Pickled Okra

This pickle is based on a traditional Iranian recipe. Okra is a fascinating vegetable, with a unique flavour and texture. Do not be alarmed if the pickling liquid thickens, it is due to the okra's glutinous sap.

INGREDIENTS

750g (1½ lb) crisp, young okra
1 tbsp salt
275g (9oz) carrots, cut into thick matchsticks
6 large garlic cloves, sliced
3–4 fresh red chillies, deseeded and sliced (optional)
small bunch of mint, coarsely chopped
For the pickling mixture
1 litre (1¼ pints) cider vinegar
4 tbsp sugar or honey
1 tbsp salt
2 tsp ground turmeric

1 Trim any dark bits from the stalk end of the okra but leave the stalks attached. Prick each okra in a few places with a wooden cocktail stick.

2 Lay the okra out on a large baking sheet and sprinkle with the salt. Leave to stand, preferably in the sun, for 1 hour.

3 Rinse the okra well under cold running water and dry on paper towels. Blanch the carrots in boiling water for 2–3 minutes (see page 46).

4 Mix together the garlic, chillies, if using, and mint. Arrange the okra and carrots in layers in the hot sterilized jars, evenly distributing the garlic mixture between the layers. The jars should be full, but loosely packed.

5 For the pickling mixture, put the vinegar, sugar or honey and salt in a non-corrosive pan. Bring to the boil and skim well. Add the turmeric and return to the boil for a few minutes.

6 Pour the hot vinegar into the jars, filling them to the top and making sure that the okra are covered. Poke the vegetables with a wooden skewer to ensure there are no air pockets, then seal. They will be ready to eat in 2 weeks.

 Degree of difficulty
Easy

 Cooking time
About 10 minutes

 Special equipment
Sterilized jars with vinegar-proof sealants (see pages 42–43)

 Yield
About 2kg (4lb)

 Shelf life
6 months

Serving suggestions
Serve on its own, or as a pickled salad to accompany cold meat

Hungarian Pickled Peppers 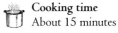 (see page 17 for illustration)

If you are lucky you will find "tomato" peppers — so named for their shape — in the shops in late summer. They are either red or pale yellow and have a dense flesh that makes them ideal for pickling. If they are unavailable, substitute small, colourful sweet peppers but do not use green ones, which lose their colour.

INGREDIENTS

1kg (2lb) red peppers
2 small dried chillies
2 bay leaves
white wine vinegar
water
sugar
salt
For the spice bag (see page 47)
2 tsp black peppercorns
1 tsp allspice berries
2 bay leaves

1 Wash the peppers thoroughly, leaving the stalks attached, then arrange them in the hot sterilized jar with the dried chillies and the bay leaves. Fill the jar with water.

2 Drain the water off into a measuring jug. Pour half of it away and replace it with vinegar. For every 1 litre (1¼ pints) liquid, add 2 tablespoons each of sugar and salt.

3 Put the vinegar, water, sugar salt and spice bag in a non-corrosive pan. Bring to the boil, reduce the heat and simmer for 10 minutes. Leave to cool slightly.

4 Pour the warm liquid into the jar, making sure that the peppers are completely covered, then seal. After a few days check that there is still enough liquid to cover the peppers — their cavities tend to absorb the vinegar. They will be ready to eat in 2 weeks.

 Degree of difficulty
Easy

Cooking time
About 15 minutes

Special equipment
2 litre (3½ pint) sterilized wide-necked jar with vinegar-proof sealant (see pages 42–43)

Yield
About 1kg (2lb)

Shelf life
1 year

Serving suggestions
Serve as an accompaniment to cold meats and cheese

Spiced Whole Oranges

(see page 29 for illustration)

Spiced oranges are a classic British preserve. In this elegant version the oranges are left whole instead of being sliced. They make a welcome addition to a festive meal.

INGREDIENTS

1kg (2lb) small, thin-skinned oranges, preferably seedless

1 litre (1¼ pints) cider vinegar or distilled malt vinegar

750g (1½ lb) sugar

juice of 1 lemon

cloves

For the spice bag (see page 47)

2 tsp cloves

2 cinnamon sticks, crushed

1 tsp cardamom pods, crushed

1 Scrub the oranges well, then remove alternate strips of rind from each one with the canelle knife and add to the spice bag.

2 Put the oranges in the preserving pan with enough cold water to cover. Bring to the boil, then simmer very gently for 20–25 minutes, or until the peel is just soft. Lift out the oranges with a slotted spoon and drain well.

3 Measure 1 litre (1¼ pints) of the cooking liquid and return to the pan. Add the vinegar, sugar, lemon juice and spice bag. Bring to the boil and boil for 10 minutes. Remove from the heat and skim well. Return the oranges to the pan and leave to stand overnight.

4 The next day, return the mixture to the boil, then simmer very gently for 20 minutes. Carefully remove the oranges from the liquid with a slotted spoon and leave to cool slightly.

5 Stud each orange with a few cloves and arrange in the hot sterilized jar. Bring the syrup to the boil and boil rapidly until it has thickened slightly. Pour the syrup into the jar, making sure that the oranges are completely covered, then seal. The oranges will be ready to eat in 1 month, but improve with keeping.

 Degree of difficulty
Moderate

 Cooking time
About 1 hour

Special equipment
Canelle knife; non-corrosive preserving pan; 2 litre (3½ pint) wide-necked, sterilized jar with vinegar-proof sealant (see pages 42–43)

 Yield
About 1kg (2lb)

 Shelf life
2 years

 Serving suggestions
Serve with cold ham (see page 134 for recipe), turkey, chicken or other poultry

Pickled Limes

(see page 29 for illustration)

A sharp, hot pickle from the Punjab in India. This recipe can also be made with lemons or oranges.

INGREDIENTS

1kg (2lb) limes

100g (3½ oz) salt

1 tsp cardamom pods

1 tsp black cumin seeds (kalajeera)

1 tsp cumin seeds

½ tsp cloves

500g (1lb) soft light brown or white sugar

1 tbsp chilli powder, or to taste

75g (2½ oz) fresh ginger root, finely shredded

1 Put the limes in a bowl and cover with cold water. Leave to soak overnight, then drain. Top and tail them and cut into slices 5mm (¼ in) thick. Put in a glass bowl and sprinkle with the salt. Mix well, cover with a clean cloth and leave to stand for 12 hours.

2 The next day, place the spices in the spice mill or coffee grinder and grind to a powder.

3 Drain the limes and put the liquid they have produced in the preserving pan with the sugar and ground spices. Bring to the boil, stirring until the sugar has dissolved, and boil for 1 minute. Remove from the heat, stir in the chilli powder and leave to cool.

4 Add the limes and ginger to the cooled syrup and mix well. Pack into the sterilized jars. Poke the limes with a wooden skewer to ensure there are no air pockets, then seal. Leave in a warm place, such as a sunny windowsill, for 4–5 days before storing. The pickle will be ready in 4–5 weeks.

 Degree of difficulty
Moderate

 Cooking time
About 5 minutes

Special equipment
Spice mill or coffee grinder; non-corrosive preserving pan; sterilized jars with vinegar-proof sealants (see pages 42–43)

 Yield
About 1kg (2lb)

 Shelf life
2 years

 Serving suggestions
Serve as a relish with a selection of appetizers or spread over whole fish or fish fillets before baking

Pickled Plums

This Central European recipe makes an unusual accompaniment to bread and cheese.

INGREDIENTS

500ml (17fl oz) cider vinegar
150ml (¼ pint) apple or pear concentrate
1 tbsp salt
1kg (2lb) plums, preferably Switzen
8 cloves
8 allspice berries
6–8 strands of finely shredded fresh ginger root
2 bay leaves

1 Put the cider vinegar, fruit concentrate and salt in a non-corrosive pan. Bring to the boil and boil for 1–2 minutes.

2 Prick the plums all over with a wooden cocktail stick and arrange in the hot sterilized jars with the spices and bay leaves. Add the boiling vinegar to cover, then seal. The plums will be ready to eat in 1 month.

 Degree of difficulty
Easy

 Cooking time
3–4 minutes

 Special equipment
Sterilized jars with vinegar-proof sealants (see pages 42–43)

 Yield
About 1kg (2lb)

Shelf life
2 years

Melon Pickled as Mango

This oddity is a 17th-century British recipe. At that time mangoes were a great luxury and many recipes were devised using cheaper, more readily available fruit, such as hot-house melons. Peppers can be prepared in the same way.

INGREDIENTS

4–5 small, underripe melons, preferably Galia or Charentais
salt
any Spiced Vinegar or Sweet Spiced Vinegar of your choice, to cover (see page 129)
For the stuffing
300g (10oz) white cabbage, finely shredded
150g (5oz) carrots, coarsely grated
2 red peppers or a few fresh red chillies, shredded
3 celery stalks, coarsely chopped
75g (2½oz) fresh ginger root, finely shredded
2 garlic cloves, sliced
100g (3½oz) salt
1 tbsp mustard seeds
2 tsp nigella seeds (optional)

1 Prepare the melons (see step 1, below) and place in a glass bowl. Cover with cold water then drain this off into a measuring jug. Add 4 tablespoons salt for every 1 litre (1¾ pints) water. Pour over the melons and leave to stand for 24 hours.

2 For the stuffing, place the vegetables, ginger and garlic in a bowl. Sprinkle with the salt, mix well, cover and leave for 24 hours.

3 Drain and rinse the stuffing and melons, then rinse and drain again. Add the spices to the stuffing and fill the melons (see steps 2–3, below). Place in the jar and add vinegar to cover. Weight down (see page 46), then seal. The melons will be ready in 5–6 weeks.

 Degree of difficulty
Advanced

 Special equipment
2 litre (3½ pint) wide-necked earthenware or glass sterilized jar with vinegar-proof sealant (see pages 42–43)

 Yield
2 litre (3½ pint) jar

 Shelf life
1 year

Serving suggestion
Serve as the centrepiece of a cold buffet

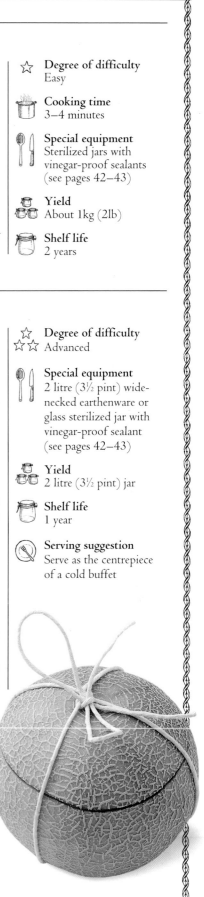

PREPARING THE MELONS

1 Cut the tops off the melons and reserve as lids. Scoop out the seeds and fibres from the centre of the fruit using a spoon.

2 Divide the drained vegetable stuffing equally between the melons, using a spoon to pack it inside carefully.

3 Place the lids on the stuffed melons and tie them in place with string or secure them with wooden cocktail sticks.

Kiwi Fruit and Red Pepper Pickle

An exotic, colourful and mild pickle. Be careful not to overcook the kiwi fruit as it softens very quickly. For extra colour, use a combination of red, yellow and orange peppers.

INGREDIENTS

1kg (2lb) hard, unripe kiwi fruit, peeled and cut into large chunks

juice of 1 lemon

3 red peppers, cut into wide strips

1 tbsp salt

1 litre (1¾ pints) cider vinegar or white wine vinegar

150g (5oz) honey, preferably single blossom

250g (8oz) light soft brown sugar or white sugar

1 tbsp black peppercorns

2 tsp juniper berries

1 tsp allspice berries

1 Put the kiwi fruit chunks in a glass bowl and sprinkle with the lemon juice. Mix gently and leave to marinate for 15 minutes. Sprinkle the red peppers with the salt and leave for 15 minutes.

2 Put the vinegar, honey, sugar and spices in the preserving pan. Bring to the boil and boil rapidly for 10 minutes, until the syrup is slightly reduced.

3 Rinse the peppers under cold water and drain well. Add them to the boiling syrup. Return to the boil, then reduce the heat and simmer for 5 minutes. Add the kiwi fruit to the pan and simmer for a further 5 minutes.

4 Using a slotted spoon, lift the kiwi fruit and peppers out of the pan and carefully pack them into the hot sterilized jars. Boil the syrup rapidly for 10 minutes, or until slightly reduced again. Pour the boiling syrup into the jars to cover, then seal. The pickle will be ready to eat in 1 week, but improves with keeping.

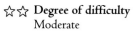 **Degree of difficulty**
Moderate

 Cooking time
About 40 minutes

 Special equipment
Non-corrosive preserving pan; sterilized jars with vinegar-proof sealants (see pages 42–43)

 Yield
About 1.5kg (3lb)

 Shelf life
1 year

 Serving suggestions
Dress with olive oil and serve as a salad or use to decorate a cold meat platter

Preserved Lemons ——— (see page 29 for illustration)

Preserved lemons are an essential ingredient in North African cooking. Salting softens the peel and gives the lemon a stronger flavour, so use with discretion.

Preserved Kaffir Limes, see Tips

INGREDIENTS

1kg (2lb) small, thin-skinned lemons

salt

about 350ml (12fl oz) lemon or lime juice or acidulated water (see method)

1–2 tbsp olive oil

1 Wash and scrub the lemons. Slice each one into quarters lengthways, from the pointed end, leaving the sections still attached at the stem end so that they resemble flowers.

2 Gently open out each lemon and sprinkle with about a teaspoon of salt, then close up. Pack the lemons tightly into the sterilized jar and weight down (see page 46). Leave to stand in a warm place, preferably on a sunny windowsill, for 4–5 days. By then some liquid should have accumulated in the jar.

3 Pour the citrus juice or acidulated water (1½ teaspoons citric acid dissolved in 500ml/ 17fl oz cold water) into the jar, making sure that the lemons are completely covered.

4 Pour the oil into the top of the jar in a thin layer: this will prevent mould from forming. Seal the jar immediately. The brine will look cloudy at first, but should clear in 3–4 weeks, when the lemons will be ready to eat.

—— **TIPS** ——

• Before using the lemons, wash them well under cold running water, then slice and prepare as directed in the recipe. You can discard the pulp and just use the peel.
• The wonderfully pungent pickling liquid can also be used to dress salads or to flavour stews.
• Limes can be preserved the same way.

 Degree of difficulty
Easy

 Special equipment
1.5 litre (2½ pint) sterilized jar with vinegar-proof sealant (see pages 42–43)

 Yield
About 1kg (2lb)

 Shelf life
2 years

Serving suggestions
Use to flavour tagines and couscous or to accompany grilled fish

Pickled Watermelon Rind

Watermelon rind is very versatile — it can be preserved in syrup, candied or fermented in brine.

INGREDIENTS

500g (1lb) watermelon rind, green skin removed, with about 5mm (¼in) of the red flesh left on

4 tbsp salt

1kg (2lb) preserving sugar

750ml (1¼ pints) water

750ml (1¼ pints) white wine vinegar or cider vinegar

For the spice bag (see page 47)

5cm (2in) piece fresh ginger root, chopped

1 cinnamon stick, broken

1 tbsp allspice berries

1 tbsp cloves

2–3 strips lemon or orange peel (optional)

1 Slice the watermelon rind into 2.5cm (1in) cubes and put in a large glass bowl with the salt. Add enough water to cover, then mix well until the salt has dissolved. Cover with a clean cloth and leave to stand overnight.

2 The next day, drain the watermelon rind. Put in the preserving pan and cover with fresh water. Bring to the boil, then reduce the heat and simmer for about 15 minutes. Drain well.

3 Put the sugar, water, vinegar and spice bag in the cleaned preserving pan. Bring to the boil and cook for about 5 minutes. Skim well, add the drained rind and return to the boil, then reduce the heat and simmer gently for 45–60 minutes, or until the rind is translucent.

4 Pack the mixture into the hot sterilized jars, then seal. The pickle will be ready to eat in about 1 month.

 Degree of difficulty
Easy

 Cooking time
1–1¼ hours

 Special equipment
Non-corrosive preserving pan; sterilized jars with vinegar-proof sealants (see pages 42–43)

 Yield
About 1.5kg (3lb)

Shelf life
2 years

Serving suggestions
Delicious with poultry and cold ham

———— TIP ————
• Always remove all of the green skin of the watermelon as it contains a laxative.

Striped Spiced Pears

(see page 30 for illustration)

This fragrant preserve is particularly attractive because of the striped appearance of the whole pears. It is especially good with game.

INGREDIENTS

juice of 1 lemon

1kg (2lb) hard pears

1.25 litres (2 pints) red wine vinegar

500ml (17fl oz) red wine

500g (1lb) sugar

250g (8oz) honey

For the spice bag (see page 47)

1 tbsp black peppercorns

2 tsp cloves

2 tsp allspice berries

1 tsp lavender flowers (optional)

2 bay leaves

1 large cinnamon stick

a few strips of lemon rind

1 Stir the lemon juice into a large bowl of cold water. Peel alternate strips of skin from the pears with the canelle knife or a vegetable peeler to give a striped effect. Put the pears in the lemon juice and water mixture.

2 Put the vinegar, wine, sugar, honey and spice bag in the preserving pan. Bring to the boil, skim well and boil for 5 minutes.

3 Add the pears, reduce the heat and simmer gently for 35–40 minutes, until they have softened a little but still show some resistance when pierced with a knife. Lift the pears out of the pan with a slotted spoon and arrange them in the hot sterilized jar.

4 Boil the syrup rapidly until it is reduced by half and slightly thickened. Remove the spice bag. Pour the hot syrup into the jar, making sure the pears are totally covered, then seal. The pears will be ready to eat in 1 month.

 Degree of difficulty
Moderate

 Cooking time
About 50 minutes

 Special equipment
Canelle knife; non-corrosive preserving pan; 1 litre (1¾ pint) wide-necked, sterilized jar with vinegar-proof sealant (see pages 42–43)

 Yield
About 1kg (2lb)

 Shelf life
2 years

 Serving suggestions
Serve with game or turkey

PRESERVES IN OIL

THE PRESERVATION OF FOOD in oil is an age-old technique that is mentioned in ancient Roman writings. It is the hot country's solution to the cold country's technique of preserving food in animal fat. The oil not only acts as a sealing agent, but also imparts a delightfully mellow flavour to the preserve, so always use the best quality oil you can afford. Cold-pressed, extra-virgin olive oil is usually too pungent for this purpose, so I usually dilute it with a mild oil, such as groundnut or refined sesame seed oil – a good-quality, fruity, virgin olive oil could be used instead. Experiment with a mixture of oils until you find the balance of flavours that suits you best.

Mushrooms Preserved in Oil

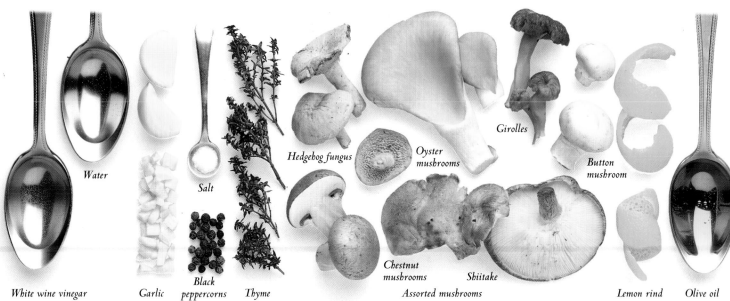

Water

White wine vinegar

Salt

Garlic

Black peppercorns

Thyme

Hedgehog fungus

Oyster mushrooms

Girolles

Button mushroom

Chestnut mushrooms

Shiitake

Assorted mushrooms

Lemon rind

Olive oil

I love mushrooms. Their flavour brings back memories of cool autumn days and the haunting scent of wood and rotting leaves. The wild mushroom season is short and one of the best ways to prolong it is to preserve a glut of mushrooms in oil.

INGREDIENTS

500ml (17fl oz) white wine vinegar
250ml (8fl oz) water
3–4 garlic cloves, coarsely chopped
1 tsp black peppercorns
2 tsp salt
4–6 sprigs thyme
1kg (2lb) assorted mushrooms
1–2 strips lemon rind
1 bay leaf (optional)
good-quality olive oil, to cover

1 Put the vinegar, water, garlic, peppercorns, salt and a few sprigs of the thyme in a deep non-corrosive pan. Bring to the boil, then reduce the heat and simmer for 30 minutes.

2 Add the mushrooms to the pan and simmer for about 10 minutes, or until they are just cooked. Remove them with a slotted spoon and drain well. Remove the thyme.

3 Arrange the mushrooms, strips of lemon rind, bay leaf, if using, and remaining thyme sprigs in the hot sterilized jar.

4 Heat the olive oil in a pan to 75°C (167°F) and pour it carefully into the jar, making sure the mushrooms are completely covered. Poke the mushrooms with a wooden skewer to ensure there are no air pockets, then seal. The mushrooms will be ready to eat in about 2 weeks.

 Degree of difficulty
Easy

 Cooking time
About 45 minutes

 Special equipment
1.5 litre (2½ pint) sterilized jar with vinegar-proof sealant (see pages 42–43); thermometer

 Yield
About 1kg (2lb)

 Shelf life
6 months

 Serving suggestions
Serve as an hors d'oeuvre, or use with a little of the oil from the jar as an instant pasta sauce

BEFORE YOU SEAL the jar, make sure that the mushrooms are totally covered with the olive oil

MUSHROOMS PRESERVED IN OIL

make a delicious appetizer. Serve them on thick slices of French bread that have been fried in a little of the mushrooms' preserving oil.

AN ASSORTMENT OF fresh wild and cultivated mushrooms will produce the best flavour combination

PIECES OF LEMON rind impart a subtle fragrance to the mushrooms

TIPS

• Mushrooms soak up water like a sponge so do not wash them unless absolutely necessary. Just trim them, brush off any dust and dirt and wipe clean with a paper towel.
• Any small edible wild mushrooms can be used as long as they are in perfect condition; ceps and morels are especially good. Small cultivated mushrooms can be prepared in the same way.

Aubergines Preserved in Oil

An adaptation of a Lebanese recipe, this makes an unusual and very fragrant preserve. Aubergines acquire an amazingly soft, melt-in-the-mouth texture when preserved this way. The oil left in the jar is superb for dressing salads.

INGREDIENTS

1kg (2lb) baby aubergines, stalks removed
salt
75g (2½oz) pecan halves
2 lemons, finely sliced into semi-circles
6 garlic cloves, cut into tiny slivers
500ml (17fl oz) olive oil, to cover

1 Steam the aubergines for 5–7 minutes or until just soft. Leave to cool.

2 Make a pocket in each aubergine by cutting a deep slit lengthways. Sprinkle the inside of the pocket with a tiny pinch of salt and place a pecan half, a slice of lemon and a sliver of garlic in each. Secure with a wooden cocktail stick.

3 Pack the aubergines into the warm sterilized jar. If there are any slices of lemon and garlic left over, arrange between the aubergines.

4 Heat the olive oil in a pan until it reaches 80°C (176°F). Pour it carefully into the jar, making sure the aubergines are completely covered, then seal. The aubergines will be ready to eat in 3–4 weeks.

 Degree of difficulty
Moderate

 Cooking time
About 10 minutes

 Special equipment
Steamer; 1.5 litre (2½ pint) wide-necked, sterilized jar with sealant (see pages 42–43); thermometer

 Yield
About 1kg (2lb)

Shelf life
6 months

 Serving suggestions
Serve as part of a *meze* or just with drinks

Chargrilled Vegetables in Oil

Chargrilling the vegetables adds a wonderfully smoky flavour to this adaptation of a classic Sicilian recipe. Many other combinations of vegetables can be prepared in the same way.

Peppers in Oil, see Variation

INGREDIENTS

500g (1lb) small aubergines halved lengthways, or large aubergines, sliced into thick batons
300g (10oz) courgettes, sliced into thick batons
3 tbsp salt
4 lemons
500g (1lb) red and yellow peppers, thickly sliced
300g (10oz) shallots, peeled
1 large head garlic, peeled
600ml (1 pint) olive oil
3 tbsp capers
2–3 sprigs rosemary
2–3 sprigs thyme

1 Put the aubergines and courgettes in a colander and sprinkle with 2 tablespoons of the salt. Mix well and leave to drain for about 1 hour. Rinse under cold running water, drain and pat dry with paper towels.

2 Grate the rind from 1 of the lemons then squeeze the juice from all of them. Put the rind and juice in a large glass bowl with the rest of the salt and stir until the salt has dissolved.

3 Brush the aubergines, courgettes, peppers, shallots and garlic with 4–5 tablespoons of the oil and cook under a hot grill or on a barbecue for about 5 minutes on each side or until lightly charred and blistered.

4 Add the chargrilled vegetables to the lemon juice. Cover the bowl with a clean cloth and leave to marinate for about 1 hour.

5 Arrange the vegetables in the hot sterilized jar with the capers and herbs. Whisk the remaining oil with the lemon juice left over from marinating the vegetables. Put in a pan and heat until it reaches 80°C (176°F).

6 Pour the hot liquid carefully into the jar, filling it to the top, making sure that all the vegetables are completely covered, then seal. The vegetables will be ready to eat in 4–6 weeks.

 Degree of difficulty
Moderate

 Cooking time
About 12 minutes

 Special equipment
2 litre (3½ pint) wide-necked, sterilized jar with sealant (see pages 42–43); thermometer

 Yield
About 2kg (4lb)

Shelf life
1 year

 Serving suggestion
Serve as part of an antipasti selection

---VARIATION---

✦ *Peppers in Oil*
Roast and skin 1.5kg (3lb) red or yellow peppers (see page 56). Marinate the warm peppers in the lemon juice with 3–4 crushed garlic cloves. Mix well, cover and refrigerate for 24 hours. Bring back to room temperature, drain and pack the whole peppers into a 1 litre (1¾ pint) sterilized jar. Finish as for the main recipe.

Preserved Artichokes

Globe artichokes are popular throughout the Mediterranean, where they are eaten raw in salads, cooked in casseroles and, of course, preserved. If you are lucky enough to find baby artichokes for this recipe, just remove any tough outer leaves and cut them in half. The tender choke can be left in.

INGREDIENTS

2 large lemons
1½ tbsp salt
1 tbsp finely chopped thyme
1.5kg (3lb) young globe artichokes
500ml (17fl oz) mild olive, groundnut or refined sesame oil

1 Grate the rind from 1 of the lemons and squeeze the juice from both of them. Keep the squeezed-out lemon halves.

2 Put the lemon juice and rind, salt and thyme in a large glass bowl and mix well until the salt has dissolved.

3 Trim the artichoke stalks and peel off the leaves, cutting back well to expose the heart (see steps 1–3, below). Rub the flesh with the reserved lemon halves to prevent it from discolouring. Using a pointed spoon, scrape out the choke (see step 4, below).

4 If the artichoke hearts are large, cut them in half lengthways. As you finish preparing each artichoke, add it to the lemon mixture, turning to coat. Leave for 30 minutes.

5 Pack the artichokes into the sterilized jar. Whisk the oil with the lemon juice left over from marinating the artichokes and pour into the jar, making sure the vegetables are covered, then seal. They will be ready in 6–8 weeks. Occasionally shake the jar to mix the ingredients.

 Degree of difficulty
Moderate

 Special equipment
1 litre (1¾ pint) wide-necked, sterilized jar with sealant (see pages 42–43)

 Yield
About 750g (1½lb)

 Shelf life
2 years

Serving suggestions
Serve as part of an antipasti selection or slice and serve with pasta

BABY ARTICHOKES are ideal for this recipe

PREPARING THE ARTICHOKES

1 Using a sharp knife, remove the tough stalk of each artichoke, cutting it off as close to the base of the head as possible.

2 Peel off the leaves, rubbing the exposed parts of the flesh with the reserved lemon half to prevent it from browning.

3 Trim the artichoke heart with a paring knife to remove any remaining tough areas. Rub the cut surfaces with the lemon.

4 Spoon out and discard the fluffy choke from the centre using a grapefruit spoon. Place the hearts in the lemon mixture.

Oven-dried Tomatoes Preserved in Oil

Tomatoes develop a strong, concentrated flavour when dried and can enhance many savoury dishes. In hot climates tomatoes can be dried in direct sun (see page 60), which takes about 2 days.

INGREDIENTS

1kg (2lb) beef or plum tomatoes, halved
2 tbsp salt
1 tbsp sugar
1 tbsp dried basil or mint
4 tbsp extra-virgin olive oil
1 sprig rosemary
1–2 dried chillies (optional)
1–2 garlic cloves, cut into slivers (optional)
olive oil, to cover

1 Arrange the tomato halves, cut-side up, on a wire rack placed over a foil-lined baking tray. Sprinkle the tomatoes with the salt, sugar and dried basil or mint and then finely drizzle the extra-virgin olive oil over the top.

2 Put the tray in an oven set to the lowest possible temperature and leave the door slightly ajar to allow the moisture to escape. Bake for 8–12 hours, or until the tomatoes are dry but still pliable.

3 Pack the dried tomatoes into the sterilized jar along with the rosemary, dried chillies and garlic, if using.

4 Pour olive oil into the jar, making sure the tomatoes are completely covered. Poke the contents of the jar with a wooden skewer to ensure there are no air pockets, then seal. The tomatoes will be ready to eat in 1–2 days, but improve with keeping.

 Degree of difficulty
Easy

 Cooking time
8–12 hours

 Special equipment
600ml (1 pint) sterilized jar with sealant (see pages 42–43)

 Yield
About 300g (10oz)

 Shelf life
2 years

Serving suggestions
Use to flavour salads, pasta sauces, stews and breads; fresh from the oven, the tomatoes make a delicious first course with a yogurt dressing

Labna (Soft Cheese)

(see page 54 for technique)

Labna is a refreshingly sharp yogurt cheese from the Middle East. Originally it was made with sheep's or goat's milk yogurt but now cow's milk yogurt is more common. Use the best virgin olive oil you can afford, as it imparts a heavenly fragrance to the cheese.

INGREDIENTS

2 litres (3½ pints) Greek-style yogurt
75ml (2½ fl oz) good-quality virgin olive oil
grated rind and juice of 1 lemon
3 tbsp dried mint (optional)
1 tbsp finely chopped thyme (optional)
1 tbsp salt
olive oil, to cover

1 Put the yogurt, virgin olive oil, lemon rind and juice, dried mint, thyme and salt in a large glass bowl. Beat with a wooden spoon until all the ingredients are thoroughly combined.

2 Line a large bowl with a double layer of sterilized muslin, leaving plenty of the material overlapping the sides. Pour in the yogurt mixture.

3 Tie the ends of the muslin together and secure with string. Hang it up over the bowl.

4 Leave the yogurt to drain in a cool place, such as a larder or an unheated room, between 6–8°C (42–46°F) for about 2–3 days in winter or 2 days in summer. On hot days, you may need to keep the mixture in the bottom of the refrigerator.

5 Chill the well-drained mixture until it is firm to the touch – this makes it easier to handle. Using your fingers, shape the resulting soft cheese into 4cm (1½ in) balls.

6 Chill the cheese balls again, if necessary, so they keep their shape, then arrange them in the sterilized jar.

7 Pour the olive oil into the jar, making sure that the cheese balls are completely covered. Rap the jar several times on a work surface to ensure there are no air pockets, then seal. The cheese balls are ready to eat immediately.

 Degree of difficulty
Moderate

 Special equipment
Sterilized muslin; 1.5 litre (2½ pint) wide-necked, sterilized jar with sealant (see pages 42–43)

 Yield
About 1.25kg (2½ lb)

 Shelf life
6 months

Serving suggestion
Serve the cheese balls drizzled with the oil from the jar as part of a *meze* selection

Mixed Seafood in Oil

(see page 27 for illustration)

You need as many colourful types of seafood as you can muster to make this strikingly beautiful preserve. Especially suitable are small squid, octopus, clams, razor clams, mussels and small crustaceans. If fresh seafood is not available, frozen mixed seafood can be used instead, though the flavour is not as good. There is no need to cook it, just pour the boiling stock over the defrosted seafood and marinate for 3 hours.

INGREDIENTS

1 large lemon, cut into thin wedges
1 tbsp salt
300g (10oz) small squid, cleaned and sliced into 1cm (½ in) rings
200g (7oz) baby octopus, cleaned and left whole, or sliced large octopus
400g (13oz) live mussels or clams
200g (7oz) queen scallops (shelled weight)
400g (13oz) shrimps or prawns, heads removed, peeled if liked
2–3 dried red chillies
2–3 sprigs rosemary
1–2 bay leaves
500ml (17fl oz) olive oil

For the stock

250ml (8fl oz) dry white wine
250ml (8fl oz) water
250ml (8fl oz) white wine vinegar
1 small fennel bulb, sliced
2–3 strips lemon or orange rind
2 tsp salt
1 tsp black peppercorns
1 tsp fennel seeds
1 bay leaf

1 Put the lemon wedges in a colander and sprinkle with the salt. Mix well and leave to stand for about 1 hour.

2 Put all the ingredients for the stock in a large non-corrosive pan. Bring to the boil, then reduce the heat and simmer for 20 minutes. Add the squid rings and octopus and simmer for 15–20 minutes or until the octopus starts to soften.

3 Add the rest of the seafood to the pan and simmer gently for 5 minutes, or until the scallops are just cooked. Drain well.

4 Arrange the warm seafood in the hot sterilized jar along with the lemon wedges, chillies, rosemary and bay leaves. Heat the olive oil in a pan until it reaches 60°C (140°F). Pour the hot oil into the jar, filling it to the top and making sure that the ingredients are completely covered, then seal. The seafood will be ready to eat in 4–6 weeks.

☆☆ **Degree of difficulty**
Moderate

Cooking time
45–55 minutes

Special equipment
1.5 litre (2½ pint) wide-necked, sterilized jar with sealant (see pages 42–43); thermometer

Yield
About 1.25kg (2½ lb)

Shelf life
3–4 months

Serving suggestions
Serve as part of an antipasti selection or spoon over hot or cold pasta for a light main course dish

TIPS

• The mussels can be removed from their shells before bottling, or left on the half shell to enhance their decorative value.
• The cooking stock can be strained and used as a base for a fish soup.

Herrings in Spiced Oil

(see page 27 for illustration)

This robust, spicy preserve is my own invention and is fast becoming a favourite amongst chilli-loving friends. Use firm-fleshed herrings such as maatjes or home-salted herrings (see Salt-curing, page 74). Salted mackerel can be prepared in the same way.

INGREDIENTS

1kg (2lb) salted herrings, or about 500g (1lb) prepared herring fillets
500ml (17fl oz) light olive, groundnut or refined sesame oil
5cm (2in) cinnamon stick, crushed
1 lemongrass stalk, chopped
3–4 dried red chillies, split open
4–5 cloves
4–5 cardamom pods

1 Soak the salted herrings in several changes of cold water for 24 hours, then drain well. Cut in half lengthways and remove all the bones. Rinse, dry well on paper towels and cut into bite-sized pieces. If using prepared herring fillets omit the soaking.

2 Put all the remaining ingredients in a pan and bring slowly to the boil. Keep at just below boiling point for about 20 minutes, then remove from the heat and leave until the mixture has cooled to 50°C (122°F).

3 Arrange the herring pieces in the warm sterilized jar. Pour the warm oil into the jar, making sure the fish are covered. Shake it gently to ensure there are no air pockets and that the spices are evenly distributed, then seal. The fish will be ready in 3–4 weeks.

☆ **Degree of difficulty**
Easy

Cooking time
About 25 minutes

Special equipment
Thermometer; wide-necked, sterilized jar with sealant (see pages 42–43)

Yield
About 500g (1lb)

Shelf life
6 months

Serving suggestions
Serve with chilled vodka; use to make open sandwiches or serve as an appetizer

RELISHES, SAUCES & SPICE MIXES

THE FOLLOWING RECIPES comprise a large and diverse family of products. Originating from various parts of the world, they are the foundation of many cuisines. Their concentrated flavour makes easy work of cooking – a dash of homemade sauce or relish will instantly lift and enhance any uninteresting dish. I always keep a selection of my own spice mixes in store as they can be used to flavour a wide variety of preserves. Make the mixes in small quantities and use as soon as possible, since once they have been ground, spices quickly lose their aroma and taste.

Tomato and Pear Relish

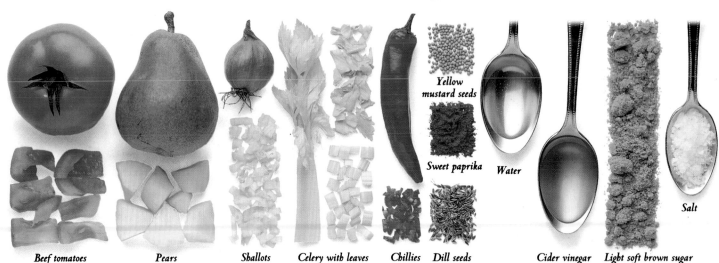

Beef tomatoes — Pears — Shallots — Celery with leaves — Chillies — Dill seeds — *Yellow mustard seeds* — *Sweet paprika* — *Water* — Cider vinegar — Light soft brown sugar — *Salt*

While the United States is the home of the relish, this particular recipe comes from the west coast of Canada, where pears are used instead of the customary apples.

INGREDIENTS

1kg (2lb) beef or plum tomatoes, skinned, deseeded and coarsely chopped
625g (1¼ lb) pears, peeled, cored and coarsely chopped
300g (10oz) shallots or onions, finely chopped
6 celery stalks with leaves, finely chopped
2–3 fresh red chillies, deseeded and finely chopped (optional)
1 tbsp yellow mustard seeds
1 tbsp sweet paprika
1 tbsp dill seeds
250ml (8fl oz) water
1 litre (1¾ pints) cider vinegar or red wine vinegar
200g (7oz) light soft brown or white sugar
1 tbsp salt

1 Put the tomatoes, pears, shallots or onions, celery, chillies, yellow mustard seeds, paprika, dill seeds and water in the preserving pan.

2 Bring to the boil and skim well. Reduce the heat and simmer, stirring frequently, for about 20 minutes or until the pears are soft and mushy.

3 Add the vinegar, sugar and salt. Simmer, stirring occasionally, for 1–1½ hours or until most of the liquid has evaporated and the relish is thick.

4 Remove the pan from the heat. Ladle the relish into the hot sterilized jars, then seal. If wished, heat process, cool and check the seals (see pages 44–45).

☆ **Degree of difficulty**
Easy

Cooking time
1½–2 hours

Special equipment
Non-corrosive preserving pan; sterilized jars with vinegar-proof sealants (see pages 42–43)

Yield
About 1.5kg (3lb)

Shelf life
6 months;
2 years, heat processed

Serving suggestions
Serve with hamburgers, in sandwiches or with grilled fish or meat

DILL SEEDS and paprika give sweetness to the relish, while chillies and mustard seeds add heat

TOMATO AND PEAR RELISH
makes a tasty accompaniment to kebabs.

USE CLAMP-TOP, heatproof jars if you wish to heat process the relish

VARIATIONS

✦ ***Tomato and Quince Relish***
Replace the chopped pears with the same quantity of quince. Increase the cooking time in step 2 to 30–35 minutes, or until the quince are soft but not mushy.

✦ ***Tomato and Apple Relish***
Replace the chopped pears with the same quantity of chopped apple and flavour with crushed coriander seeds instead of the dill.

Corn and Pepper Relish
(see page 17 for illustration)

Even more American than apple pie, Corn and Pepper Relish is often served with a good hamburger. It tastes clean, sweet and sharp. If you like your relish hotter, add some sliced chillies to the chopped vegetables.

INGREDIENTS
300g (10oz) white cabbage, hard core removed, coarsely chopped
300g (10oz) onions, roughly sliced
6 celery stalks, coarsely chopped
2 green peppers, coarsely chopped
2 red peppers, coarsely chopped
10 fresh corn cobs, kernels sliced off
1.25 litres (2 pints) cider vinegar
500g (1lb) light soft brown sugar
2 tbsp yellow mustard seeds
1 tbsp salt

1 Finely chop the cabbage, onions, celery and peppers in a food processor. Put all the ingredients in the preserving pan. Bring to the boil, then simmer for 45–60 minutes, until the corn is tender and the sauce thick.

2 Pour into the hot sterilized jars, pushing the mixture down with a spoon, so that the vegetables are covered by the sauce. Ensure there are no air pockets, then seal. The relish is ready immediately, but improves with keeping.

☆ **Degree of difficulty**
Easy

Cooking time
45–60 minutes

Special equipment
Food processor; non-corrosive preserving pan; sterilized jars with vinegar-proof sealants (see pages 42–43)

Yield
About 2½ kg (5lb)

Shelf life
1 year

Fresh Cranberry and Orange Relish
(see page 28 for illustration)

Fresh cranberries have a refreshingly sour flavour. I use them to add colour and a sharp note to many dishes, such as stuffings, salads and fish. This recipe is the perfect accompaniment to Christmas turkey and ham.

INGREDIENTS
500g (1lb) fresh cranberries
2 oranges, coarsely chopped, pips removed
3–4 tbsp honey
2–3 tbsp orange-flavoured liqueur, such as Grand Marnier or Triple Sec
1 tsp coriander seeds, freshly ground
1 tsp salt

1 Put all the ingredients in the food processor and process, using the pulse button, until the cranberries and oranges are coarsely chopped.

2 Pack into the sterilized jars, then seal and refrigerate. The relish is ready immediately, and if you are using it within 2–3 days, there is no need to bottle it.

☆ **Degree of difficulty**
Easy

Special equipment
Food processor; sterilized jars and sealants (see pages 42–43)

Yield
About 750g (1½ lb)

Shelf life
1 month, refrigerated

Tomato Sauce
(see page 15 for illustration)

Tomato sauce is one of the most popular standbys of the modern kitchen, loved by children and adults alike. Although there are plenty of ready-made sauces to choose from, none can compare with the fresh, full-flavour of a homemade one. Make sure you use ripe, fleshy tomatoes, preferably vine-ripened. If you do not want to heat process the sauce, keep it refrigerated and use within 3 months.

INGREDIENTS
4 tbsp olive oil
300g (10oz) onions, chopped
6 garlic cloves, chopped
6 celery stalks with leaves, chopped
2kg (4lb) beef or plum tomatoes, skinned, deseeded and coarsely chopped
250ml (8fl oz) water or dry white wine
2 tsp salt
2 tsp honey or sugar (optional)
For the herb bundle (see page 47)
3–4 sprigs thyme
4 sage leaves
2 bay leaves
2 strips orange or lemon rind (optional)

1 Heat the olive oil in a large heavy-based pan, add the onions, garlic and celery and fry gently for about 10 minutes or until the onion is translucent.

2 Add the remaining ingredients to the pan. Bring to the boil, then simmer, uncovered, for 30–45 minutes, until most of the liquid has evaporated.

3 Remove the herbs. Pour the sauce into the hot sterilized bottles or jars; seal. Heat process, cool, check the seals and dip corks in wax (see pages 43–45). The sauce is ready immediately.

☆ **Degree of difficulty**
Easy

Cooking time
45–50 minutes

Special equipment
Sterilized bottles or jars with corks or sealants (see pages 42–43)

Yield
About 1.25 litres (2 pints)

Shelf life
1 year, heat processed

Serving suggestions
Use as a base for stews, pasta sauces and pizzas

Red Pepper Ketchup

(see page 56 for technique)

In the past, ketchup was made from a variety of fruit and vegetables. This recipe uses red peppers to create an original sauce with an elusive smoky flavour. Yellow or orange peppers can be used instead. If you don't want to heat process the ketchup, keep it refrigerated and use within 3 months.

INGREDIENTS

2kg (4lb) red peppers
500g (1lb) shallots or onions, peeled
250g (8oz) cooking apples, cored and coarsely chopped
2–3 fresh red chillies, deseeded and coarsely chopped (optional)
1.5 litres (2½ pints) water
750ml (1¼ pints) red wine vinegar or cider vinegar
150g (5oz) white or light soft brown sugar
1 tbsp salt
1 tbsp arrowroot or cornflour
For the herb bundle (see page 47)
1 sprig tarragon
2 sprigs each mint, thyme, sage and parsley
2 strips lemon rind
For the spice bag (see page 47)
1 tbsp coriander seeds
1 tbsp black peppercorns
1 tsp cloves

1 Roast and skin the peppers (see steps 1 and 2, page 56). Rinse well, then core and deseed.

2 Put the peppers, shallots or onions, apples and chillies, if using, in the food processor and process until finely chopped.

3 Transfer to the preserving pan, add the herb bundle, spice bag and water. Bring to the boil, reduce the heat and simmer for 25 minutes. Remove from the heat and leave to cool.

4 Discard the herbs and spice bag. Press the mixture through a sieve or food mill, and put the resulting purée in the cleaned pan. Add the vinegar, sugar and salt. Bring to the boil, stirring to dissolve the sugar, then simmer for 1–1½ hours, until the sauce is reduced by half its volume.

5 Mix the arrowroot to a paste with some vinegar. Stir into the ketchup and boil for 1–2 minutes. Pour into the hot sterilized bottles, then seal. Heat process, cool, check the seals and dip corks in wax (see pages 43–45). The ketchup is ready immediately.

 ✩✩ **Degree of difficulty**
Moderate

 Cooking time
1½–2 hours

 Special equipment
Food processor; non-corrosive preserving pan; sterilized bottles with vinegar-proof sealants or corks (see pages 42–43)

 Yield
About 1 litre (1¾ pints)

Shelf life
2 years, heat processed

Serving suggestions
Serve with grilled or fried fish or as a sauce for pasta

Mushroom Ketchup

This is an adaptation of an 18th-century recipe recorded in The Country Housewife and Lady's Director by Richard Bradley, who was the first professor of botany at Cambridge University. This makes a flavoursome ketchup but it is important to use only flat, fully matured mushrooms.

INGREDIENTS

2kg (4lb) large flat-cap mushrooms
60g (2oz) dried ceps (optional)
150g (5oz) salt
300g (10oz) shallots, unpeeled, quartered
5cm (2in) piece dried ginger root, bruised
125ml (4fl oz) port
1 tbsp cloves
2 tsp crumbled mace blades

1 Put the fresh mushrooms in the food processor and coarsely chop. Arrange in thin layers with the dried ceps, if using, in the casserole dish, sprinkling each layer with some of the salt. Cover and leave to stand for 24 hours.

2 Bake in an oven preheated to 140°C/275°F/gas 1 for 3 hours. Cool and strain through the jelly bag, squeezing to extract all the liquid. Put the liquid in the preserving pan with the remaining ingredients. Bring to the boil, then simmer for 45 minutes, or until the mixture has reduced by a third.

3 Strain again, then return the liquid to the pan and bring back to the boil. Pour into the hot sterilized bottles, then seal. Heat process, cool, check the seals and dip corks in wax (see pages 43–45). The ketchup will be ready to use in 1 month, but improves with keeping.

 ✩✩ **Degree of difficulty**
Moderate

 Cooking time
3½–4½ hours

Special equipment
Food processor; sterilized jelly bag; non-corrosive preserving pan; sterilized bottles with sealants or corks (see pages 42–43)

 Yield
About 750ml (1¼ pints)

 Shelf life
2 years, heat processed

Serving suggestions
Use in small amounts to flavour soups and stews

Mexican Chilli Sauce

Chipotle chillies give this fiery sauce its characteristic smoky flavour. Chipotles are smoked jalapeño chillies and can be bought in many shops that stock Mexican foods. If they are not available, replace with double the quantity of chargrilled fresh chillies (see Chargrilled Vegetables in Oil, page 106).

TIPS
- When deseeding or chopping chillies, wash your hands well afterwards and do not touch your eyes; alternatively, wear disposable household gloves.
- For an extra smooth sauce, pass the mixture through a fine sieve after step 3.

INGREDIENTS
75–100g (2½–3½oz) chipotle chillies
1kg (2lb) plum tomatoes or other tomatoes, skinned and deseeded
300g (10oz) onions, sliced
4 garlic cloves, sliced
750ml (1¼ pints) cider vinegar or distilled malt vinegar
2 tbsp dark soft brown sugar
1 tbsp salt
1 tbsp ground coriander
1 tbsp arrowroot or cornflour
large bunch of coriander, chopped

1 Put the chillies in a bowl and pour over enough boiling water to cover them. Leave until the water is cold. Drain, reserving the water. Slit the chillies open lengthways, and remove the seeds with a knife.

2 Purée the chillies, tomatoes, onions and garlic in the food processor. Place in the preserving pan, adding the water from soaking the chillies. Bring to the boil, then simmer for 30 minutes, or until slightly reduced.

3 Stir in the vinegar, sugar, salt and ground coriander. Return to the boil, then simmer for 25–30 minutes, stirring, until the mixture has reduced by half.

4 Mix the arrowroot to a paste with a little water and stir into the pan. Add the coriander and cook for 1–2 minutes, stirring. Pour into the hot sterilized bottles, then seal. Heat process, cool, check the seals and dip corks in wax (see pages 43–45). The sauce is ready immediately, but improves after 3–4 weeks.

 ☆☆ **Degree of difficulty**
Moderate

 Cooking time
About 1 hour

 Special equipment
Food processor; non-corrosive preserving pan; sterilized bottles with vinegar-proof sealants or corks (see pages 42–43)

 Yield
About 1 litre (1¾ pints)

 Shelf life
1 year, heat processed

 Serving suggestions
Use to add flavour to stews, soups and dips; especially good with chicken dishes

---

Spicy Tomato Ketchup

This recipe produces a thick, wonderfully rich and not too sweet ketchup. If you prefer a sweeter taste, increase the amount of sugar to 100g (3½oz) per 1 litre (1¾ pints) of pulp and omit the chillies.

TIP
- The best celery to use is the leafy "cutting" celery; if it is not available use a head of celery instead.

INGREDIENTS
2kg (4lb) tomatoes
500g (1lb) shallots or onions, peeled
75g (2½oz) fresh ginger root, peeled
6 garlic cloves, peeled
3–4 chillies, deseeded (optional)
6 celery stalks with leaves
For the spice bag (see page 47)
2 tbsp coriander seeds
1 tsp cloves
1 tsp crumbled mace blades
For every 1 litre (1¾ pints) pulp
250ml (8fl oz) cider vinegar
75g (2½oz) soft brown or white sugar
2 tsp salt
1 tbsp sweet paprika

1 Coarsely chop the tomatoes, shallots or onions, ginger, garlic and chillies, if using, in the food processor.

2 Put the mixture in the preserving pan. Tie the celery stalks together with string and add to the pan with the spice bag. Bring to the boil, then simmer for 25 minutes, or until the shallots or onions are translucent.

3 Remove the celery and spice bag. Press the mixture through a sieve or food mill, then return to the cleaned pan. Bring to the boil and cook for ¾–1 hour, or until the purée has reduced by half.

4 Measure the purée and add the vinegar, sugar, salt and paprika. Boil for 1 hour, stirring frequently, until reduced and thick. Pour into the hot sterilized bottles, then seal. Heat process, cool, check the seals and dip corks in wax (see pages 43–45). The ketchup is ready immediately, but improves with keeping.

 ☆☆ **Degree of difficulty**
Moderate

Cooking time
2¼–2½ hours

Special equipment
Food processor; non-corrosive preserving pan; sterilized bottles and vinegar-proof sealants or corks (see pages 42–43)

Yield
About 1 litre (1¾ pints)

Shelf life
2 years, heat processed

Serving suggestions
Use to flavour soups, stews and sauces or serve with pasta

VARIATION
♦ **Damson Ketchup**
Replace the tomatoes with 2kg (4lb) damsons, pitted.

Cooked Tomato and Pepper Salsa

Salsa, *meaning sauce, is Mexican in origin. As a variation, this salsa can be eaten uncooked: add the tomatoes and herbs to the chopped ingredients and marinate for 2–3 hours before using. Keep refrigerated and eat within 2 weeks.*

INGREDIENTS

750g (1½ lb) mixed coloured peppers
2–3 fresh red or green chillies, deseeded
1 large red onion
2 garlic cloves, peeled
3 tbsp olive, corn or groundnut oil
3 tbsp red wine vinegar or lemon juice
2 tsp salt
500g (1lb) firm red tomatoes, skinned, deseeded and finely chopped
3 tbsp chopped coriander or parsley

1 Coarsely chop the vegetables, then finely chop in the food processor with the garlic, oil, vinegar or lemon juice and salt.

2 Put in the preserving pan with the tomatoes and herbs. Bring to the boil, then simmer for 5 minutes. Pour into the hot sterilized jars, then seal. Heat process, cool and check the seals (see pages 44–45). The salsa is ready immediately.

☆ **Degree of difficulty**
Easy

Cooking time
About 5 minutes

Special equipment
Food processor; non-corrosive preserving pan; sterilized jars with vinegar-proof sealants (see pages 42–43)

Yield
About 1kg (2lb)

Shelf life
6 months, heat processed

Chinese-style Plum Sauce

Sweet, sour and hot, this Chinese sauce is a suitable accompaniment to roast duck as well as a flavouring for soups and stews.

INGREDIENTS

2kg (4lb) red plums, or half plums and half damsons
1 litre (1¾ pints) red wine vinegar or rice vinegar
2 tsp salt
250ml (8fl oz) dark soy sauce
300g (10oz) honey or dark brown sugar
1 tbsp arrowroot or cornflour
For the spice bag (see page 47)
1 tbsp star anise, crushed
2 tsp Sichuan pepper, crushed
1 tsp small dried red chillies, crushed

1 Put the plums, vinegar, salt and spice bag into the preserving pan. Bring to the boil, then reduce the heat and simmer for about 25 minutes, or until the plums are soft and mushy.

2 Discard the spice bag. Pass the plums through a sieve. Put the purée in the cleaned pan and stir in the soy sauce and honey or sugar. Bring to the boil, then simmer for 45 minutes, or until the purée has reduced by a quarter.

3 Mix the arrowroot to a paste with water. Stir into the pan and cook for 1–2 minutes, stirring. Pour into the hot sterilized bottles, then seal. Heat process, cool, check the seals and dip corks in wax (see pages 43–45). The sauce is ready immediately, but improves with keeping.

☆ **Degree of difficulty**
Easy

Cooking time
About 1¼ hours

Special equipment
Non-corrosive preserving pan; sterilized bottles with vinegar-proof sealants or corks (see pages 42–43)

Yield
About 1 litre (1¾ pints)

Shelf life
2 years, heat processed

Serving suggestion
Use to dress salads instead of oil and vinegar

Harissa
(see page 17 for illustration)

Here is the basic recipe for this famous, fiercely hot Moroccan paste. Before using it, you can soften its flavour with a little tomato purée or puréed fresh tomatoes. Some garlic, coriander and cumin can be added too.

INGREDIENTS

500g (1lb) dried red chillies, deseeded
150ml (¼ pint) olive oil, plus a little more to cover
2 tbsp salt

1 Put the deseeded chillies in a bowl. Add enough hot water to cover and leave to stand for 15–20 minutes, until soft.

2 Drain the chillies and place in the food processor with 125ml (4fl oz) of the soaking water. Process to a paste. Stir in the oil and salt. Pack into the sterilized jars.

3 Cover the paste with a thin layer of oil, then seal and refrigerate. The harissa is ready to use immediately.

☆ **Degree of difficulty**
Easy

Special equipment
Food processor; sterilized jars and sealants (see pages 42–43)

Yield
About 500g (1lb)

Shelf life
6 months, refrigerated

Harrief

This Moroccan speciality is my favourite hot sauce. I make it in large quantities and use it to add instant piquancy to sauces, soups, stews, salads and pasta, or brush it on meat before barbecuing.

---TIP---

• It is difficult to give an exact quantity of chillies, since different varieties vary greatly in heat. For this recipe I use the large red Westland, which gives a hot but not scorching result.

INGREDIENTS

2kg (4lb) red peppers
250g (8oz) fresh red chillies, deseeded
250g (8oz) garlic cloves, peeled
150ml (¼ pint) fruity olive oil
250ml (8fl oz) cider vinegar
3 tbsp salt
1–2 tbsp chilli powder (optional)
2 tbsp cumin seeds, freshly ground
2 tsp arrowroot

1 Roast and skin the peppers (see steps 1 and 2, page 56). Rinse well, then core and deseed. Put in the food processor with the chillies, garlic and oil.

2 Process until the vegetables are finely chopped. Transfer to the preserving pan and add the vinegar, salt and spices. Bring to the boil, then reduce the heat and simmer for 1–1½ hours, until the mixture is reduced by a third.

3 Mix the arrowroot to a paste with a little vinegar and stir into the sauce. Raise the heat and boil the sauce rapidly for 1 minute, stirring constantly.

4 Pour the sauce into the hot sterilized jars, then seal. The sauce is ready immediately, but improves with keeping.

☆☆ **Degree of difficulty**
Moderate

 Cooking time
1–1½ hours

 Special equipment
Food processor; non-corrosive preserving pan; sterilized jars with vinegar-proof sealants (see pages 42–43)

 Yield
About 1kg (2lb)

 Shelf life
1 year

Serving suggestion
Use as a condiment

Schug — (see page 17 for illustration)

This is a fiercely hot chilli paste from Yemen, where it is used in a wide range of dishes. Extra chopped fresh coriander should be added just before serving. If you prefer a milder version, replace half or more of the chillies with green peppers.

INGREDIENTS

1 large head garlic, peeled
750g (1½lb) fresh green chillies
150g (5oz) coriander (about 2 bunches)
1 tbsp coriander seeds
2 tsp cumin seeds
2 tsp black peppercorns
1 tsp cardamom pods
1 tsp cloves
1½ tbsp salt
a little olive oil, to cover

1 Finely mince or chop the garlic, chillies and fresh coriander in the mincer or food processor.

2 Grind all the spices to a fine powder in the spice mill or coffee grinder. Sieve into the chilli and garlic mixture, then stir in the salt and mix well.

3 Pack tightly into the sterilized jars. Cover with a thin layer of oil, then seal. Keep refrigerated. The schug is ready immediately.

☆ **Degree of difficulty**
Easy

 Special equipment
Mincer or food processor; spice mill or coffee grinder; sterilized jars and sealants (see pages 42–43)

 Yield
About 1kg (2lb)

 Shelf life
3 months, refrigerated

 Serving suggestion
Use as a condiment

Date Blatjang (Date Sauce) — (see page 35 for illustration)

I came across this recipe in South Africa, where it had been introduced in the 17th century by Malay slaves. It has a hot, sharp, sweet flavour. Serve it with rice or oily fish. Other fruit, such as fresh or dried apricots, peaches and mango, can be used instead of dates.

INGREDIENTS

150g (5oz) tamarind block
350ml (12fl oz) boiling water
500g (1lb) pitted dates, coarsely chopped
5cm (2in) piece fresh ginger root, peeled and chopped
8 garlic cloves, chopped
3–4 dried red chillies, deseeded and chopped
1 litre (1¾ pints) red wine vinegar
2 tsp salt

1 Soak the tamarind in the boiling water for 30 minutes. Strain, then pour the liquid into the preserving pan with the rest of the ingredients. Bring to the boil, simmer for 10 minutes, then cool.

2 Purée in the food processor. Return to the cleaned pan and boil for 1–2 minutes. Pour into the hot sterilized bottles, then seal. The sauce is ready immediately, but improves with keeping.

☆ **Degree of difficulty**
Easy

 Cooking time
About 15 minutes

 Special equipment
Non-corrosive preserving pan; food processor; sterilized bottles with vinegar-proof sealants or corks (see pages 42–43)

 Yield
About 1 litre (1¾ pints)

 Shelf life
2 years

Masalas and Spice Mixes

I have borrowed the word masala *from India but the following recipes come from all over the world. A masala is a mixture of spices, which Indian cooks use to give a rich, subtle range of flavours to their cooking. There are as many masalas as there are cooks. The whole spices are sometimes roasted, then pounded or ground to a powder and used as fresh as possible. Use these recipes as a blueprint and create your own favourite combinations for adding to pickles and other preserves.*

— TIPS —

• Dried rose petals are available from some herbalists or from healthfood shops in the form of tea. Do check that they have not been treated with chemicals. Alternatively, dry your own.
• To toast whole spices, put them in a dry frying pan and stir constantly over the heat until they become aromatic and start to pop.

1. CHAWAGE (YEMENITE SPICE MIX)

3 tbsp black peppercorns
3 tbsp cumin seeds
2 tbsp coriander seeds
1 tsp cloves
1 tsp green cardamom pods
2 tsp ground turmeric

2. GARAM MASALA

1 tbsp cumin seeds, toasted
1 tbsp coriander seeds, toasted
2 tsp black peppercorns
5cm (2in) cinnamon stick, crushed
1 tsp crumbled mace blades
1 tsp black cumin seeds (kalajeera)
½ nutmeg, broken into pieces

3. MY FAVOURITE SAVOURY MASALA

2 tbsp coriander seeds
2 tsp black peppercorns
2 tsp cumin seeds
2 tsp caraway seeds
1 tsp green cardamom pods

4. MY FAVOURITE SWEET MASALA

2 tbsp coriander seeds
1 tbsp allspice berries
1 tbsp cloves
1 tbsp cardamom pods
2 tsp caraway seeds
1 tsp anise (optional)

5. BRITISH MIXED SPICE

5cm (2in) cinnamon stick, crushed or 1½ tbsp ground cinnamon
1 tbsp allspice berries
2 tsp cloves
2 tsp coriander seeds
1 nutmeg, broken into pieces
1–2 strips dried orange rind (optional)

6. MOROCCAN MEAT SPICING

1 tbsp black peppercorns
1 tbsp allspice berries
2 tsp crumbled mace blades
1 nutmeg, broken into pieces
2.5cm (1in) cinnamon stick, crushed
1 tbsp sweet paprika (optional)
2 tsp ground turmeric

7. RAS EL HANOUT

2 tsp black peppercorns
1 tsp coriander seeds
1 tsp cumin seeds
1 tsp allspice berries
5cm (2in) cinnamon stick, crushed
½ nutmeg, broken into pieces
½ tsp cloves
½ tsp cardamom pods
1 tbsp dried rose petals, crumbled (optional)
1 tsp ground ginger
½ tsp hot chilli powder

1 For each masala or spice mix, put all the ingredients (except any ready-ground spices), in the spice mill, coffee grinder or mortar. Grind them to a fine powder then mix in any ready-ground spices.

2 For an extra-fine powder, pass through a fine sieve, re-grind the debris left in the mesh, then sieve again. Discard any bits that remain in the sieve. Transfer to a small airtight jar and seal.

☆ **Degree of difficulty**
Easy

🍴 **Special equipment**
Spice mill, coffee grinder or pestle and mortar; airtight jar

🍯 **Shelf life**
3 months

🍽 **Serving suggestions**
(1) goes well with meat, especially chicken; (2) may be used in pickles or added to Pickled Venison (see page 132); (3) and (6) add savour to burgers, koftas and meat balls; use (4) or (5) to flavour mincemeat (see page 169); (7) can be added to sweet and savoury dishes

CHUTNEYS

CHUTNEYS CAN BE SWEET, hot, sour or spicy, smooth or chunky. Whatever their individual characteristics, all use sugar and vinegar as a preservative. In India, where the chutney originated, the name also encompasses fresh marinated salads with a short shelf life, so I have included a few recipes for these too (even though they are not preserves as such). I like my chutney to have lots of texture, so I cut the ingredients into large chunks. If you prefer a smoother product, slice fruit and vegetables into smaller pieces. Chutneys are traditionally served with meat, and their role is, perhaps, most accurately summed up by the author of the recipe for Ginger Chutney, below: "Chutneys are intended to act upon the taste in direct contrast to the meat with which they are eaten, and therefore spices, aromatics and acid assume the ascendant." Use mellow vinegars for chutneys: cider, wine or citrus vinegars are best – malt vinegar produces too harsh a result. Keep chutneys for at least a month before using them, to allow time for their flavours to blend and mellow.

Ginger Chutney

Fresh ginger root   *Red peppers*   *Cucumber*   *Raisins*   *Onions*   *Lemons*   *Cider vinegar*   *Salt*   *Sugar*

This is adapted from a recipe for Indian chutney that I found in an undated pickling book, by Marion Harris Neil, probably published about 90 years ago.

INGREDIENTS

300g (10oz) fresh ginger root, shredded
300g (10oz) red peppers, diced
250g (8oz) cucumber, quartered lengthways and thickly sliced
250g (8oz) raisins
250g (8oz) onions, coarsely chopped
4 lemons, halved lengthways, pips removed, thinly sliced
1 litre (1¾ pints) cider vinegar or white wine vinegar
500g (1lb) preserving or granulated sugar
2 tsp salt

1 Put all the ingredients, except the sugar and salt, into the preserving pan. Bring the mixture to the boil, then reduce the heat and simmer gently for about 30 minutes, until the fruit and vegetables have softened.

2 Add the sugar and salt to the pan, stirring until they have dissolved. Simmer for a further 30–45 minutes, until most of the liquid has evaporated and the chutney is thick.

3 Ladle the mixture into the hot sterilized jars, then seal. The chutney will be ready to eat in 1 month, but improves with keeping.

 Degree of difficulty
Easy

 Cooking time
1–1¼ hours

 Special equipment
Non-corrosive preserving pan; sterilized jars with vinegar-proof sealants (see pages 42–43)

 Yield
About 1.5kg (3lb)

 Shelf life
2 years

 Serving suggestions
Serve with game, cheese or grilled fish

GINGER CHUTNEY *makes a delicious accompaniment to grilled tuna steak. Serve the fish with a spicy tomato coulis and a mixture of wild and white rice.*

THICKLY CUT VEGETABLES, sliced lemons and whole raisins give this chutney a coarse texture

FRESH GINGER ROOT mellows in flavour with long cooking, and produces an intensely aromatic chutney

TIPS

• When buying fresh ginger root, choose firm pieces with a smooth, silky skin. Store in the refrigerator.

• Any leftover pieces of fresh ginger can be frozen and used in another recipe. To use, simply grate it straight from the freezer.

• Pieces of ginger can also be preserved in dry sherry, vodka or brandy and used to flavour drinks and desserts.

• Do not throw ginger peel away; wash it well, cover with vinegar and steep for 3 months. Filter and use the vinegar to flavour salads and rice dishes.

Green Tomato Chutney

(see page 15 for illustration)

This sweet and sour version of a classic colonial recipe is well worth trying. Green tomatoes are notoriously difficult to peel so if, like me, you do not mind skin in your chutney, there is no need to peel them.

INGREDIENTS

750g (1½ lb) green tomatoes
500g (1lb) cooking apples
250g (8oz) onions, coarsely chopped
1 tbsp salt
125g (4oz) raisins
500g (1lb) light soft brown or white sugar
250ml (8fl oz) cider vinegar
grated rind and juice of 2 large lemons
2 tbsp black or yellow mustard seeds
2–3 fresh red chillies, deseeded and chopped (optional)
For the spice bag (see page 47)
1 tbsp coriander seeds
2 tsp black peppercorns
2 tsp allspice berries
1 tsp cloves
2 cinnamon sticks, crushed

1 Skin the tomatoes, if desired (see page 46), then coarsely chop. Peel, core and chop the apples. Add the peel and cores to the spice bag. Put the tomatoes, apples, onions and salt in the preserving pan. Bring the mixture slowly to the boil, then simmer for 20 minutes.

2 Add the raisins, sugar, vinegar, lemon rind and juice and spice bag. Return to the boil, stirring until the sugar has dissolved, then simmer for 30 minutes, until most of the liquid has evaporated and the mixture is thick.

3 Add the mustard seeds and chillies, if using. Ladle the mixture into the hot sterilized jars, then seal. The chutney will be ready to eat in 1 month.

Degree of difficulty
Easy

Cooking time
About 1 hour

Special equipment
Non-corrosive preserving pan; sterilized jars with vinegar-proof sealants (see pages 42–43)

Yield
About 1.5kg (3lb)

Shelf life
1 year

Serving suggestions
Serve as an accompaniment to mature cheese or add to sandwiches

Pumpkin Chutney

(see page 58 for technique)

Pumpkin makes a superb, rich golden chutney. If, like me, you prefer a crunchy texture, cook the mixture for less time than recommended in step 2, so that the pumpkin still has some bite to it. Leave the chutney to mature for up to 6 weeks.

INGREDIENTS

1.25kg (2½ lb) pumpkin, peeled, deseeded and cut into 2.5cm (1in) chunks
750g (1½ lb) apples, peeled, cored and coarsely chopped
75g (2½ oz) fresh ginger root, finely shredded
3–4 fresh red chillies, deseeded and sliced
2 tbsp white mustard seeds
2 tbsp black mustard seeds
1 litre (1¾ pints) cider vinegar or distilled malt vinegar
500g (1lb) white or light soft brown sugar
1 tbsp salt

1 Put all the ingredients, except the sugar and salt, in the preserving pan and mix well.

2 Bring to the boil, then reduce the heat and simmer for 20–25 minutes, or until the pumpkin is just tender.

3 Add the sugar and salt. Return to the boil, stirring until they have dissolved. Simmer, stirring frequently, for about 1 hour, until most of the liquid has evaporated and the mixture is thick.

4 Ladle into the hot sterilized jars, then seal. The chutney will be ready to eat in 1 month, but improves with keeping.

--- VARIATION ---

✦ Pineapple Chutney
Substitute 1 medium pineapple and 625g (1¼ lb) cooking apples, peeled, cored and chopped, for the pumpkin. Put in a non-corrosive preserving pan with 250ml (8fl oz) water, bring to the boil, then simmer until very soft. Add 350ml (12fl oz) vinegar, 300g (10oz) sugar and 1 tablespoon each of black and white mustard seeds, and continue as in step 3. Add 6 finely sliced green chillies and 2 teaspoons caraway seeds just before potting.

Degree of difficulty
Easy

Cooking time
1¼–1½ hours

Special equipment
Non-corrosive preserving pan; sterilized jars with vinegar-proof sealants (see pages 42–43)

Yield
About 2kg (4lb)

Shelf life
2 years

Serving suggestions
Mix a few large tablespoons of chutney with plain boiled rice, or serve with cold meats and cheese

Fresh Onion Chutney

(see page 18 for illustration)

This recipe belongs to a large family of fresh, salad-like chutneys that are served to refresh the palate and revive the appetite. Grated apples, quince, carrots and turnips can be used instead of the onions.

INGREDIENTS

500g (1lb) large, sweet purple or white onions, sliced into thin rings
1 tbsp salt
1–2 fresh green or red chillies, deseeded and finely chopped
3 tbsp white wine vinegar or cider vinegar
2 tbsp chopped mint or coriander
1 tsp nigella seeds (optional)

1 Put the onion rings in a colander and sprinkle with the salt. Mix well and leave to drain for about 1 hour.

2 Squeeze the onion to extract as much moisture as possible, then mix with the rest of the ingredients and leave to stand for 1 hour, to let the flavour develop. The chutney is ready immediately.

☆ **Degree of difficulty**
Easy

Yield
About 250g (8oz)

Shelf life
1 week, refrigerated

Serving suggestions
Serve with curries, as an appetizer or as a refreshing salad

Carrot and Almond Chutney

(see page 23 for illustration)

My adaptation of angel hair jam, a Middle Eastern classic made with long, thin strands of carrot. The carrot strands look translucent, which makes it particularly attractive. Full-flavoured, sweet and sour, this chutney goes well with mature cheese, and my friend Ron can't eat his Scotch eggs without it.

INGREDIENTS

1.25kg (2½lb) carrots, grated lengthways
125g (4oz) fresh ginger root, shredded
250ml (8fl oz) white wine vinegar
grated rind and juice of 2 large lemons
150ml (¼ pint) water
400g (13oz) white or light brown sugar
4 tbsp honey
2 tbsp coriander seeds, freshly ground
1 tbsp salt
3–4 dried bird's eye chillies
3 tbsp flaked almonds

1 Put all the ingredients, except the chillies and almonds, in a glass bowl. Mix well, cover and leave to stand overnight.

2 The next day, transfer the mixture to the preserving pan. Bring to the boil, then simmer for 20 minutes. Raise the heat and boil hard for 10–15 minutes, until most of the liquid has evaporated and the mixture is thick.

3 Grind the chillies to a powder in the spice mill or coffee grinder. Stir into the pan with the almonds. Ladle into the hot sterilized jars, then seal. The chutney will be ready in 1 month, but improves with keeping.

☆ **Degree of difficulty**
Easy

Cooking time
30–35 minutes

Special equipment
Non-corrosive preserving pan; spice mill or coffee grinder; sterilized jars with vinegar-proof sealants (see pages 42–43)

Yield
About 1.5kg (3lb)

Shelf life
2 years

Serving suggestions
Serve with cold meats or just spread on bread

Marrow Chutney

A simple and delicious chutney that turns the humble marrow into a delicacy. If using a very large marrow, remember to remove the seeds and soft centre.

INGREDIENTS

1kg (2lb) marrow, peeled, cored and cut into 2.5cm (1in) cubes
2 tbsp salt
2 large onions, coarsely chopped
300g (10oz) carrots, coarsely grated
100g (3½oz) crystallized ginger, coarsely chopped
1–2 fresh red chillies, finely chopped
2 tbsp black mustard seeds
1 tbsp ground turmeric
750ml (1¼ pints) cider vinegar
250g (8oz) sugar

1 Put the marrow in a colander and sprinkle with half the salt. Leave for 1 hour. Rinse and dry. Put in the preserving pan with the rest of the ingredients, except the sugar and remaining salt. Bring to the boil, then simmer for 25 minutes, or until just soft.

2 Add the sugar and salt, stirring until they have dissolved, then simmer for 1–1¼ hours, until most of the liquid has evaporated and the mixture is thick. Ladle into the hot sterilized jars, then seal. The chutney will be ready in 1 month.

☆ **Degree of difficulty**
Easy

Cooking time
1½–2 hours

Special equipment
Non-corrosive preserving pan; sterilized jars with vinegar-proof sealants (see pages 42–43)

Yield
About 1.5kg (3lb)

Shelf life
2 years

Serving suggestion
Good with cheese

Aubergine and Garlic Chutney

A soft, melt-in-the-mouth chutney that combines the mild taste of aubergine with the wonderful aroma of garlic. Use large, firm, light-purple aubergines if possible.

INGREDIENTS

1kg (2lb) aubergines, cut into 2.5cm (1in) cubes
2 tbsp salt
3 tbsp groundnut, olive or sesame oil
1 tbsp nigella seeds
3 tbsp sesame seeds
4 heads garlic, peeled
250g (8oz) shallots, quartered
2–3 red or green chillies, deseeded and coarsely chopped
750ml (1¼ pints) cider vinegar or white wine vinegar
150g (5oz) soft brown sugar
3 tsp sweet paprika
small bunch of mint, chopped (optional)

1 Put the aubergine cubes in a colander and sprinkle with half the salt. Mix well and leave to drain for 1 hour. Rinse well and pat dry with paper towels.

2 Heat the oil in the preserving pan, add the nigella and sesame seeds and cook for a minute or two, until the sesame seeds start to pop.

3 Add the aubergine, garlic, shallots and chillies to the pan and cook, stirring frequently, for about 5 minutes.

4 Add the vinegar and bring to the boil, then reduce the heat and simmer for 15 minutes, until the aubergines are soft. Add the sugar, paprika and remaining salt, stirring until they have dissolved.

5 Increase the heat slightly and cook, stirring frequently, for 45 minutes–1 hour, until most of the liquid has evaporated and the mixture is thick. Add the mint, if using, and remove the pan from the heat.

6 Ladle the mixture into the hot sterilized jars, then seal. The chutney is ready to eat in 1 month, but improves with keeping.

 Degree of difficulty
Easy

 Cooking time
1–1¼ hours

 Special equipment
Non-corrosive preserving pan; sterilized jars with vinegar-proof sealants (see pages 42–43)

 Yield
About 1.5kg (3lb)

 Shelf life
1 year

Serving suggestions
Especially good with chicken curry, cheese or in sandwiches

Red Tomato Chutney

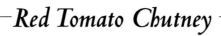

A mild and fragrant chutney. Originally jaggery (unrefined Indian sugar) was used, but since it is hard to obtain brown sugar can be substituted.

INGREDIENTS

3 tbsp groundnut or sesame oil
300g (10oz) onions, coarsely chopped
1 head garlic, peeled and coarsely chopped
90g (3oz) fresh ginger root, finely shredded
2–3 fresh red chillies, deseeded and cut into thick strips (optional)
1kg (2lb) firm, red plum or beef tomatoes, skinned, deseeded and chopped
125g (4oz) jaggery or soft brown sugar
250ml (8fl oz) red wine vinegar
6 cardamom pods
90g (3oz) basil or mint, coarsely chopped

1 Heat the oil in the preserving pan and add the onions, garlic, ginger and chillies, if using. Fry gently for 5 minutes, or until the onions just start to colour. Add the tomatoes and cook for about 15 minutes or until they are soft.

2 Add the sugar and vinegar, stirring until the sugar has dissolved. Bring to the boil, then simmer for 25–30 minutes, stirring frequently, until most of the liquid has evaporated and the mixture is thick. Remove the pan from the heat.

3 Grind the cardamom pods in the spice mill or coffee grinder. Add to the chutney through a sieve and stir in the basil or mint. Ladle into the hot sterilized jars, then seal. The chutney will be ready to eat in 1 month, but improves with keeping.

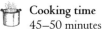 **Degree of difficulty**
Easy

Cooking time
45–50 minutes

Special equipment
Non-corrosive preserving pan; spice mill or coffee grinder; sterilized jars with vinegar-proof sealants (see pages 42–43)

 Yield
About 1kg (2lb)

Shelf life
1 year

Serving suggestion
Spread a few tablespoons over the bottom of a flan case before adding a savoury filling

Hot Mango Chutney

This recipe is from Bihar in India, and produces a hot, richly flavoured, golden preserve. Although turmeric can be used, saffron gives the chutney a unique flavour.

INGREDIENTS

2kg (4lb) unripe mangoes, peeled and cut into 2.5cm (1in) chunks (see page 175)

2 limes or lemons, sliced into semi-circles

3–4 fresh red chillies, deseeded and coarsely chopped

750ml (1¼ pints) white wine vinegar or distilled white vinegar

500g (1lb) light soft brown sugar

1 tbsp salt

1 tbsp green cardamom pods

1 tsp cumin seeds

1 tsp chilli powder (optional)

½ tsp saffron strands or 1 tsp ground turmeric

1 Put the mangoes, limes or lemons, chillies and vinegar in the preserving pan. Bring to the boil, then reduce the heat and simmer for 10–15 minutes, or until the mango is just tender. Add the sugar and salt, stirring until they have dissolved. Simmer for 50–60 minutes, until most of the liquid has evaporated and the mixture is thick.

2 Grind the cardamom and cumin to a powder in the spice mill or coffee grinder. Add to the chutney through a sieve, together with the chilli powder. Soak the saffron strands in a little hot water for a few minutes. Stir into the chutney or add the turmeric.

3 Ladle into the hot sterilized jars, then seal. The chutney will be ready to eat in 1 month.

 Degree of difficulty
Easy

 Cooking time
1–1¼ hours

 Special equipment
Non-corrosive preserving pan; spice mill or coffee grinder; sterilized jars with vinegar-proof sealants (see pages 42–43)

 Yield
About 1.5kg (3lb)

 Shelf life
2 years

Serving suggestions
Serve with poppadoms or with plain boiled rice for a light supper dish

Plum Chutney

A dark red, superbly flavoured chutney. The original recipe, which comes from Assam, includes 15 chillies and several spoons of chilli powder. I tried it and it was wonderfully hot — a real treat for chilli lovers. This is a toned-down version but you can add more chillies if you want to spice it up.

INGREDIENTS

500g (1lb) dark red plums

500g (1lb) light plums

6 large garlic cloves, coarsely chopped

6 fresh red chillies, coarsely chopped

75ml (3fl oz) water

125g (4oz) tamarind block or 2 tbsp tamarind paste

750ml (1¼ pints) malt vinegar

400g (13oz) light soft brown or white sugar

2 tsp salt

1 tsp cloves

1 tsp allspice berries

1 cinnamon stick, broken

½ tsp black cumin seeds (kalajeera)

1 Cut the plums in half and remove the stones. Crack the stones with a hammer or nutcracker and tie them in a piece of muslin.

2 Put the plums, muslin bag, garlic, chillies and water in the preserving pan. Bring to the boil, then simmer gently, stirring frequently, for 15–20 minutes or until the plums are soft.

3 If using a tamarind block, soak it in 125ml (4fl oz) hot water for 20 minutes, then sieve out and discard the large seeds.

4 Add the vinegar, sieved tamarind or tamarind paste, sugar and salt to the pan. Bring to the boil, stirring until they have dissolved. Simmer for 25–30 minutes, stirring frequently, until most of the liquid has evaporated and the mixture is thick. Remove from the heat and take out the muslin bag.

5 Grind the cloves, allspice and cinnamon to a powder in the spice mill or coffee grinder. Stir into the chutney with the cumin seeds. Ladle into the hot sterilized jars, then seal. The chutney will be ready to eat in 1 month.

 Degree of difficulty
Easy

 Cooking time
About 1¼ hours

Special equipment
Hammer or nutcracker; muslin; non-corrosive preserving pan; spice mill or coffee grinder; sterilized jars with vinegar-proof sealants (see pages 42–43)

 Yield
About 1kg (2lb)

 Shelf life
2 years

 Serving suggestions
Serve with cold meat and cheese or simply spread on bread

—— TIP ——
• Select firm, fleshy plums with a good colour. I use a mixture of Victoria and dark red plums, but you can use just red plums if you cannot obtain Victorias.

Apple Chutney

This is a classic, mild, fruity British chutney. You can make it with a combination of apples and pears instead of just apples. It is delicious served with cheese or can be used as an unusual sandwich filling.

INGREDIENTS

1.25kg (2½ lb) underripe cooking apples (windfalls are good), peeled, cored and coarsely chopped
625g (1¼ lb) onions, coarsely chopped
2 lemons, finely sliced into semi-circles
300g (10oz) raisins
2 garlic cloves, finely chopped (optional)
500ml (17fl oz) cider vinegar
400g (13oz) dark molasses sugar
1 tbsp salt
1 tsp ground ginger
1 tsp ground cinnamon
1 tsp ground turmeric

1 Put the apples, onions, lemons, raisins, garlic, if using, and vinegar in the preserving pan. Bring to the boil, then simmer for 15–20 minutes, until the apples soften but still retain some texture.

2 Add the sugar, stirring until it has dissolved. Simmer for 30–45 minutes, until most of the liquid has evaporated and the mixture is thick. Remove from the heat. Add the salt and spices.

3 Ladle into the hot sterilized jars, then seal. The chutney will be ready to eat in 1 month.

☆ **Degree of difficulty**
Easy

Cooking time
45 minutes–1 hour

Special equipment
Non-corrosive preserving pan; sterilized jars with vinegar-proof sealants (see pages 42–43)

Yield
About 2kg (4lb)

Shelf life
1 year

Serving suggestions
Serve with cheese or spread on bread and butter

Exotic Fruit Chutney

A delightfully fresh-tasting chutney. I tend to make it in winter and sometimes add a combination of pawpaw, kiwi fruit and lychees to the kumquats, apples and sweetcorn.

INGREDIENTS

250g (8oz) kumquats or oranges
1 small pineapple, peeled, cored and cut into 2.5cm (1in) chunks
500g (1lb) cooking or dessert apples, peeled, cored and coarsely chopped
300g (10oz) dried apricots, soaked if necessary and coarsely chopped
250g (8oz) baby sweetcorn, cut into 2.5cm (1in) lengths
1 litre (1¾ pints) cider vinegar or white wine vinegar
500g (1lb) sugar
3–4 fresh red chillies, deseeded and chopped
2 tbsp black mustard seeds
2 tbsp salt
1 tbsp green peppercorns
100g (3½oz) mint, coarsely chopped

1 If using kumquats, leave them whole; slice oranges in half, then cut into medium-thick slices. Put all the fruit in the preserving pan with the sweetcorn and vinegar. Bring to the boil, then simmer for 15 minutes.

2 Add the sugar, chillies, mustard seeds, salt and peppercorns. Stir until the sugar has dissolved. Simmer, stirring frequently, for 50–60 minutes, until most of the liquid has evaporated and the mixture is thick.

3 Remove from the heat and stir in the mint. Ladle into the hot sterilized jars, then seal. The chutney will be ready in 1 month, but improves with keeping.

☆ **Degree of difficulty**
Easy

Cooking time
1–1¼ hours

Special equipment
Non-corrosive preserving pan; sterilized jars with vinegar-proof sealants (see pages 42–43)

Yield
About 3kg (6lb)

Shelf life
1 year

Serving suggestions
Serve with poultry, cheese or curries

Fig Chutney

I found this unusual recipe in an anonymous Victorian cookery book. It makes a dark and delicious chutney and is an ideal way to use up unripe figs.

INGREDIENTS

1.25 litres (2 pints) red wine vinegar
500g (1lb) light soft brown sugar
2 tbsp salt
1kg (2lb) firm, slightly underripe black figs, sliced into rounds 1cm (½in) thick
500g (1lb) onions, sliced into thin rings
250g (8oz) pitted dates, coarsely chopped
150g (5oz) fresh ginger root, finely shredded
2 tbsp sweet paprika
1 tbsp white mustard seeds
3 tbsp chopped fresh tarragon or 1 tbsp dried tarragon

1 Put the vinegar, sugar and salt in the preserving pan, stirring until the sugar and salt have dissolved. Bring to the boil, then simmer for about 5 minutes.

2 Add the figs, onions, dates and spices. Bring to the boil, then simmer for 1 hour, until most of the liquid has evaporated and the mixture is thick.

3 Remove from the heat, add the tarragon and mix well. Ladle into the hot sterilized jars, then seal. The chutney will be ready to eat in 1 month.

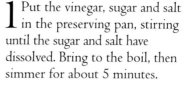

☆ **Degree of difficulty**
Easy

Cooking time
About 1¼ hours

Special equipment
Non-corrosive preserving pan; sterilized jars with vinegar-proof sealants (see pages 42–43)

Yield
About 2kg (4lb)

Shelf life
1 year

Serving suggestions
Serve with cheese and cold meats or add to hot curries

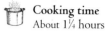
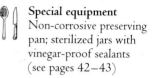

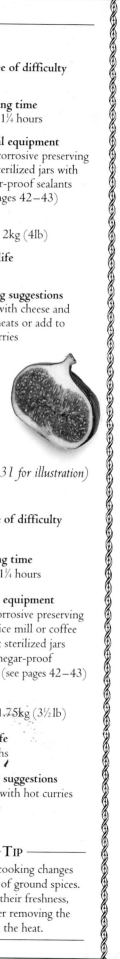

Peach Chutney

(see page 31 for illustration)

A light, elegant and refreshing chutney. Peaches sometimes produce a pale chutney; to correct this you can, as I do, add 2 tablespoons of sweet paprika, which gives it a pinkish hue, or 2 teaspoons of ground turmeric, which adds a golden yellow tint. They are added with the other ground spices.

INGREDIENTS

1kg (2lb) peaches, skinned, stoned and sliced 2.5cm (1in) thick
300g (10oz) cooking apples, peeled, cored and chopped
250g (8oz) seedless grapes
2 lemons, finely sliced into semi-circles
275g (9oz) shallots, coarsely chopped
3 garlic cloves, finely shredded
75g (2½oz) fresh ginger root, finely shredded
500ml (17fl oz) cider vinegar or white wine vinegar
250g (8oz) sugar
1 tsp cloves
1 tsp cardamom pods
5cm (2in) piece cinnamon stick
2 tsp caraway seeds

1 Put all the fruit, the shallots, garlic, ginger and vinegar in the preserving pan. Bring to the boil, then reduce the heat and simmer for about 25 minutes, until the apples are just soft and the shallots translucent.

2 Add the sugar, stirring until it has dissolved. Simmer for 35–40 minutes, until most of the liquid has evaporated and the mixture is thick. Remove the pan from the heat.

3 Grind the cloves, cardamom pods and cinnamon stick to a powder in the spice mill or coffee grinder.

4 Add the ground spices to the chutney through a sieve (this will remove any fibres from the cardamom pods), then add the caraway seeds and mix well.

5 Ladle the mixture into the hot sterilized jars, then seal. The chutney will be ready to eat in 1 month.

☆ **Degree of difficulty**
Easy

Cooking time
About 1¼ hours

Special equipment
Non-corrosive preserving pan; spice mill or coffee grinder; sterilized jars with vinegar-proof sealants (see pages 42–43)

Yield
About 1.75kg (3½lb)

Shelf life
6 months

Serving suggestions
Superb with hot curries or game

— TIP —
• Prolonged cooking changes the character of ground spices. To maintain their freshness, add them after removing the chutney from the heat.

FLAVOURED VINEGARS, OILS & MUSTARDS

OILS AND VINEGARS readily absorb flavours: simply by adding herbs, spices and soft fruit to oil or vinegar you can make superb condiments to dress and finish all kinds of dishes. For this purpose, do not use a strong-tasting oil, such as extra-virgin olive oil or nut oil, as it tends to mask the flavour of the steeped ingredients. I also prefer to use a clear, mild vinegar, such as cider or white wine, as its fruitiness complements the added flavourings. If you are lucky enough to have a small oak cask, you can mature vinegar in it for 2–3 years with the most wonderful results. Salad Vinegar, below, is particularly suited to this method. Mustard is one of the most ancient condiments. In the past, people would chew a few mustard seeds with a mouthful of meat to produce a mild, aromatic flavour. It is only when dry mustard powder is mixed with cold water that mustard generates the hot sensation we are used to today.

— Salad Vinegar —

White wine vinegar *Tarragon* *Thyme* *Chillies* *Garlic* *Peppercorns*

As its name suggests, this mild and fragrant vinegar is perfect for making vinaigrettes and salad dressings. It improves greatly with long maturation, about 2–3 years, after which it should be filtered (see page 47) and used sparingly.

INGREDIENTS

1 litre (1¾ pints) white wine vinegar or cider vinegar
2 sprigs tarragon
2 sprigs thyme
2 fresh or dried red chillies (optional)
2 garlic cloves, peeled and bruised
2 tsp black peppercorns

1 Put the vinegar in a non-corrosive pan. Bring to the boil and boil rapidly for 1–2 minutes. Remove from the heat and leave to cool to 40°C (104°F).

2 Wash the herbs only if necessary, then dry well and bruise by crushing them lightly with the flat side of a wide-bladed knife. Make a long slit in each chilli, if using.

3 Divide the tarragon, thyme, chillies, garlic and black peppercorns evenly between the sterilized bottles. Pour in the warm vinegar, then seal. Shake the bottles occasionally during storage to blend the ingredients. The vinegar will be ready to use in about 3 weeks.

☆ **Degree of difficulty**
Easy

Cooking time
3–4 minutes

Special equipment
Thermometer; 2x500ml (17fl oz) sterilized bottles with vinegar-proof sealants (see pages 42–43)

Yield
About 1 litre (1¾ pints)

Shelf life
2 years

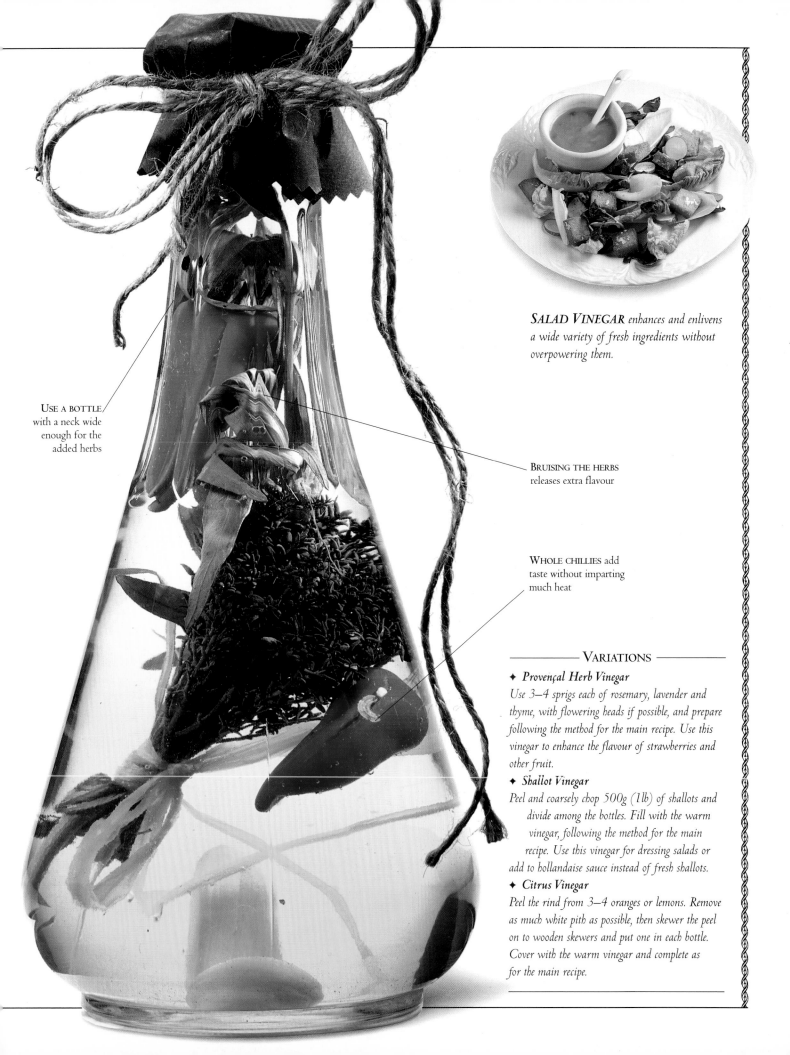

USE A BOTTLE
with a neck wide
enough for the
added herbs

SALAD VINEGAR *enhances and enlivens
a wide variety of fresh ingredients without
overpowering them.*

BRUISING THE HERBS
releases extra flavour

WHOLE CHILLIES add
taste without imparting
much heat

VARIATIONS

✦ *Provençal Herb Vinegar*

*Use 3–4 sprigs each of rosemary, lavender and
thyme, with flowering heads if possible, and prepare
following the method for the main recipe. Use this
vinegar to enhance the flavour of strawberries and
other fruit.*

✦ *Shallot Vinegar*

*Peel and coarsely chop 500g (1lb) of shallots and
divide among the bottles. Fill with the warm
vinegar, following the method for the main
recipe. Use this vinegar for dressing salads or
add to hollandaise sauce instead of fresh shallots.*

✦ *Citrus Vinegar*

*Peel the rind from 3–4 oranges or lemons. Remove
as much white pith as possible, then skewer the peel
on to wooden skewers and put one in each bottle.
Cover with the warm vinegar and complete as
for the main recipe.*

Gooseberry Vinegar

Pale, yellow-green in colour, this vinegar is especially delicious with fish.

INGREDIENTS
1.25 litres (2 pints) cider vinegar

1kg (2lb) tart gooseberries

150g (5oz) sorrel or spinach

a few strips of lemon rind

1 Bring the vinegar to the boil in a non-corrosive pan and boil rapidly for 1–2 minutes. Remove from the heat and leave to cool.

2 Wash the gooseberries and sorrel or spinach, then drain well. Put them in the food processor and coarsely chop.

3 Transfer to a large jar and add the lemon rind. Pour in the vinegar, then cover with a clean cloth and leave in a warm place for 3–4 weeks, shaking the jar from time to time.

4 Strain through the jelly bag, then filter (see page 47). Pour into the sterilized bottles, then seal. The vinegar may be cloudy at first but the sediment should settle after a few weeks.

— VARIATION —
✦ *Blueberry Vinegar*
Substitute blueberries for the gooseberries, omit the sorrel or spinach and lemon rind. Increase the vinegar to 1.5 litres (2½ pints). Use for salads or dilute and serve as a drink.

☆ **Degree of difficulty**
Easy

Cooking time
3–4 minutes

Special equipment
Food processor; sterilized jelly bag; sterilized bottles with vinegar-proof sealants (see pages 42–43)

Yield
About 2 litres (3½ pints)

Shelf life
2 years

Serving suggestions
Add to fish dishes and sauces as a finishing touch

Strawberry Vinegar

— (see page 33 for illustration)

This delightfully pink vinegar with a concentrated strawberry flavour is an ideal way to use up overripe fruit. Remember to discard any damaged berries.

— TIPS —
• Although the flavour of fruit vinegars improves with keeping, their colour will eventually fade and turn brown.
• Sometimes fruit vinegars can be cloudy. When left undisturbed in a cool, dark place the sediment will settle to the bottom and the clear vinegar can be siphoned off. If the vinegar is still cloudy, clarify it by beating 2 egg whites with a little of the vinegar until frothy. Gradually add the mixture to the vinegar, stirring well. Bottle and leave to stand in a cool place for about a week. The sediment will settle at the bottom and the clear liquid can be siphoned off.

INGREDIENTS
1.25 litres (2 pints) cider vinegar or white wine vinegar

1kg (2lb) ripe, full-flavoured strawberries

a few wild or small cultivated strawberries and a few basil leaves (optional)

1 Bring the vinegar to the boil in a non-corrosive pan and boil rapidly for 1–2 minutes. Remove from the heat and leave to cool to 40°C (104°F).

2 Hull the strawberries, then finely chop in the food processor. Transfer to a large glass jar or bowl.

3 Pour the warm vinegar over the chopped berries and mix well. Cover with a clean cloth and leave to stand in a warm place (a sunny windowsill is ideal) for 2 weeks, stirring occasionally.

4 Strain the vinegar through the jelly bag, then filter (see page 47). Pour into the sterilized bottles, then seal.

5 To intensify the flavour of the vinegar, skewer a few wild or small cultivated strawberries and some basil leaves alternately on to thin wooden skewers. Insert a skewer into each bottle and seal. The vinegar is ready to use immediately, but the flavour improves with keeping.

— VARIATIONS —
✦ *Blackberry* or *Blackcurrant Vinegar*
Substitute blackberries or blackcurrants for the strawberries and increase the vinegar to 1.5 litres (2½ pints). Omit the wild strawberries and basil. Follow the method as for the main recipe. Blackberry or Blackcurrant vinegar makes a superb salad dressing or can be diluted and served as a refreshing drink.

☆ **Degree of difficulty**
Easy

Cooking time
3–4 minutes

Special equipment
Thermometer; food processor; sterilized jelly bag; sterilized bottles with vinegar-proof sealants (see pages 42–43)

Yield
About 2 litres (3½ pints)

Shelf life
2 years

Serving suggestions
Use to dress salads, finish meat sauces or sprinkle over fresh strawberries

Spiced Vinegars

Basic flavoured vinegars like these are very easy to make and can be stored until needed. They mature and mellow with time. Any type of vinegar can be used but make sure it has an acidity of no less than 5%. I like the fruitiness of cider vinegar, which complements pickles well. To make a sweet version, add 2–4 tablespoons of white or soft brown sugar or honey to every 1 litre (1¾ pints) of vinegar. Experiment with different combinations of spices to suit your own taste.

Perfumed Vinegar

INGREDIENTS

2 litres (3½ pints) vinegar

1. SIMPLE SPICED VINEGAR

2 tbsp peppercorns

2 tbsp mustard seeds

1 tbsp cloves

2 tsp crumbled mace blades

2 nutmegs, broken into pieces

2–3 dried chillies, crushed (optional)

1 cinnamon stick, crushed

2–3 bay leaves

1 tbsp salt

2. HOT AND SPICY VINEGAR

90g (3oz) shallots, chopped

75g (2½oz) fresh ginger root, crushed

5–6 dried red chillies, crushed

1 tbsp black peppercorns

1 tbsp allspice berries

2 tsp cloves

1 cinnamon stick, crushed

2 tsp salt

3. PERFUMED VINEGAR

5cm (2in) piece fresh ginger root, sliced

2 tbsp coriander seeds

1 tbsp black peppercorns

1 tbsp cardamom pods

1 tbsp allspice berries

2 cinnamon sticks, crushed

2 nutmegs, broken into pieces

1 tsp aniseed

a few strips of lemon or orange rind

1 tbsp salt

4. MILD EUROPEAN VINEGAR

1 tbsp black peppercorns

1 tbsp juniper berries

1 tbsp allspice berries

1 tbsp caraway seeds

2 tsp dill or celery seeds

2–3 bay leaves

2–3 garlic cloves, crushed

2–3 dried red chillies (optional)

2 tbsp salt

5. SPICY EUROPEAN VINEGAR

100g (3½oz) shallots or onions, coarsely chopped

small bunch fresh tarragon

4 garlic cloves, crushed

2 tsp black peppercorns

1 tsp cloves

2 tbsp salt

6. MELLOW TRADITIONAL BRITISH VINEGAR

90g (3oz) fresh horseradish root, sliced

1 tbsp black peppercorns

1 tbsp mustard seeds

1 tbsp allspice berries

2 tsp cloves

2 pieces dried ginger root

1 cinnamon stick, crushed

2 tbsp salt

1 For each vinegar, tie all the flavourings, except the salt, in a piece of muslin (see spice bags, page 47). Place in a non-corrosive pan with the salt and vinegar. Bring to the boil and boil for about 10 minutes.

2 Leave to cool, then remove the spice bag. Filter the vinegar if it is cloudy (see page 47). Pour into the sterilized bottles, then seal. The vinegar is ready immediately, but improves with keeping.

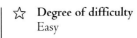

☆ **Degree of difficulty**
Easy

Cooking time
About 12 minutes

Special equipment
Muslin; sterilized bottles with vinegar-proof sealants (see pages 42–43)

Yield
About 2 litres (3½ pints)

Shelf life
2 years

Serving suggestions
Try (1) or (2) with Pickled Onions (page 92); (3) with Pickled Garlic (page 92); (4) with Pickled Baby Vegetables (page 98); (5) with Olive Oil Pickle (page 97); or (6) with Chow-chow (page 95)

Simple Spiced Vinegar

Sugar-free Sweet Vinegar

Useful for general pickling, this vinegar is sweetened with concentrated fruit juice (available from most healthfood shops) rather than sugar. I make large quantities of it at the beginning of winter so it will mature and be ready for use in the summer.

INGREDIENTS

4 litres (7 pints) cider vinegar or distilled malt vinegar

300ml (½ pint) concentrated apple or pear juice

2 tbsp black peppercorns

1 tbsp allspice berries

2 tsp cloves

2 tbsp coriander seeds

3 cinnamon sticks

a few fresh or dried chillies (optional)

1 Put the vinegar and fruit juice in a non-corrosive pan. Bring to the boil and skim well. Make a spice bag with the remaining ingredients (see page 47). Add to the boiling vinegar and boil for 10 minutes.

2 Remove the spice bag, pour the vinegar into the hot sterilized bottles, then seal. The vinegar is ready to use immediately, but improves with keeping.

☆ **Degree of difficulty**
Easy

Cooking time
About 12 minutes

Special equipment
Large sterilized bottles with vinegar-proof sealants (see pages 42–43)

Yield
About 4.3 litres (7 pints)

Shelf life
Almost indefinitely

Malay Chilli and Shallot Oil

In Malaysia this condiment appears on every table and has a wonderfully nutty, hot taste. Add to anything that needs extra flavour. Use in moderation to finish soups, stews and rice dishes.

INGREDIENTS

100g (3½oz) dried chillies, stalks removed

325g (11oz) shallots, peeled

8–10 garlic cloves, peeled

1 litre (1¾ pints) groundnut or refined sesame oil

1 Put the dried chillies, whole shallots and garlic in the food processor and process until finely chopped.

2 Transfer the mixture to a pan and add the groundnut oil. Heat gently and cook for about 20 minutes, or until the shallots are nicely browned.

3 Remove the pan from the heat and leave until the oil is cool. Filter the oil (see page 47), pour it into the sterilized bottle, then seal. The oil is ready to use immediately.

☆ **Degree of difficulty**
Easy

Cooking time
About 23 minutes

Special equipment
Food processor; sterilized bottle with sealant (see pages 42–43)

Yield
About 1 litre (1¾ pints)

Shelf life
6 months

Basil Oil

Herb-flavoured oils are indispensable condiments in my kitchen. I use them to flavour salads or add them to soups and stews just before serving to give an extra lift. Basil oil is particularly fragrant, but many herbs — alone or with spices and other flavourings — are equally good, especially thyme with lemon and rosemary with coriander.

INGREDIENTS

1 litre (1¾ pints) light olive oil

150g (5oz) basil

1 Heat the oil gently in a pan until it reaches 40°C (104°F).

2 Lightly bruise the basil and put it in the warm sterilized jar or bottle. Pour the warm oil into the jar, then seal. The oil will be ready to use in 3–4 weeks.

——— TIP ———

• If you plan to keep the oil for longer than a few weeks, it is best to filter it (see page 47), since the basil leaves tend to become slimy after 3–4 months' maceration. Re-bottle the oil and seal before storing.

☆ **Degree of difficulty**
Easy

Cooking time
3–4 minutes

Special equipment
Thermometer; 1 litre (1¾ pint) sterilized jar or bottle with sealant (see pages 42–43)

Yield
About 1 litre (1¾ pints)

Shelf life
1 year, filtered

Serving suggestions
Use to flavour salads, sauces and soups

Chilli Oil

Red hot and wonderfully versatile, a few drops of this oil will add fire to any dish.

INGREDIENTS

100g (3½ oz) red chillies

1 litre (1¾ pints) groundnut, refined sesame or corn oil

2 tbsp sweet or hot paprika

1 Remove the stalks from the chillies. Put them in the food processor and process until chopped finely. Transfer the chillies to a pan and add the oil.

2 Heat the oil gently until it nearly reaches 120°C (248°F), then simmer for 15 minutes without letting the mixture get any hotter.

3 Remove from the heat, cool slightly and stir in the paprika. Leave to cool completely, then filter (see page 47). Pour into the sterilized bottle and seal. The oil is ready to use immediately.

☆ **Degree of difficulty**
Easy

Cooking time
About 18 minutes

Special equipment
Food processor; thermometer; sterilized bottle with sealant (see pages 42–43)

Yield
About 1 litre (1¾ pints)

Shelf life
1 year

Orange and Tarragon Mustard

This coarse-grained mustard is particularly good for coating meat before roasting. If you plan to use it immediately, there is no need to boil the orange juice.

INGREDIENTS

finely grated rind and juice of 2 oranges

250g (8oz) yellow mustard seeds

100ml (3½ fl oz) white wine vinegar

2 tsp salt

1 tbsp chopped fresh tarragon or 1 tsp dried tarragon

a little brandy or whisky

1 Put the orange rind and juice in a small pan. Bring to the boil, then reduce the heat and simmer for a few seconds. (This improves the keeping qualities of the mustard.) Remove from the heat and leave to cool completely.

2 Coarsely grind 200g (7oz) of the mustard seeds in the spice mill or coffee grinder. Place in a glass bowl with the remaining whole mustard seeds, add the boiled orange juice and rind and mix well. Leave to stand for about 5 minutes, then stir in the vinegar, salt and tarragon.

3 Pack the mustard into the sterilized jars. Cover each one with a waxed paper disc that has been dipped in brandy or whisky, then seal. The mustard will be ready to eat in a few days (this gives the whole mustard seeds time to swell and soften).

☆ **Degree of difficulty**
Easy

Cooking time
1–2 minutes

Special equipment
Spice mill or coffee grinder; small sterilized jars with vinegar-proof sealants (see pages 42–43)

Yield
About 500g (1lb)

Shelf life
6 months

Serving suggestion
Serve with cold meat

Dark Spicy Mustard

Making homemade mustard is an economical way of utilizing this traditional spice. A versatile product, it can be served simply as a condiment, included in a wide variety of sauces, or used to form a tasty crust for roasted meat.

INGREDIENTS

100g (3½ oz) yellow mustard seeds

3 tbsp brown or black mustard seeds

250g (8oz) tamarind block, soaked in 300ml (½ pint) water for 25 minutes

1 tbsp honey

1 tsp salt

1 tsp ground allspice

¼ tsp ground cinnamon

¼ tsp ground cloves

¼ tsp ground cardamom

a little brandy or whisky

1 Grind the mustard seeds in the spice mill or coffee grinder, then mix together in a bowl.

2 Strain the tamarind and add to the seeds with the honey, salt and spices. Mix very well.

3 Pack into the sterilized jars, making sure there are no air pockets. Cover each one with a waxed paper disc that has been dipped in brandy or whisky, then seal. The mustard will be ready to eat in a few days.

☆ **Degree of difficulty**
Easy

Special equipment
Spice mill or coffee grinder; sterilized jars with vinegar-proof sealants (see pages 42–43)

Yield
About 500g (1lb)

Shelf life
6 months

Serving suggestions
Use in dressings and sauces

PRESERVED MEAT

PRESERVING MEAT at home is not difficult, but it does require patience, common sense and attention to detail. It is a rewarding skill that turns fresh meat into a superb, long-lasting delicacy. Follow each recipe closely and once a technique is mastered, you can experiment with different flavourings and ingredients — the results are worthwhile. Please read page 42 before starting.

Pickled Venison

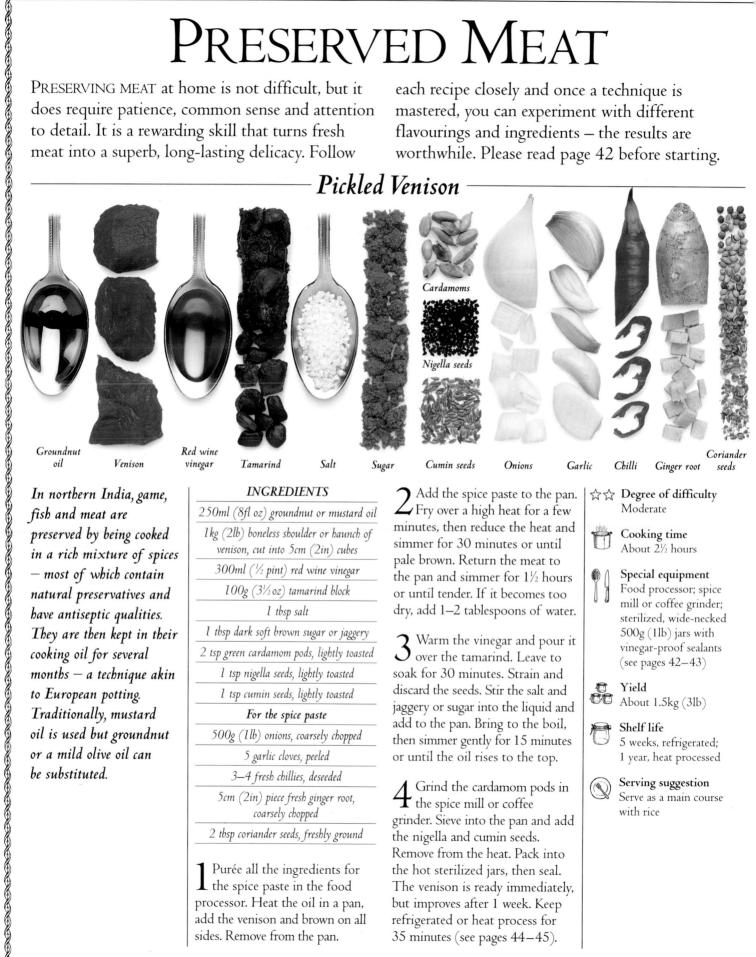

Groundnut oil	Venison	Red wine vinegar	Tamarind	Salt	Sugar	Cumin seeds	Onions	Garlic	Chilli	Ginger root	Coriander seeds

Cardamoms

Nigella seeds

In northern India, game, fish and meat are preserved by being cooked in a rich mixture of spices — most of which contain natural preservatives and have antiseptic qualities. They are then kept in their cooking oil for several months — a technique akin to European potting. Traditionally, mustard oil is used but groundnut or a mild olive oil can be substituted.

INGREDIENTS

250ml (8fl oz) groundnut or mustard oil

1kg (2lb) boneless shoulder or haunch of venison, cut into 5cm (2in) cubes

300ml (½ pint) red wine vinegar

100g (3½ oz) tamarind block

1 tbsp salt

1 tbsp dark soft brown sugar or jaggery

2 tsp green cardamom pods, lightly toasted

1 tsp nigella seeds, lightly toasted

1 tsp cumin seeds, lightly toasted

For the spice paste

500g (1lb) onions, coarsely chopped

5 garlic cloves, peeled

3–4 fresh chillies, deseeded

5cm (2in) piece fresh ginger root, coarsely chopped

2 tbsp coriander seeds, freshly ground

1 Purée all the ingredients for the spice paste in the food processor. Heat the oil in a pan, add the venison and brown on all sides. Remove from the pan.

2 Add the spice paste to the pan. Fry over a high heat for a few minutes, then reduce the heat and simmer for 30 minutes or until pale brown. Return the meat to the pan and simmer for 1½ hours or until tender. If it becomes too dry, add 1–2 tablespoons of water.

3 Warm the vinegar and pour it over the tamarind. Leave to soak for 30 minutes. Strain and discard the seeds. Stir the salt and jaggery or sugar into the liquid and add to the pan. Bring to the boil, then simmer gently for 15 minutes or until the oil rises to the top.

4 Grind the cardamom pods in the spice mill or coffee grinder. Sieve into the pan and add the nigella and cumin seeds. Remove from the heat. Pack into the hot sterilized jars, then seal. The venison is ready immediately, but improves after 1 week. Keep refrigerated or heat process for 35 minutes (see pages 44–45).

☆☆ **Degree of difficulty**
Moderate

Cooking time
About 2½ hours

Special equipment
Food processor; spice mill or coffee grinder; sterilized, wide-necked 500g (1lb) jars with vinegar-proof sealants (see pages 42–43)

Yield
About 1.5kg (3lb)

Shelf life
5 weeks, refrigerated; 1 year, heat processed

Serving suggestion
Serve as a main course with rice

TAMARIND AND JAGGERY or dark soft brown sugar give the gravy an appetizing colour

PICKLED VENISON makes a delicious instant meal: simply reheat the meat and serve with warmed chapatis. Garnish with sprigs of fresh coriander and a few sliced chillies, if wished.

THE TOASTED SPICES complement the rich flavour of the venison

TIPS

• Lightly toasting whole spices releases their flavour. Put them in a small heated frying pan, without any oil, and cook them briefly, shaking the pan frequently, until they are slightly coloured and start to pop. Remove from the heat immediately and tip on to a plate. (If the seeds are left in the pan they will carry on cooking in the residual heat and may burn.)

• Skim off the fat from the top of the jar before reheating the meat.

Cured Ham

(see page 64 for technique)

This recipe produces a mild-flavoured ham that can be matured for a short period and then cooked. For a more pronounced flavour, dry further and smoke, if desired, before cooking (see Tip, below). Instead of pork you could use mutton or lamb. First-timers may find these meats easier, as the joints are smaller and more manageable. Mutton is fairly hard to come by but it has much more flavour than lamb. A good butcher will order it for you.

IMPORTANT NOTE

Before starting this recipe, please read the information on pages 42 and 64.

TIP

• If wished, the ham can be cold-smoked before cooking. Smoke after step 4 or 5, at or below 30°C (86°F) for 18–24 hours or longer, according to taste (see page 66).

INGREDIENTS

1 leg of pork, weighing 5–6kg (11–13lb)
500g (1lb) coarse salt
For the brine
3 litres (5 pints) water or 2 litres (3½ pints) water and 1 litre (1¾ pints) strong ale
750g (1½lb) salt
250g (8oz) molasses sugar or soft brown sugar
1 tbsp saltpetre
small bunch thyme
3 sprigs rosemary
3 bay leaves
2 tbsp juniper berries, crushed
2 tsp cloves
For the paste
150g (5oz) plain flour
150g (5oz) salt
8–10 tsp water

1 Rub the pork all over with some of the salt, pushing it well into the crevices. Sprinkle a layer of salt about 1cm (½ in) deep in a large, non-corrosive dish. Set the meat on top and sprinkle with the rest of the salt. Cover and refrigerate for 24–48 hours.

2 Make the brine (see page 47) and cool completely. Brush the salt off the meat and place it in the crock. Strain the brine over, making sure it covers the meat.

3 Weight down the meat (see page 46). Cover and refrigerate or store between 6–8°C (42–46°F) for 2–2½ weeks. Check the brine every day. Discard it if any "off" odours develop and cover the meat with fresh brine. (See Information Box, page 64.)

4 Remove the meat from the brine, rinse, then dry. Hang in a cool, dry, dark, airy place between 6–8°C (42–46°F) for 2–3 days. The ham can be cooked now, if desired (see steps below), or dried further for a stronger flavour, see step 5.

5 Mix the paste ingredients together and spread over the exposed meat, in a layer 1cm (½ in) thick. Hang the meat for a further 2–2½ weeks, covering it with the calico when the surface has dried out. Cook as below.

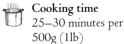

Degree of difficulty
☆
☆☆ Advanced

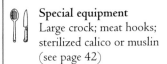

Cooking time
25–30 minutes per 500g (1lb)

Special equipment
Large crock; meat hooks; sterilized calico or muslin (see page 42)

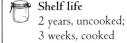

Yield
3.75–4.5kg (8¼–9¾ lb)

Shelf life
2 years, uncooked; 3 weeks, cooked

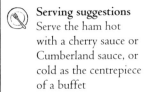

Serving suggestions
Serve the ham hot with a cherry sauce or Cumberland sauce, or cold as the centrepiece of a buffet

✳ Warning
This recipe contains saltpetre, see page 42

SERVE THE HAM cold with Spiced Whole Oranges (see page 100) and Spiced Cherry Tomatoes (see page 93)

TO COOK THE HAM

SOAK THE HAM before cooking

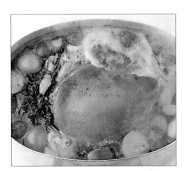

1 Soak the ham in water for 24 hours. Place in a large pan with cold water to cover. Add a herb bundle (rosemary, thyme, citrus peel), some bay leaves, parsley, apple, carrot, onion, courgette, peppercorns and cloves.

2 Bring the ham slowly to the boil, then cover and simmer for 25–30 minutes per 500g (1lb). Top up with more water if necessary.

3 If serving the ham hot, remove it from the pan. To serve cold, leave to cool in the water. Peel off the skin with the help of a knife.

Smoked Chicken

(see page 24 for illustration)

Good smoked chicken is a rare delicacy — flavourful and succulent. But do be sure to use only firm, fresh, free-range chicken for the best results. Many other kinds of poultry and game birds can be prepared in the same way, but you need to vary the curing time according to the size of the bird: add or subtract 1 hour from the curing time for every 500g (1 lb) over or under the given weight.

— IMPORTANT NOTE —
Before starting this recipe, please read the information on pages 42 and 64.

INGREDIENTS

1.5–2kg (3–4lb) chicken
1 tbsp olive or groundnut oil
4–5 sprigs thyme
4–5 sprigs tarragon
1 bay leaf
For the brine
2 litres (3½ pints) water
600g (1¼ lb) salt
5–6 sprigs tarragon
4–5 strips lemon rind

1 To make the brine, put all the ingredients in a non-corrosive pan. Bring to the boil, stirring until the salt has dissolved, then reduce the heat and simmer for about 10 minutes. Strain and leave to cool completely.

2 Wash and dry the chicken, then trim off any loose skin or cavity fat. Tie the bird's legs together with string, then prick all over with a sharp wooden skewer.

3 Put the chicken in a deep glass dish and cover with the brine. Weight down (see page 46), then refrigerate for 6–8 hours.

4 Drain the chicken well. Insert a wooden skewer through the trussed wings and tie a loop of string to it. Hang up to dry in a cool, dry, dark, airy place (between 6–8°C/42–46°F) for 24 hours.

5 Brush the chicken with the oil and hang, legs down, in the smoker or place on a smoker tray. Hot-smoke for 3–3½ hours at 110–125°C (225–240°F). Half-way through smoking, add the herbs to the smoking tray.

6 To check if cooked, insert a skewer into the thickest part of the thigh — the juices should run clear without any sign of pinkness. The chicken can be served hot, but is best left until cold, then wrapped in waxed paper and refrigerated until needed.

 Degree of difficulty
Advanced

 Cooking time
About 15 minutes, simmering; 3–3½ hours, smoking

 Special equipment
String; smoker, meat hook

 Yield
About 1.5kg (3lb)

 Shelf life
1 month, refrigerated; 3 months, frozen

Serving suggestions
Serve thinly sliced with a mixed leaf salad; with fresh mango as a canapé; or skewered with Striped Spiced Pears (see page 103)

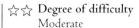

Pastrami

New York just wouldn't be the same without pastrami on rye. This lightly smoked, deliciously piquant, cured meat originated in Romania but its roots probably lie in Turkey. Traditionally, the meat is only lightly smoked for 4 hours but for a more intense flavour, smoke it for up to 12 hours over some fragrant fruit wood.

— IMPORTANT NOTE —
Before starting this recipe, please read the information on pages 42 and 64.

INGREDIENTS

3kg (6lb) lean beef brisket
250g (8oz) coarse salt
6 garlic cloves, crushed
4 tbsp soft brown sugar
4 tbsp coarsely ground black pepper
2 tbsp coriander seeds, coarsely ground
1 tbsp ground ginger
1 tsp saltpetre

1 Put the beef in a deep glass dish. Rub 100g (3½ oz) of the salt into the meat. Cover and leave for 2 hours, then rinse the meat and dry well.

2 Mix the remaining ingredients together, including the rest of the salt, and rub well into the meat. Return the meat to the cleaned dish. Cover and refrigerate for 1½–2 weeks, turning the meat every few days.

3 Lift the meat out and pat dry. Insert a meat hook into the beef and hang up to dry in a cool, dry, dark, airy place (between 6–8°C/42–46°F) for 1 day. Cold-smoke below 50°C/100°F for 4–6 hours (see page 66).

4 Cook the pastrami in simmering, unsalted water for 2½–3 hours or until it is tender. Remove from the cooking liquid, drain well, then serve. To serve cold, drain well and weight down (see page 46). Leave to cool, then refrigerate until needed.

 Degree of difficulty
Moderate

 Cooking time
4–6 hours, smoking; 2½–3 hours, simmering

 Special equipment
Meat hook; smoker

 Yield
About 2–2½ kg (4–5 lb)

 Shelf life
4–6 weeks, refrigerated; 6 months, frozen

Serving suggestions
Serve hot or cold, or as a sandwich filling

* **Warning**
This recipe contains saltpetre, see page 42

Preserved Toulouse Sausages

(see page 25 for illustration)

These simple, versatile sausages can be flavoured with different herbs and spices. Traditionally, they are seasoned with just salt and pepper – white pepper rather than black, because flecks of black pepper are considered unsightly. However, I much prefer the taste of black pepper.

IMPORTANT NOTE

Before starting this recipe, please read the information on pages 42 and 62.

VARIATIONS

♦ **Herb Sausages**
Add 2 tablespoons chopped parsley or a mixture of parsley and thyme in step 2.

♦ **Garlic Sausages**
Add 3 garlic cloves, crushed, and 2 tablespoons chopped herbs in step 2.

♦ **Cumberland Sausages**
Add ¼ teaspoon grated nutmeg in step 2.

INGREDIENTS

2.1kg (4¼lb) lean shoulder of pork, cubed
900g (1¾lb) pork back fat, cubed
60g (2oz) salt
1 tsp freshly ground white or black pepper
½ tsp saltpetre
3–4 metres (3¼–4¼ yards) hog casing
For each jar
2 garlic cloves, blanched for 2 minutes (see page 46)
2 sprigs thyme
1 sprig rosemary
olive oil or lard, to cover

1 Put the meat through the coarse disc of the mincer and the fat through the fine disc.

2 Put the minced meat and fat in a glass bowl with the salt, pepper and saltpetre. Knead the mixture well with your hands to ensure the meat and fat are evenly distributed. Cover and refrigerate for at least 4 hours.

3 Prepare the casing (see steps 4 and 5, page 68). Stuff with the meat and divide into 5cm (2in) links (see step 6, page 69).

4 Fry, grill or barbecue the sausages for 8–10 minutes per side, or until they are completely cooked through but still slightly pink and moist inside. Immediately arrange the sausages in the hot sterilized jars, along with the garlic and herbs.

5 If using olive oil to cover, heat until it reaches 90°C (194°F), pour into the jars, making sure the sausages are covered, then seal.

6 If using lard to cover, melt it then leave to cool slightly before pouring over the sausages in the jar. Refrigerate until the fat sets, top up with more melted lard so that it covers the sausages by at least 1cm (½in), then seal.

7 Store in a cool, dark place (between 6–8°C/42–46°F) or the bottom of the refrigerator. The sausages will be ready to eat in 1 month. The oil or lard from the jars can be used in cooking.

 Degree of difficulty
Moderate

 Cooking time
About 20 minutes

Special equipment
Mincer; sausage maker or sausage filler; sterilized wide-necked jars with sealants (see pages 42–43); thermometer

Yield
About 3kg (6lb)

Shelf life
1 year

Serving suggestions
Add to stews, bean casseroles or cassoulet

✳ **Warning**
This recipe contains saltpetre, see page 42

TIP

• To eat the sausages fresh, omit the saltpetre and leave them in a coil, or divide into 10cm (4in) links. Keep refrigerated and cook within 2 days (see step 4).

Dried Lamb Sausages

(see page 25 for illustration)

Different versions of this recipe are made all over the Muslim world, where pork is not eaten. The sausages may be consumed after 4 weeks when they are still very aromatic, or hung until they are hard and dry to be used for cooking.

IMPORTANT NOTE

Before starting this recipe, please read the information on pages 42 and 62.

INGREDIENTS

1.5kg (3lb) boned shoulder or leg of lamb, cut into large cubes
300g (10oz) lamb or beef fat, cut into large cubes
6 garlic cloves, crushed
4 tbsp olive oil
1½ tbsp salt
1 tbsp fennel seeds
2 tbsp sweet paprika
1 tsp dried mint
1–2 tsp chilli powder
½ tsp freshly ground black pepper
½ tsp saltpetre
3.5 metres (3¾ yards) beef runners (casing)

1 Put the lamb and fat through the coarse disc of the mincer. Add all the remaining ingredients, except the runners, and mix well. Pack into a glass bowl, making sure there are no air pockets. Cover and refrigerate for 12 hours.

2 Prepare the beef runners (see steps 4 and 5, page 68). Stuff with the meat and divide into 15cm (6in) links (see step 6, page 69). Hang in a cool, dry, dark, airy place (between 6–8°C/42–46°F) for 4–5 weeks, or until they have lost about 50% of their original weight. Wrap in greaseproof paper and refrigerate.

 Degree of difficulty
Moderate

 Special equipment
Mincer; sausage maker or sausage filler; meat hooks

 Yield
About 1kg (2lb)

Shelf life
6 months, refrigerated

Serving suggestions
Either barbecue the sausages or add to stews, couscous or tagines

✳ **Warning**
This recipe contains saltpetre, see page 42

Wind-dried Duck Sausages
— (see page 25 for illustration)

These unusual sweet and spicy sausages were inspired by an ancient Chinese recipe. In China, sausages like these are hung to dry in the cool, breezy mountain air, which is the ideal curing place. I hang them in my cool larder and the results are almost as good. The same technique can be used with pork or a mixture of pork fat and beef or venison.

— IMPORTANT NOTE —
Before starting this recipe, please read the information on pages 42 and 62.

INGREDIENTS
3kg (6lb) duck, boned, skin left on
300g (10oz) veal or pork tenderloin, cubed
3 tbsp sake or fortified rice wine
3–4 fresh Thai chillies, deseeded and chopped
1 tbsp salt
4–5 star anise, finely ground
1 tsp Sichuan pepper, finely ground
1 tsp fennel seeds, finely ground
about 3.8 metres (4 yards) sheep casing
a little groundnut oil

For the cure
250ml (8fl oz) soy sauce
4 tbsp honey or molasses sugar
3 garlic cloves, crushed
5cm (2in) piece fresh ginger root, shredded
½ tsp saltpetre

1 Put all the meat in a glass bowl. Mix together all the ingredients for the cure and pour over the meat, rubbing it in well. Cover with clingfilm. Refrigerate for 24 hours, turning occasionally.

2 Put the duck breasts through the coarse disc of the mincer. Put the rest of the meat through the fine disc. Mix in the remaining ingredients, except the casing and oil. Pack into a bowl, making sure there are no air pockets. Cover and refrigerate for 12 hours.

3 Prepare the casing (see steps 4 and 5, page 68). Stuff with the meat and divide into 10cm (4in) links (see step 6, page 69).

4 Hang up in a cool, dry, dark, airy place (between 6–8°C/ 42–46°F) for 4–5 weeks, or until they have lost about 50% of their original weight. After 10 days, or when the sausages reduce in size, rub with the oil.

Degree of difficulty
Moderate

Special equipment
Mincer; sausage maker or sausage filler; meat hooks

Yield
About 1kg (2lb)

Shelf life
6 months

Serving suggestions
Serve as a part of a sausage platter, or add to stir-fries and slow-cooked Chinese dishes

* **Warning**
This recipe contains saltpetre, see page 42

— TIP —
• To store the sausages, wrap in greaseproof or waxed paper and store in a cool, dry, dark place (between 6–8°C/42–46°F), or freeze for up to 3 months.

Landjäger
— (see page 25 for illustration)

Landjäger *is the German word for hunter and these flat, spicy sausages used to be the favourite food to take on a hunt. If possible, use cherry tree chips when smoking the sausages.*

— IMPORTANT NOTE —
Before starting this recipe, please read the information on pages 42 and 62.

INGREDIENTS
1.25kg (2½lb) lean beef, such as chuck, shoulder or rump, cut into large cubes
1kg (2lb) streaky bacon, rind removed
5 garlic cloves, crushed
1 tbsp salt
1 tbsp soft brown sugar
½ tsp saltpetre
2 tsp coriander seeds, finely ground
1 tsp freshly ground black pepper
2 tsp caraway seeds
75ml (2½fl oz) kirsch
3.5 metres (3¾ yards) beef runners (casing)
a little groundnut oil

1 Put the beef through the coarse disc of the mincer and the bacon through the fine disc.

2 Add all the remaining ingredients, except the beef runners and oil, and mix well. Pack the mixture tightly into a bowl, making sure there are no air pockets. Cover and refrigerate for 48 hours.

3 Prepare the beef runners (see steps 4 and 5, page 68). Stuff with the meat and divide into 15cm (6in) links (see step 6, page 69). Place between two wooden boards and weight down (see page 46). Refrigerate for 48 hours.

4 Hang up in a cool, dry, dark, airy place (between 6–8°C/ 42–46°F) for 24 hours, then cold-smoke for 12 hours at 30°C/86°F (see page 66).

5 Rub the sausages with a little oil. Hang up to dry as before for 2–3 weeks, or until they have lost 50% of their original weight.

Degree of difficulty
Moderate

Special equipment
Mincer; sausage maker or sausage filler; meat hooks; smoker

Yield
About 1.5kg (2½lb)

Shelf life
4–5 months, refrigerated

Serving suggestion
Wonderful for picnics

* **Warning**
This recipe contains saltpetre, see page 42

— TIPS —
• To speed up the drying process, hang the sausages in front of an electric fan switched to the cold setting.
• To store, wrap in greaseproof or waxed paper and keep refrigerated or freeze for up to 3 months.

Garlic and Herb Salami

(see page 68 for technique)

Do not worry if a white deposit grows on the sausages: it is a harmless mould that helps to preserve them.

— **IMPORTANT NOTE** —
Before starting this recipe, please read the information on pages 42 and 62.

INGREDIENTS

1kg (2lb) lean shoulder, hand or blade of pork, trimmed, all sinew removed, and cut into large cubes

1½ tbsp salt

½ tsp saltpetre

75ml (3fl oz) vodka

350g (11½ oz) pork back fat, cut into large cubes

5 garlic cloves, finely chopped

3 tbsp finely chopped thyme

2 tsp black peppercorns

2 tsp coriander seeds, coarsely ground

½ tsp freshly ground black pepper

¼ tsp allspice, freshly ground

about 2 metres (2 yards) medium hog casing

1 Put the pork in a glass bowl, sprinkle with the salt, saltpetre and vodka and mix well. Cover and refrigerate for 12 hours.

2 Put the meat through the fine disc of the mincer. Mince the back fat through the coarse disc. Mix together, adding any marinating liquid left in the bowl.

3 Add all the remaining ingredients, except the casing, and mix thoroughly but lightly. Refrigerate for at least 2 hours.

4 Prepare the casing (see steps 4 and 5, page 68). Stuff with the meat and divide into 20cm (8in) links (see step 6, page 69).

5 Hang up to dry in a cool, dry, dark, airy place (between 6–8°C/42–46°F) for 5–6 weeks, or until they have lost about 50% of their original weight. Wrap well in greaseproof or waxed paper and store in a cool, dry, dark place or in the bottom of the refrigerator.

 Degree of difficulty
Moderate

 Special equipment
Mincer; sausage maker or sausage filler; meat hooks

 Yield
About 750g (1½ lb)

 Shelf life
4–5 months, refrigerated

Serving suggestion
Remove the skin and bake in a brioche dough

* **Warning**
This recipe contains saltpetre, see page 42

A selection of salami

Chilli Salami

(see page 25 for illustration)

These spicy sausages are similar to Spanish chorizo, and can be used in cooking or eaten raw. To make milder sausages, simply reduce the number of chillies. For convenience, you can mince the fat on the coarse disc of a mincer instead of chopping it by hand, but you will lose the sausages' wonderful marbled appearance. Before serving raw, the sausages should be brought to room temperature.

— **IMPORTANT NOTE** —
Before starting this recipe, please read the information on pages 42 and 62.

INGREDIENTS

1kg (2lb) pork shoulder, hand or blade, cut into large cubes

1½ tbsp salt

1 tbsp soft brown sugar

½ tsp saltpetre

75ml (3fl oz) brandy

350g (11½ oz) pork back fat, cut into small, rough chunks

4–5 large, mild red chillies, very finely chopped

2 garlic cloves, crushed

2 tbsp sweet paprika

1 tsp chilli powder, or to taste

1 tsp aniseed

about 2 metres (2 yards) hog casing

1 Put the pork in a large glass bowl, sprinkle with the salt, sugar, saltpetre and brandy. Mix together with your hands. Cover and refrigerate for 12–24 hours.

2 Put the meat through the coarse disc of the mincer. Mix well with all the remaining ingredients, except the casing. Prepare the casing (see steps 4 and 5, page 68). Stuff with the meat and divide into 50cm (20in) links (see step 6, page 69).

3 Tie the ends of each sausage together to form a horseshoe. Hang up in a cool, dry, dark, airy place (between 6–8°C/42–46°F) for 4–6 weeks, or until they have lost about 50% of their original weight. Wrap in greaseproof paper and refrigerate until needed.

— **VARIATION** —

◆ Smoked Chilli Salami

Dry for 1–2 days or until the surface is just moist, then cold-smoke for 6–8 hours at 30°C/86°F (see pages 66–67). Dry as above. The smoked sausages will be ready to eat in 4–5 weeks.

 Degree of difficulty
Moderate

 Special equipment
Mincer; sausage maker or sausage filler; meat hooks

 Yield
About 750g (1½ lb)

 Shelf life
4–5 months, refrigerated

Serving suggestions
Slice and serve raw, or add to bean stews and casseroles

* **Warning**
This recipe contains saltpetre, see page 42

Jerky

Jerky conjures up images of the Wild West, yet it was eaten by Native Americans for generations before then. Pounded with fat and wild cherries, it was made into cakes called pemmican, which were taken on long journeys to provide an instant source of energy. Unlike Biltong (see below), Jerky is not cured before drying.

IMPORTANT NOTE
Before starting this recipe, please read the information on pages 42 and 62.

INGREDIENTS

1kg (2lb) silverside of beef or rump steak
2 tsp coarse salt
2 tbsp coarsely ground black pepper
1 tsp chilli powder

1 To slice the meat easily, put it in the freezer for 2–3 hours. Using a large, sharp cook's knife, cut the meat into 5mm (¼in) slices, along the grain, then cut into 5cm (2in) strips.

2 Mix the salt, pepper and chilli powder together, sprinkle over the meat and rub in well.

3 Arrange the meat on a wire rack, leaving small gaps between slices. Put in an oven on the lowest possible setting, leaving the door slightly ajar.

4 After about 5 hours, turn the meat over and leave for a further 5–8 hours, or until it has lost about 75% of its original weight. The Jerky should be dry and stiff. Leave to cool, then store in jars or wrap in waxed paper. Keep in a cool, dry, dark place (between 6–8°C/42–46°F).

VARIATION

♦ Mix together 4 tablespoons soy sauce, 4 tablespoons tomato sauce, 1 tablespoon paprika, 1 teaspoon ground chilli and rub this mixture over the meat instead of the salt, pepper and chilli. Dry as above. This is especially good made with turkey.

☆ **Degree of difficulty**
Easy

Cooking time
10–13 hours

Yield
About 250–300g (8–10oz)

Shelf life
6 months

Serving suggestions
Serve as a snack, grate over an omelette, or rehydrate in warm water and use in stews

TIP
• Beef, venison and turkey can be prepared in the same way.

Biltong
(see page 62 for technique)

Biltong is a South African speciality, made from venison, ostrich or beef.

IMPORTANT NOTE
Before starting this recipe, please read the information on pages 42 and 62.

INGREDIENTS

2kg (4lb) piece of top side, sirloin or silverside of beef or venison
250g (8oz) coarse salt
3 tbsp soft brown sugar
1 tsp saltpetre
3 tbsp coriander seeds, toasted and crushed
2 tbsp black peppercorns, crushed
4 tbsp malt vinegar

1 To slice the meat easily, put it in the freezer for 2–3 hours. Using a large, sharp cook's knife, slice the meat into long steaks 5cm (2in) thick, cutting along the grain. Cut off any sinew or loose fat.

2 Mix together the salt, brown sugar, saltpetre, coriander seeds and peppercorns. Sprinkle a layer into a large earthenware or glass dish, then add the meat. Sprinkle the beef with the rest of the dry mix in an even layer, rubbing it in well.

3 Sprinkle the vinegar evenly over both sides of the meat and rub it in. Cover and refrigerate for 6–8 hours, turning the meat occasionally and rubbing the salt mixture into it after 2–3 hours.

4 Lift the meat out of the dish and shake off any loose salt. Hang it from meat hooks or hang it up with string (see step 6, page 63). Leave to dry in a cool, dry, dark, airy place (between 6–8°C/42–46°F) for 1½ weeks, until it is semi-dried and has lost 40–50% of its weight. Wrap well in waxed paper and keep refrigerated.

5 To fully dry the Biltong, line the bottom of an oven with foil and place a shelf at the top position. Hang the meat from it and dry at the very lowest setting for 8–16 hours, until it is fully-dried, dark and splinters when bent in two. Wrap in waxed paper and store between 6–8°C (42–46°F) or keep refrigerated.

☆ **Degree of difficulty**
Easy

Cooking time
8–16 hours, oven-dried

Special equipment
String and larding needle, or meat hooks

Yield
About 1kg (2lb)

Shelf life
3 weeks, semi-dried; 2 years, fully-dried

Serving suggestion
Serve as a tasty snack

✳ **Warning**
This recipe contains saltpetre, see page 42

PATES & POTTED GOODS

IN THE PAST, using fat as a preservative was a convenient way to keep those cuts of meat that could not be used for roasting; flavoured mince, offal and other scraps were cooked and sealed in fat to last throughout the winter. Today, this technique has become a skill that gives the cook an opportunity to be creative, transforming different cuts of meat into spectacular, luxurious products. Meat, when combined with herbs, spices, alcohol and other flavourings, is ideal for making pâtés. These are delicious served simply with a relish, a glass of wine and a chunk of bread. Always use the best raw ingredients you can afford – a cheap brandy might be less expensive but you will need to add more of it to achieve the depth of flavour required. These products, by the nature of their ingredients, have a high fat content. After mastering the technique, you can always try reducing the fat content by replacing some of it with vegetables, such as carrots, fine beans, sweet potatoes or even fruit, to retain the moisture.

Confit of Duck

Pickling salt   Saltpetre   Duck legs   Goose fat   Peppercorns   Garlic   Cloves

This speciality of south-west France is an indispensable item in the country's larders. It is easy to make and absolutely delicious. Traditionally, goose is used, but the rich flavour of duck lends itself perfectly to this technique. Turkey, chicken and rabbit can be preserved in the same way.

INGREDIENTS

2 tbsp pickling salt
¼ tsp saltpetre
6 duck legs, any loose skin removed
750g (1½lb) lard, goose or duck fat
4 garlic cloves
1 tsp black peppercorns
½ tsp cloves

1 Mix the salt and saltpetre together and rub well all over the duck. Refrigerate for 24 hours.

2 Brush the salt off the duck, then dry well but do not wash. Gently heat the fat in a large, heavy pan. Add the duck, garlic, peppercorns and cloves. Ensure that the fat completely covers the duck. If not, melt some more fat and add to the pan to cover.

3 Cook very gently for 2 hours, or until no liquid comes out of the meat when pierced with a skewer. Lift out and allow to cool completely. Strain the fat through the muslin (see page 47).

4 Cover the bottom of the sterilized crock or jar with a little of the fat. Pack the duck into the jar and cover with the remaining fat. Allow to solidify, adding more fat if necessary to cover the meat by at least 1cm (½in). Seal the jar or cover the crock with waxed paper or a double layer of foil. The duck is ready to eat immediately.

☆ **Degree of difficulty**
Easy

Cooking time
About 2 hours

Special equipment
Sterilized muslin; sterilized earthenware crock or large jar with airtight sealant (see pages 42–43)

Yield
About 1.5–2kg (3–4lb)

Shelf life
6 months, refrigerated

Serving suggestion
Heat and serve with sauté potatoes

✱ **Warning**
This recipe contains saltpetre, see page 42

TIP

• To serve the confit, lift the duck out of the sealing fat and place in a dry frying pan. Heat thoroughly and serve either hot or cold, accompanied by salad or mashed potatoes.

THE FAT SHOULD COVER the duck in a thick layer to seal it

CONFIT OF DUCK or goose is traditionally used in cassoulet. This delicacy of the Toulouse and Castelnaudary regions of France combines confit with haricot beans and sausages (use Preserved Toulouse Sausages, page 136) to produce a hearty winter dish.

COVER THE DISH with waxed paper or a double layer of foil

Rabbit Pâté

(see page 25 for illustration)

Traditional pâtés owe their moist texture to their high fat content. Some time ago, however, I was challenged to produce a low-fat pâté and devised this light, healthy version using lean meat and plenty of fresh vegetables to provide moisture. The lard used to seal the pâté is removed before eating.

INGREDIENTS

1 large rabbit, boned, saddle fillets removed
400g (13oz) lean pork, cut into large cubes
150g (5oz) shallots, coarsely chopped
1 tbsp oil
200g (7oz) carrots, finely diced
3 eggs (size 2)
1 tbsp green peppercorns in brine, drained
2 tbsp salt
½ tsp freshly ground black pepper
2 tbsp finely chopped parsley
1 tbsp finely chopped thyme
1 tbsp finely chopped sage
a piece of caul fat or 250g (8oz) streaky bacon rashers, rind removed
about 500g (1lb) lard, melted
For the marinade
75ml (3fl oz) slivovitz, kirsch or brandy
3–4 sprigs thyme
3–4 sage leaves
1 tsp coarsely ground black pepper
2 bay leaves, lightly toasted and crumbled (see Tips, right)
1 tsp finely grated lemon rind

1 Put the rabbit fillets, the rest of the rabbit and the pork in a bowl and mix in all the ingredients for the marinade. Cover and refrigerate for 12 hours.

2 Fry the shallots in the oil for a few minutes until softened. Blanch the carrots for 1 minute, then drain, refresh and drain again (see page 46).

3 Remove the rabbit fillets from the marinade and pat dry. Put the rest of the meat and the shallots through the fine disc of the mincer. Strain the marinade and add to the minced meat, together with the carrots, eggs, peppercorns, salt and pepper. Mix very well, then cover and refrigerate for 2–3 hours.

4 Mix together the chopped herbs and spread them out on a baking tray. Roll the rabbit fillets in the herbs until they are evenly coated.

5 Line the terrine with the caul fat or bacon (see step 2, page 70). Spoon half the meat mixture into the terrine and smooth the surface with a palette knife.

6 Put the herb-coated rabbit fillets on top of the meat, in the centre. Spoon in the remaining meat mixture, making sure there are no air pockets, and smooth the top level with a palette knife. Fold over the ends of the caul fat or bacon and cover the pâté with the lid or a double layer of foil.

7 Place the terrine in a roasting tin filled with enough warm water to come about half-way up the sides of the dish. Bake in an oven preheated to 160°C/ 325°F/gas 3 for 1½–2 hours, or until the pâté has shrunk from the sides of the dish and is surrounded by liquid.

8 Remove the dish from the roasting tin. Weight down the pâté (see page 46). Leave to cool, then refrigerate for 12 hours.

9 Turn out the pâté from the terrine and wipe off the jelly or any liquid with paper towels.

10 Pour a 1cm (½in) layer of the melted lard into the bottom of the cleaned terrine and refrigerate until set. Place the pâté on top of the set fat and pour over the remaining lard, making sure it fills the gaps down the sides and covers the pâté by about 1cm (½in). Cover and refrigerate. The pâté will be ready to eat in 2 days.

 Degree of difficulty
 Advanced

Cooking time
1½–2 hours

Special equipment
Mincer; 1.5 litre (2½ pint) terrine

Yield
About 1.25kg (3lb)

Shelf life
3 weeks, refrigerated

Serving suggestions
Serve with Carrot and Almond Chutney (see page 121) or Striped Spiced Pears (see page 103)

TIPS

• To toast the bay leaves, place in a small frying pan and heat for a few minutes or until they start to colour. They can then be easily crumbled or pounded.
• Check the balance of flavours when making pâté before you put the meat mixture in the terrine. Fry a spoonful in a little oil, leave to cool and taste.
• To judge if the pâté is cooked, insert a meat thermometer into the centre; it should register 75°C (167°F).
• Instead of covering the pâté with lard, you could remove it from the terrine and wrap it tightly in aluminium foil. Before serving, decorate with bay leaves, fresh sage and thyme, then brush with melted aspic.
• Pâtés should always be brought to room temperature before serving.

TIP

• When using fresh herbs in a marinade, bruise them first by crushing with the flat side of a large cook's knife or a cleaver.

Quail and Pheasant Terrine

(see page 25 for illustration)

This is just about the most complicated recipe in the whole book — a tour de force consisting of boned, stuffed quail embedded in a rich, gamey forcemeat. A good butcher should be able to bone the birds for you.

INGREDIENTS

4 quails, boned, with the skin left on
2 tbsp honey
¼ tsp salt
4 tsp brandy

For the forcemeat

1 large, old cock pheasant, boned, all skin and sinew removed
300g (10oz) pork tenderloin or veal, cubed
100ml (3½fl oz) brandy
200g (7oz) shallots, chopped
2 garlic cloves, chopped
a little oil or butter
500g (1lb) skinless mild bacon or salt belly of pork, cut into small pieces
250ml (8fl oz) dry white wine
2 eggs (size 2)
1½ tsp freshly ground black pepper
1½ tsp salt
2 tbsp finely chopped thyme
15 juniper berries, coarsely ground
finely grated rind ½ lemon

For the green forcemeat

100g (5oz) baby spinach
2 tbsp finely chopped parsley

For the terrines

2 pieces of caul fat or 300g (10oz) streaky bacon rashers, rinds removed

1 Lay the boned quails skin-side down on a board and spread evenly with the honey, salt and brandy. Tightly roll up the birds and put in a bowl. Cover and refrigerate for 12 hours.

2 For the forcemeat, combine the pheasant and tenderloin. Add the brandy and mix well. Cover and refrigerate for 12 hours.

3 Sweat the shallots and garlic in a little oil or butter for a few minutes until softened, then leave to cool. Combine with the pheasant and pork and bacon or belly pork in the food processor.

4 Process for 1–2 minutes, adding some of the wine and any liquid left in the bowl, until smooth. Add the eggs, seasoning, thyme, juniper and lemon rind. Mix in well. Weigh 100g (3½oz) of the mixture and reserve. Cover the rest and refrigerate for 2 hours.

5 For the green forcemeat, blanch the spinach in boiling water for 2 minutes (see page 46) and squeeze dry. Put in the food processor and purée. Mix with the reserved forcemeat and parsley. Refrigerate for 2 hours.

6 Unroll the quails, skin-side down, on a board. Divide the green forcemeat between them, placing it in the centre of each one. Fold over the skin flaps to encase it and reshape the quails.

7 Line the terrines with the caul fat or bacon (see step 2, page 70). Spoon a quarter of the forcemeat into each terrine and smooth the surface over with a palette knife. Arrange the quails on top, pressing them lightly into the mixture. Spoon in the remaining forcemeat making sure there are no air pockets, then smooth the surface level.

8 Fold over the ends of the caul fat or bacon and cover each dish with the lid or a double layer of foil. Place the terrines in a roasting tin filled with enough warm water to come half-way up the sides of the dishes. Bake in an oven preheated to 160°C/325°F/ gas 3, for 2 hours, or until each pâté has shrunk from its dish and is surrounded by liquid.

9 Remove the dishes from the roasting tin and leave to cool. Weight down each pâté (see page 46), then refrigerate overnight. The pâtés are ready immediately.

 Degree of difficulty
 ☆☆ Advanced

 Cooking time
About 2 hours

 Special equipment
Food processor; 2x1 litre (1¾ pint) terrines

 Yield
About 2kg (4lb)

 Shelf life
3–4 weeks, sealed with lard, refrigerated

 Serving suggestions
Serve decorated as the centrepiece of a buffet or accompany with a rocket salad and Peach Chutney (see page 125) for an elegant first course

TIPS

• To serve the pâtés, decorate them with bay leaves and cranberries or brush with melted aspic or fruit jelly.
• To keep longer than a few days, seal the top of the pâté with melted lard or wrap tightly in foil.

Pâté de Campagne

(see page 70 for technique)

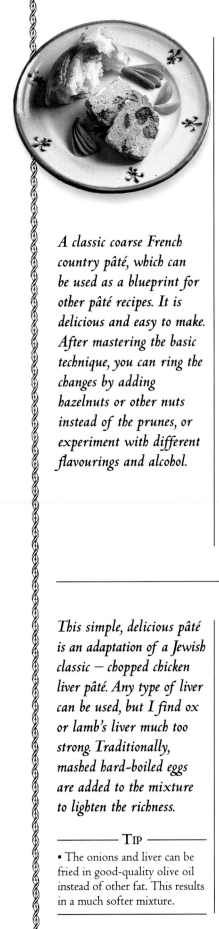

A classic coarse French country pâté, which can be used as a blueprint for other pâté recipes. It is delicious and easy to make. After mastering the basic technique, you can ring the changes by adding hazelnuts or other nuts instead of the prunes, or experiment with different flavourings and alcohol.

INGREDIENTS

500g (1lb) skinless, boneless belly of pork, cut into large cubes
500g (1lb) lean pork such as shoulder, tenderloin or leg, cut into large cubes
500g (1lb) pig's or calf's liver, sliced
150g (5oz) streaky bacon rashers
1–2 garlic cloves, finely chopped
1 tsp juniper berries, crushed
½ tsp freshly ground black pepper
1 tbsp finely chopped thyme
2 tsp salt
100g (3½oz) pitted prunes soaked in 5 tsp warm brandy for 2 hours
150ml (¼ pint) dry white wine
2 tbsp brandy
For the terrines
2 pieces of caul fat or 500g (1lb) streaky bacon rashers, rind removed
6 thin slices of lemon or orange
4–6 bay leaves
500–750g (1–1½lb) lard, melted
juniper berries, bay leaves and cranberries, to garnish (optional)

1 Mix together all the meat and put through the fine plate of the mincer. Add the remaining ingredients and mix well. Cover and refrigerate for 3–4 hours.

2 Line the terrines with the caul fat or bacon (see step 2, page 70). Spoon half the meat mixture into each, making sure there are no air pockets. Fold over the caul or bacon and put the citrus slices and bay leaves on top. Cover with the lids or a double layer of foil.

3 Place the terrines in a roasting tin filled with enough warm water to come half-way up the sides of the dishes. Bake in an oven preheated to 160°C/325°F/ gas 3 for 1½–2 hours, or until each pâté has shrunk from its dish and is surrounded by liquid. Allow to cool, then weight down (see page 46) and refrigerate overnight.

4 Remove the citrus slices and bay leaves, unmould each pâté and wipe off the jelly. Set the pâtés in the melted lard (see step 7, page 71). Garnish, if desired, then cover and refrigerate. The pâtés will be ready in 2–3 days.

 Degree of difficulty
Moderate

 Cooking time
1½–2 hours

 Special equipment
Mincer; 2x1 litre (1½ pint) terrines

 Yield
About 2kg (4lb)

 Shelf life
1 month, refrigerated

Serving suggestion
Serve with crusty bread, pickles and a glass of wine

TIP

• The meat for this pâté is minced to give a coarse texture. If you prefer a smoother result, use a food processor.

Smooth Liver Pâté

(see page 24 for illustration)

This simple, delicious pâté is an adaptation of a Jewish classic — chopped chicken liver pâté. Any type of liver can be used, but I find ox or lamb's liver much too strong. Traditionally, mashed hard-boiled eggs are added to the mixture to lighten the richness.

TIP

• The onions and liver can be fried in good-quality olive oil instead of other fat. This results in a much softer mixture.

INGREDIENTS

250g (8oz) chicken fat, goose fat or clarified butter (see page 73)
250g (8oz) onions or shallots, chopped
500g (1lb) chicken, duck or calf's liver, trimmed and washed
1 tsp salt
½ tsp freshly ground black pepper
2 tbsp brandy (optional)
2 tbsp finely chopped parsley (optional)
½ tsp finely grated orange or lemon rind (optional)
1 clove garlic, finely mashed (optional)

1 Heat 150g (5oz) of the fat in a heavy frying pan, add the onions or shallots and fry gently for 15–20 minutes, until browned. Add the liver and fry for 2 minutes on each side, or until cooked but still pink inside. Cool briefly.

2 Transfer the mixture to the food processor and process until smooth. Add the remaining ingredients and mix well.

3 Press the mixture into the dish or individual ramekins. Leave to cool completely, then cover and refrigerate for a few hours. Melt the remaining fat and pour over the pâté to seal. Refrigerate for at least 12 hours before serving.

 Degree of difficulty
Easy

 Cooking time
About 25 minutes

 Special equipment
Food processor; 500ml (¾ pint) sterilized earthenware dish or 5x175ml (6fl oz) ramekins (see pages 42–43)

 Yield
About 500g (1lb)

 Shelf life
2 weeks, refrigerated

 Serving suggestions
Serve on toast or baked en croûte in puff pastry

Duck Pâté with Pistachio Nuts and Kumquats

The addition of kumquats in this classic French recipe produces a spectacular pâté. You do need to use a large, mature bird — the young, intensively reared, oven-ready ducklings commonly available just do not have the depth of flavour. Keep the duck bones to make stock and use the skin to make delicious crackling (see Tips, right).

INGREDIENTS

3kg (6lb) duck with its liver, skinned and boned

300g (10oz) pork tenderloin or lean pink veal, cut into large cubes

500g (1lb) boned and skinned belly of pork, cut into large cubes

2 eggs (size 2)

100g (3½oz) very green pistachio nuts, skinned (see Tips, right)

1 tbsp salt

1 tsp freshly ground black pepper

1 tbsp finely chopped tarragon

2 pieces of caul fat or 300g (10oz) streaky bacon rashers, rind removed

about 16 kumquats

about 500–750g (1–1½lb) lard, melted

For the marinade

100ml (3½fl oz) brandy

2 garlic cloves, crushed

rind and juice of 1 large orange

a few sprigs of thyme, bruised

1 Put the duck meat and liver and pork tenderloin or veal in a bowl. Add all the ingredients for the marinade and mix well. Cover and refrigerate for 12 hours.

2 Remove the duck breasts and liver from the marinade and cut into 1cm (½in) cubes. Put the remaining meat and the belly of pork through the fine disc of the mincer.

3 Add the cubed duck breast and liver to the minced meat, together with the marinating liquid and the eggs, nuts, salt, pepper and tarragon. Mix well.

4 Line the terrines with the caul fat or the bacon, (see step 2, page 70). Spoon a quarter of the meat mixture into each terrine and smooth the surface.

5 Arrange a row of whole kumquats down the centre of each dish. Divide the remaining meat mixture between the dishes, making sure there are no air pockets, then smooth the surface. The mixture should be about 2.5cm (1in) from the rim of each terrine. Fold over the ends of the caul fat or bacon and cover each dish with its lid or a double layer of foil.

6 Place the terrine in a roasting tin filled with enough warm water to come about half-way up the sides of the dishes. Bake in an oven preheated to 160°C/325°F/gas 3, for 2 hours, or until each pâté has shrunk from its dish and is surrounded by liquid.

7 Remove the dishes from the roasting tin and leave to cool. Weight down each pâté (see page 46), then refrigerate for about 12 hours. Turn out each pâté and wipe off any jelly or liquid with paper towels.

8 Set each pâté in the melted lard (see step 7, page 71), then cover and refrigerate for at least 12 hours before serving.

☆ **Degree of difficulty**
☆☆ Advanced

Cooking time
About 2 hours

Special equipment
Mincer; 2x1 litre (1¾ pint) terrines

Yield
About 2kg (4lb)

Shelf life
3 weeks, refrigerated

Serving suggestion
Serve as a first course with a salad and Shallot Confiture (see page 161) or Onion Marmalade (see page 164)

TIPS
• To skin pistachio nuts, blanch them in boiling water, then leave until cool enough to handle and rub off the skins.
• If you prefer a smoother pâté, mince the meat twice, or process in a food processor.
• To make crackling with the duck skin, cut it into large pieces and place in a pan with 250ml (8fl oz) of water. Bring to the boil, then simmer very slowly until most of the water has evaporated and all the fat has melted. Increase the heat and cook until the skin is golden and crisp. Drain well, reserving the fat for future use. Serve the skin hot, sprinkled with salt and pepper. It can also be potted in its own fat and heated before serving.

Rillettes

(see page 25 for illustration)

Rillettes is the French equivalent of British potted meat, except the meat is not pounded or minced but shredded. Each region of France has its own favourite recipe and most of them are only lightly flavoured to allow the natural taste of the pork to come through. Goose, duck and rabbit can all be prepared in the same way.

INGREDIENTS

1kg (2lb) boneless belly of pork, cut into 1 x 5cm (½ x 2in) strips
500g (1lb) back fat, cut into small pieces
125ml (4fl oz) water or dry white wine
2–3 sprigs thyme
2 garlic cloves, peeled
1½ tsp salt
1 tsp freshly ground black or white pepper
1 blade mace
about 250g (8oz) lard, melted, to seal

1 Put all the ingredients, except the melted lard, in a heavy pan or a deep casserole and bring slowly to the boil.

2 Cook, covered, over a very low heat for about 3 hours, stirring frequently to prevent it from sticking. Uncover the pan and continue to cook for about 1 hour, or until the meat is very soft and falling apart.

3 Transfer the contents of the pan to a colander placed over a deep bowl. Remove the thyme, garlic and mace and lightly squeeze the meat to extract the fat. With the aid of two forks, shred the meat until it resembles a fine, fibrous mass.

4 Put the meat in a clean pan and add the strained off fat and cooking juices. Heat gently for about 10 minutes, mixing well to achieve a homogeneous mass. Taste and adjust the seasoning, then pack into the dish or terrine. Leave to cool, then pour over the melted lard to seal. Cover and refrigerate. The rillettes is ready to eat immediately.

 Degree of difficulty
Moderate

 Cooking time
About 4½ hours

 Special equipment
1 litre (1½ pint) sterilized earthenware dish or terrine (see pages 42–43)

 Yield
About 1kg (2lb)

 Shelf life
6 weeks, refrigerated

Serving suggestion
A wonderful picnic dish served with crusty bread

Potted Venison

(see page 72 for technique)

Venison makes the most delicious potted meat. The addition of bacon is important as it provides moisture. When using bacon always select dry-cured.

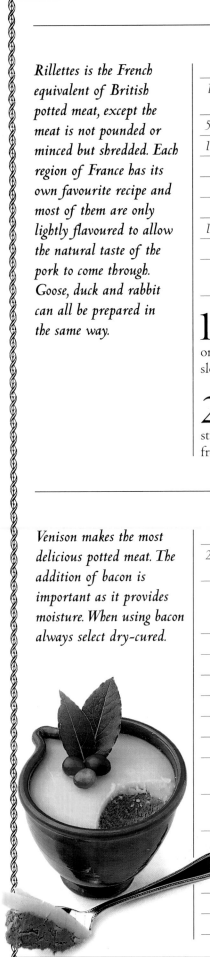

INGREDIENTS

250g (8oz) bacon rashers, rinds removed and tied together with string
750g (1½lb) boned shoulder or leg of venison, trimmed well and cut into 2.5cm (1in) cubes
100g (3½oz) butter
2 garlic cloves, finely chopped
250ml (8fl oz) port or good red wine
1 tsp juniper berries, crushed
1 tsp freshly ground black pepper
2 blades mace
100–250g (3½–8oz) clarified butter, to seal (see page 73)
a few bay leaves and cranberries, to garnish (optional)
For the herb bundle (see page 47)
2 sprigs thyme
1 bay leaf
2–3 sage leaves
a strip of lemon rind

1 Coarsely chop the bacon and put in a deep casserole with the herb bundle and all the remaining ingredients, except the clarified butter and garnish. Cover and bake in an oven preheated to 160°C/325°F/gas 3 for 2½–3 hours, until the meat is very tender.

2 Remove the mace, herb bundle and bacon rinds from the dish. Put the meat in the food processor and process to a smooth paste. Pack into the dish or individual ramekins. Leave to cool completely. Cover and refrigerate for 2–3 hours.

3 Pour the melted clarified butter over the meat to seal (see step 5, page 73), using the larger quantity if covering the individual ramekins. Garnish with a few bay leaves and cranberries, if desired. The venison is ready immediately.

☆☆ **Degree of difficulty**
Moderate

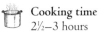 **Cooking time**
2½–3 hours

Special equipment
Food processor; 1 litre (1¾ pint) sterilized dish or 6x175ml (6fl oz) ramekins (see pages 42–43)

Yield
About 1kg (2lb)

Shelf life
1 month, refrigerated

Serving suggestion
Traditionally served in a ramekin, with watercress, and accompanied by toast

VARIATION

♦ *Before filling the ramekins, pour 1 tablespoon melted redcurrant or blackcurrant jelly over the base of each and leave to set.*

Potted Meat

Potted meats were a useful standby in Victorian Britain and a prudent way to extend leftovers. Cooked and raw meat were simmered with gravy and seasoning, then mixed with butter and pounded to a fine paste. The following is made with raw meat but any leftover cooked beef can also be used.

INGREDIENTS

1kg (2lb) beef (rump or shoulder), all fat and sinew removed, cut into small pieces
250ml (8fl oz) good beef stock
3–4 anchovy fillets, chopped
150g (5oz) butter
2–3 sprigs of thyme
2 bay leaves
2 blades mace
1 tsp salt
½ tsp grated lemon rind
100g (3½oz) clarified butter (see page 73)

1 Put all the ingredients, except the lemon rind and clarified butter, in a casserole. Bring to the boil, cover tightly, then simmer on the lowest heat. Alternatively, bake in an oven preheated to 160°C/325°F/gas 3, for 2 hours, or until the meat is tender.

2 Remove the herbs and mace and drain the meat. Pour the cooking liquid into a pan and boil until reduced to 250ml (8fl oz).

3 Process the meat and reduced liquid to a paste in the food processor. Mix in the lemon rind and season. Pack into the ramekins or dish and refrigerate for 2–3 hours. Seal the top with the melted clarified butter (see step 5, page 73). Cover and refrigerate. The meat will be ready in 2 days.

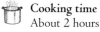 **Degree of difficulty**
Easy

 **Cooking time**
About 2 hours

Special equipment
Food processor; 6x175ml (6fl oz) sterilized ramekins or a 1 litre (1¾ pint) earthenware dish (see pages 42–43)

Yield
About 750g (1½lb)

Shelf life
5 weeks, refrigerated

Serving suggestion
Serve as a first course with a watercress salad

Potted Cheese

Potting is a wonderful way to use up odd bits of good leftover cheese. Blended with butter, the cheese makes a flavourful paste that keeps for over a month. Any kind of mature hard cheese is suitable, including blue cheese.

INGREDIENTS

500g (1lb) mature Cheddar or Cheshire cheese, or a mixture, finely grated
75g (2½oz) softened unsalted butter
1 tbsp pale dry sherry
1 tsp English mustard
¼ tsp finely grated lemon rind
large pinch freshly grated nutmeg
large pinch cayenne pepper or chilli powder
150g (5oz) clarified butter (see page 73)

1 Put all the ingredients, except the clarified butter, in a large bowl. Beat together until smooth. Pack into the ramekins or dish, filling them to within 1cm (½in) of the rim. Smooth the top and refrigerate for 2–3 hours.

2 Seal the top with the melted clarified butter (see step 5, page 73). Cover and refrigerate. The cheese will be ready in 2 days.

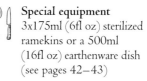 **Degree of difficulty**
Easy

Special equipment
3x175ml (6fl oz) sterilized ramekins or a 500ml (16fl oz) earthenware dish (see pages 42–43)

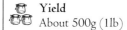 **Yield**
About 500g (1lb)

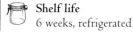 **Shelf life**
6 weeks, refrigerated

Potted Shrimps

This classic British delicacy is tasty and easy to make. It is essential to use freshly boiled shrimps, preferably small brown ones, for their fresh, sweet flavour. The shells are usually removed but I like their crunchiness and therefore only remove the heads.

INGREDIENTS

1kg (2lb) raw shrimps
300g (10oz) clarified butter (see page 73)
1 tsp salt
½ tsp freshly ground white or black pepper
½ tsp ground mace
large pinch cayenne pepper or chilli powder

1 Cook the shrimps in boiling water for no more than 2 minutes. Drain, refresh under cold water, drain again, then peel.

2 Place the shrimps in a bowl and mix with 200g (7oz) of the melted clarified butter and all the remaining ingredients. Divide between the ramekins and bake in an oven preheated to 190°C/375°F/gas 5 for 15 minutes.

3 Leave to cool, then refrigerate for 2–3 hours. Seal the tops with the remaining melted clarified butter (see step 5, page 73). Cover and refrigerate. The shrimps will be ready to eat in 24 hours.

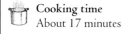 **Degree of difficulty**
Easy

Cooking time
About 17 minutes

Special equipment
6x175ml (6fl oz) ramekins

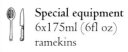 **Yield**
About 1kg (2lb)

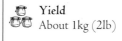 **Shelf life**
1 month, refrigerated

PRESERVED FISH

FISH MAKE EXCELLENT preserves: they can be cured, pickled, or smoked to produce the most tasty delicacies. Do not attempt to salt-cure fish unless you have a good fishmonger who can supply you with very fresh fish; they can deteriorate quickly, especially in hot weather. Many of the following recipes use whole salted herrings, which are sometimes difficult to obtain. If you are unable to find them, use prepared salted fillets instead. These are usually sold loose, in brine or oil, in supermarkets or fishmongers, or can be bought ready-prepared in jars or cans.

Pickled Fish

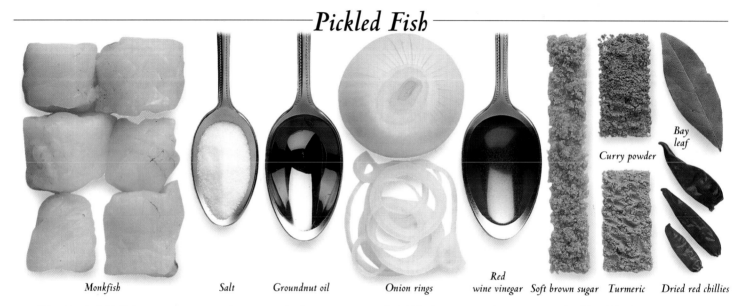

Monkfish   Salt   Groundnut oil   Onion rings   Red wine vinegar   Soft brown sugar   Curry powder   Turmeric   Dried red chillies   Bay leaf

This delicious, piquant recipe is from the Cape of South Africa. According to the writer Laurens van der Post, it used to be made by Transvaal farmers on their summer holidays in the Cape, then taken to the interior and eaten during the winter. Traditionally, Cape salmon, cod or snoek are used but monkfish, haddock, conger eel and mackerel make good substitutes.

INGREDIENTS

1kg (2lb) firm, very fresh fish fillets, cut into 5cm (2in) chunks
5 tsp salt
6–7 tbsp groundnut or refined sesame oil
500g (1lb) onions, sliced into thin rings
1 litre (1¾ pints) red or white wine vinegar
2 tbsp soft brown sugar
1 tbsp mild curry powder
1 tsp ground turmeric
2.5cm (1in) piece fresh ginger root, shredded
2–3 dried red chillies
1–2 bay leaves

1 Put the fish in a bowl. Sprinkle with 3 teaspoons of the salt, mixing well. Leave for 2 hours. Drain and dry on paper towels.

2 Heat 4 tablespoons of the oil in a large, heavy frying pan.

Add the fish, a few pieces at a time, and fry over a high heat for 3 minutes on each side, or until evenly browned and just cooked through. Drain on paper towels.

3 Put the sliced onions, vinegar, sugar, curry powder, turmeric, ginger and remaining salt in a non-corrosive pan. Bring to the boil, skim well and boil for 5–6 minutes, until the onion is cooked but still slightly crunchy. Remove the onion with a slotted spoon and drain well.

4 Arrange the fish and onion in alternate layers in the hot sterilized jar, adding the chillies and bay leaves, and finishing with a layer of onion. Bring the vinegar back to the boil and pour into the jar. Add the remaining oil to cover, then seal. The fish will be ready to eat in 2 days.

☆ **Degree of difficulty**
Easy

Cooking time
About 30 minutes

Special equipment
2 litre (3½ pint) sterilized glass or earthenware jar with vinegar-proof sealant (see pages 42–43)

Yield
About 1.5kg (3lb)

Shelf life
3–4 months, refrigerated

PICKLED FISH *make a delicious appetizer simply garnished with fresh parsley and lime wedges. For a more substantial dish, accompany with a mixed leaf salad and crusty bread and butter.*

FISH SUCH AS MONKFISH or cod produce the best results as they have a firm texture

ONIONS, GINGER AND CURRY POWDER give additional flavour to the pickling vinegar, while ground turmeric adds colour

VARIATIONS

✦ *Pickled Fish with Lemon*
Thinly slice 2 lemons, sprinkle with 2 tablespoons salt and leave to stand for 2 hours. Drain well, then add to the onion mixture.

✦ *Pickled Fish with Herbs*
Add 4 tablespoons chopped fresh dill to the onion mixture.

Pickled Salmon

— see page 27 for illustration

In the past, when salmon was cheap and plentiful, pickled salmon was the food of the poor and was prepared in large barrels. This recipe comes from the west coast of Canada and can also be made using pike or whitefish. The bones are left in as they become soft and edible with pickling.

INGREDIENTS

4 onions, thinly sliced
1kg (2lb) salmon fillets, cut into slices 2.5cm (1in) thick
2½ tsp salt
juice of 1 lemon
200ml (7fl oz) white wine vinegar
2 tbsp sugar
2 bay leaves
1 tsp black peppercorns
½ tsp mustard seeds
½ tsp dill seeds
¼ tsp cloves

1 Put half of the sliced onions in a fish kettle or large saucepan and arrange the salmon fillets on top in a single layer.

2 Add 1 teaspoon of the salt, the lemon juice and enough cold water to cover. Bring slowly to the boil, then reduce the heat and simmer for 1 minute. Remove from the heat and leave the salmon to cool in the liquid.

3 Arrange alternate layers of the remaining raw onion and salmon in the hot sterilized jar, finishing with a layer of onion.

4 Strain the cooking liquid into a non-corrosive pan and boil until it has reduced to about 750ml (1¼ pints).

5 Add the vinegar, sugar, bay leaves, peppercorns, mustard seeds, dill seeds, cloves and the remaining salt and boil for 2–3 more minutes.

6 Pour into the jar, making sure that the ingredients are totally covered, then seal. The fish will be ready to eat in 3–4 days.

 Degree of difficulty
Easy

 Cooking time
4–5 minutes

 Special equipment
Fish kettle or large non-corrosive saucepan; 2 litre (3½ pint) sterilized jar with vinegar-proof sealant (see pages 42–43)

 Yield
About 1.25kg (2½ lb)

 Shelf life
3 months, refrigerated

Serving suggestion
Serve with a beetroot salad as a light main course

Rollmops

— see page 27 for illustration

The best kind of fish to use for this pickle are maatjes *or* schmaltz *herrings, although other salted herrings will do. Butterflied herrings are boned with the fillets still joined together.*

TIPS

• To fillet herring, first cut off the head and tail. Lay the fish, skin-side up, on a work surface and spread the belly flaps out to the side. Press down firmly along the length of the backbone with a thumb, to loosen it. Turn the fish over and pull the bone out in one piece.
• If there is not enough marinade to cover the rollmops, top up the jar with cold vinegar.

INGREDIENTS

8 whole salted herrings or 8 filleted butterflied herrings
6 tbsp strong mustard
4 large dill-pickled gherkins, sliced into thick batons as long as the width of the herrings
1 large onion, thinly sliced into rings, blanched for a few seconds (see page 46)
2 tbsp capers
For the marinade
500ml (17fl oz) white wine vinegar or cider vinegar
500ml (17fl oz) water or dry white wine
2 tsp juniper berries, crushed
1 tsp allspice berries, crushed
2–3 cloves, crushed

1 To prepare the whole herrings, pour over water to cover and refrigerate for at least 12 hours, changing the water once or twice.

2 Put all the ingredients for the marinade in a non-corrosive pan. Bring to the boil, then simmer for 10 minutes. Leave to cool completely.

3 Drain and dry the herrings, then fillet (see Tips, left). Rinse and dry the prepared fillets, if using. Lay the fillets skin-side down on a board and spread with the mustard. Place a piece of gherkin at the wide end of each, scatter with a few onion rings and capers. Roll up like a Swiss roll, securing with 2 wooden skewers.

4 Layer the fish rolls with the remaining onion in the sterilized jar, finishing with a layer of onion. Pour in the marinade, making sure the onion is totally covered, then seal and refrigerate. The fish will be ready in 1 week.

 Degree of difficulty
Easy

 Cooking time
About 12 minutes

 Special equipment
2 litre (3½ pint) sterilized wide-necked jar with vinegar-proof sealant (see pages 42–43)

 Yield
About 1.5kg (3lb)

 Shelf life
6 months, refrigerated

 Serving suggestions
Serve as an appetizer with chilled schnapps or vodka; as part of a buffet; or with a warm potato salad as a light main course

Herrings in Mustard Sauce

I found this recipe on a yellowing piece of paper between the pages of an old cookery book. Although its origins are unknown, I would guess it probably came from somewhere in northern or central Europe. Select large, salted herrings, which should be soaked overnight to remove the excess salt.

TIPS

• Do not allow the egg mixture to boil or it will curdle.
• Before sealing the jar, tap it on a work surface to ensure there are no air pockets.

INGREDIENTS

6 whole salted herrings or 12 prepared fillets

250ml (8fl oz) white wine vinegar or distilled malt vinegar

¼ tsp cloves

2 bay leaves

1 tsp black peppercorns

3 onions, thinly sliced

4 eggs (size 2)

1½ tbsp sugar

2 tbsp mustard powder

large pinch ground turmeric

1 To prepare the whole herrings, pour over water to cover and refrigerate for at least 12 hours, changing the water once or twice.

2 Put the vinegar, cloves, bay leaves and peppercorns in a non-corrosive pan. Bring to the boil, reduce the heat and simmer for a few minutes. Leave to cool.

3 Blanch the onion for 2 minutes (see page 46). Drain and dry the whole herrings, then fillet (see Rollmops, Tips, opposite). Rinse and dry the prepared fillets, if using. Cut into bite-sized pieces.

4 Beat the eggs with the sugar, mustard and turmeric, and add to the vinegar mixture. Transfer to the double boiler or a bowl placed over a pan of hot water. Cook gently, stirring, until the mixture is thick enough to coat the back of a spoon. Pour over the onion and leave to cool.

5 Add the herring and mix well. Pack into the sterilized jars, then seal and refrigerate. The fish will be ready to eat in 3 days.

 Degree of difficulty
Moderate

 Cooking time
35–40 minutes

 Special equipment
Double boiler; 2x500ml (17fl oz) sterilized jars with vinegar-proof sealants (see pages 42–43)

 Yield
About 1kg (2lb)

 Shelf life
1–2 weeks, refrigerated

Serving suggestion
Serve with buttered rye bread, accompanied by chilled vodka or aquavit

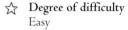

Herrings in Cream Sauce

This recipe was given to me by Penny Stonfield, one of the best traditional Jewish cooks I know. She makes large quantities of this delicious salad for special occasions.

INGREDIENTS

6 whole salted herrings or 12 prepared fillets

2 large onions, sliced into thin rings

6–8 allspice berries, crushed

2–3 dried bay leaves, crumbled

350ml (12fl oz) double cream

250ml (8fl oz) white wine vinegar

1 tbsp sugar

1 To prepare the whole herrings, pour over water to cover and refrigerate for at least 12 hours, changing the water once or twice.

2 Drain and dry the whole salted herrings, then fillet (see Rollmops, Tips, opposite). Rinse and dry the prepared fillets, if using. Cut the fish into bite-sized pieces.

3 Blanch the sliced onions for 2 minutes (see page 46). Mix the onion with the crushed allspice berries and bay leaves. Layer with the herring in the sterilized jar, finishing with a layer of onion.

4 Stir together the cream, wine vinegar and sugar. Pour into the jars, making sure there are no air pockets, then seal and refrigerate. The fish will be ready to eat in 2–3 days.

 Degree of difficulty
Easy

 Special equipment
2x500ml (17fl oz) sterilized jars with vinegar-proof sealants (see pages 42–43)

 Yield
About 1kg (2lb)

 Shelf life
1 week, refrigerated

Serving suggestion
Serve with rye bread as a first course

TIP

• If the whole herrings are still too salty after being soaked for 12 hours, rinse, cover with fresh water and soak for a further 12 hours.

Smoked Salmon

(see page 66 for technique)

Freshly smoked, cured salmon is a rare delicacy. After curing, the salmon can be cold-smoked in the traditional way, or hot-smoked, the way it is often served in North America. Oak is most commonly used, but exotic woods, like mesquite, hickory and cherry, also produce good results.

VARIATION

♦ Smoked Trout

Do not bone the trout. Sprinkle the trout both inside and out with a thick layer of the curing mixture and refrigerate for 3–4 hours. Dry as for the salmon, then hot-smoke for 1½–2 hours. Finish as for salmon.

INGREDIENTS

2–3kg (4–6lb) fresh salmon, cleaned
375g (12oz) sea salt
125g (4oz) light soft brown or demerara sugar
1–2 tsps whisky

1 Fillet the salmon and remove all the remaining bones with tweezers (see steps 1 and 2, page 66). Wash and dry the fillets.

2 Mix together the salt and sugar. Sprinkle some into a large, non-corrosive dish in a layer 5mm (¼ in) thick. Lay one fillet on top, skin-side down. Sprinkle with another layer of salt and sugar about 1cm (½ in) thick, making it thinner towards the tail end.

3 Put the second fillet, skin-side down, on top and sprinkle with the remaining salt mix. Cover and refrigerate for 3–3½ hours.

4 Remove the fish from the salt, wash under running water and dry well with paper towels. Brush with the whisky and insert a wooden skewer into the back of each fillet (see step 5, page 66).

5 Hang up in a cool, dry, dark, airy place (between 6–8°C/42–46°F) for 24 hours, or until the salmon is almost dry to the touch and has a shiny salt glaze.

6 Put the fish in the smoker and hot-smoke, between 105–110°C (215–225°F), for 2–3 hours; or cold-smoke, below 30°C (86°F), for 3–4 hours. Leave until cold, then wrap in waxed paper or foil and refrigerate. The fish is ready in 24 hours.

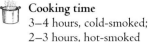

Degree of difficulty
Moderate

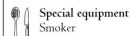

Cooking time
3–4 hours, cold-smoked; 2–3 hours, hot-smoked

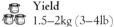

Special equipment
Smoker

Yield
1.5–2kg (3–4lb)

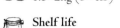

Shelf life
3 weeks, refrigerated; 3 months, frozen

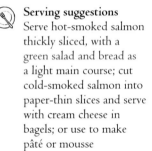

Serving suggestions
Serve hot-smoked salmon thickly sliced, with a green salad and bread as a light main course; cut cold-smoked salmon into paper-thin slices and serve with cream cheese in bagels; or use to make pâté or mousse

Smoked Prawns

Smoking gives a new dimension to prawns, adding to their flavour and shelf life. I find oak smoke too strong for delicate shellfish and prefer to use lighter, more fragrant woods such as apple or citrus. Shrimps can be substituted for prawns, and other types of seafood, such as squid, octopus, oysters and clams, are equally good.

INGREDIENTS

1.5kg (3lb) raw prawns
2 litres (3½ pints) water
1 tbsp salt
1 bunch of fresh dill or fennel flowers and stems, or 2 tbsp dried dill
2–3 tbsp olive or groundnut oil
For the brine
1.5 litres (2½ pints) water
350g (11½ oz) salt

1 Remove the heads from the prawns and discard. Wash the prawns well and leave to drain for 30–45 minutes.

2 Make the brine by mixing together the water and salt until the salt has dissolved. Pour over the prawns and weight down (see page 46) so that they are completely submerged. Leave for 30 minutes and then drain well.

(This produces mildly salted prawns; for a saltier flavour, leave for up to 1 hour.)

3 Put the first measure of water and salt in a large pan and bring to the boil. Add the dill or fennel and simmer for 15 minutes, then add the prawns. Simmer for 2–5 minutes or until the prawns are just cooked.

4 Lift out the prawns and cool on a wire rack for 1–2 hours, or until just dry to the touch.

5 Brush the prawns with the oil and cold-smoke below 25°C (77°F) for 2 hours (see page 66).

6 Wrap the prawns in waxed or greaseproof paper and refrigerate. Alternatively, you could preserve them in oil (see Mixed Seafood in Oil, page 109).

Degree of difficulty
Moderate

Cooking time
About 20 minutes, simmering; 2 hours, smoking

Special equipment
Smoker

Yield
About 1kg (2lb)

Shelf life
1 month, refrigerated; 3 months, frozen

Serving suggestions
Serve as a snack with drinks or as a first course; add to fish stews, risotto and pasta dishes just before serving

Gravad Lax

(see page 26 for illustration)

This delicious Scandinavian recipe is the simplest and most enjoyable way to cure fish. Although salmon is almost always used, trout, mackerel and even very fresh halibut can be prepared in the same way. Alcohol is not a traditional ingredient but it adds flavour and helps to preserve the fish.

TIP

• Brown sugar gives the fish a delightful flavour and an appetizing dark colour.

INGREDIENTS

1kg (2lb) middle-cut of salmon, filleted, all bones removed (see steps 1 and 2, page 66)
4 tbsp coarse pickling salt
3 tbsp soft brown or white sugar
1 tbsp coarsely ground black pepper
1 large bunch dill, coarsely chopped
2–3 tbsp aquavit or vodka

1 Place one fillet of the salmon skin-side down on a large piece of aluminium foil. Mix together the salt, sugar and pepper. Sprinkle half of the salt mixture evenly over the salmon.

2 Sprinkle with the chopped dill, remaining salt mixture and the aquavit or vodka. Place the other fillet of salmon, skin-side up, over the top. Fold the foil over and wrap well.

3 Put the foil-wrapped salmon in a shallow dish. Cover with a board or plate and weight down (see page 46). Refrigerate for 24–36 hours, turning the parcel over every 12 hours.

4 Unwrap the salmon and carefully remove each fillet from the foil. Gently brush off all the salt, dill and spices. To serve the salmon, cut it into very thin slices with a long-bladed, serrated knife, angling the knife at 45 degrees.

 Degree of difficulty
Easy

 Yield
About 1kg (2lb)

 Shelf life
1 week, refrigerated; to keep longer, see Herrings in Spiced Oil (page 109)

 Serving suggestion
Serve with a dill and mustard sauce, accompanied by a potato or beetroot salad

Salt-cured Sprats

(see page 74 for technique)

Salt-cured fish develop a characteristic flavour and smell and are a somewhat acquired taste. Sardines, herrings and anchovies can be cured in the same way.

TIPS

• Choose young, fresh, even-sized fish with a good, shiny, silvery skin.
• Leaving the heads on results in a stronger, more gamey taste, as they contain a lot of oil. You can remove them if you prefer.
• Other flavourings, such as juniper, allspice and aromatic wood chips, can be added with the peppercorns and bay leaves.
• For longer keeping, the sprats can also be kept in salt. At the end of step 6, remove the fish from the brine and layer alternately with coarse salt in a new wooden box.
• When you want to use the sprats, remove them from the brine or salt and soak for a few hours in water or a mixture of milk and water.

INGREDIENTS

1kg (2lb) sprats
500g (1lb) fine sea salt
1–1.5kg (2–3lb) pickling salt
3–4 bay leaves
1 tbsp black peppercorns

1 Clean and gut the fish. With a small pair of scissors, snip each fish just below the gills. Make a cut down the belly, then with your fingers carefully pull out and discard the stomach contents (see steps 1–3, page 74).

2 Sprinkle a little of the fine sea salt in the cavity of each fish and all over the outside, rubbing it in thoroughly.

3 Arrange the fish in layers in a shallow dish, adding a fine sprinkling of the sea salt to each layer. Leave in a cool place (between 6–8°C/42–46°F) or refrigerate for 4–5 hours to draw out some of the moisture. Remove the fish and dry on paper towels.

4 Sprinkle a layer of the pickling salt over the base of a large glass or earthenware container.

5 Arrange a layer of fish on top and add a bay leaf and a few peppercorns. Cover with an even layer of pickling salt about 5mm (¼in) thick and continue to arrange the ingredients in this way until all the sprats are used, finishing with a layer of salt.

6 Weight down (see page 46), cover and refrigerate or leave in a cool, dark place (between 6–8°C/42–46°F). The sprats will be ready to eat in 1 week.

7 To keep the fish for longer, remove the oil that has formed at the top of the container. If not enough brine has formed to cover the fish, top up with a strong salt solution made of equal quantities of salt and water. Seal the container and refrigerate or store in a cool, dark place (between 6–8°C/42–46°F).

 Degree of difficulty
Easy

 Special equipment
Sterilized earthenware or glass container with non-corrosive sealant (see pages 42–43)

 Yield
About 750g (1½lb)

 Shelf life
2 years, refrigerated

Serving suggestion
Serve with a fruit vinegar and olive oil dressing, accompanied with thinly sliced raw onion and chilled vodka

VARIATIONS

◆ *The salt-cured sprats can be filleted and preserved in oil (see Herrings in Spiced Oil, page 109).*
◆ **Anchovies in Oil**
Salt-cure the anchovies like the sprats, then fillet. Roll each fillet around a caper and skewer on to a wooden cocktail stick. Arrange in a small jar and cover with olive oil.

JAMS & OTHER SWEET PRESERVES

SUMMER IS THE TIME for making sweet preserves, with its long, warm days and abundance of sweet, juicy fruit. This large family of products is divided into a number of distinct types that all use sugar as the only means of preservation. The most popular is jam, pulped fruit cooked together with sugar until it reaches a setting point, while jelly is clear and sparkling and made from fruit juice and sugar. In the past marmalade was made from many different kinds of fruit other than citrus fruit. I use the term for a preserve that is chunkier than jam, though not necessarily citrus based. Confiture consists of whole fruit preserved in fruit jelly. The terms preserve and conserve are interchangeable and refer to semi-candied fruit preserved in a heavy sugar syrup. Freezing destroys some of the pectin in fruit, so if you use frozen fruit to make sweet preserves, adjust the pectin content as necessary with a homemade pectin stock (see page 47) or commercial pectin; alternatively add oranges or lemons.

Grape Jam

Grapes   *Lemon*   *Preserving sugar*   *Pecan nuts*   *Brandy*

This is a rich confection, crunchy with nuts. Jams like this are an essential part of the traditional Middle Eastern welcoming ceremony, when they are eaten with a spoon and accompanied by a glass of cold water.

INGREDIENTS

1kg (2lb) seedless green or red grapes
2 lemons, thinly sliced
750g (1½lb) preserving or granulated sugar
100g (3½oz) pecan nuts, lightly toasted
75ml (3fl oz) brandy

1 Put the grapes, lemon slices and sugar in the preserving pan. Mix well, cover and leave to stand for a few hours, until the juices start to run.

2 Bring to the boil, then cook over a moderate heat for 1–1½ hours, stirring frequently to prevent it from sticking to the bottom of the pan.

3 There is no need to test this jam for the setting point; it is ready when it is thick enough for a wooden spoon drawn through the centre of the mixture to leave a clear channel.

4 Remove the pan from the heat and leave the jam to settle for a few minutes. (This stops the fruit sinking to the bottom of the jar.) Stir in the pecan nuts and brandy. Ladle the jam into the hot sterilized jars, then seal.

☆ **Degree of difficulty**
Easy

Cooking time
1¼–1¾ hours

Special equipment
Preserving pan; sterilized jars and sealants (see pages 42–43)

Yield
About 1.25kg (2½lb)

Shelf life
2 years

GRAPE JAM *makes a delicious topping for a steamed sponge pudding: the jam melts over it to form a sauce, and the nuts, grapes and lemon are a wonderful contrast to the moist sponge.*

TOASTED PECAN NUTS
add a crunchy texture

THIN SLICES OF
LEMON give the jam
a tangy note

VARIATIONS

✦ *Other fruit, such as figs, fresh dates, plums, peaches and apricots, can be prepared in the same way.*

✦ *Toasted walnuts or whole almonds can be used instead of pecan nuts.*

✦ *Use 3 oranges instead of the lemon and add rum or an orange-flavoured liqueur in place of the brandy.*

✦ *For extra flavour add 2–3 tablespoons orange-flower water.*

Povidle (Eastern European Plum Jam)

Strictly speaking, Povidle is not a jam but a soft fruit cheese. This recipe was given to me by my mother. The amount of sugar seems small but it results in a sharp, sweet and sour jam.

INGREDIENTS

2kg (4lb) purple plums, preferably Switzen

1kg (2lb) preserving or granulated sugar

1 Remove the stones from the plums, then chop them coarsely. Layer the plums and sugar in the preserving pan, cover with a clean cloth and leave to stand for a few hours, until the juices start to run.

2 Bring the mixture to the boil, stirring until the sugar has dissolved. Reduce the heat and simmer for 1½–2 hours, stirring occasionally, until the mixture is dark red and thick (there is no need to test for the setting point).

3 Ladle the jam into the hot sterilized jars, then seal. The jam is ready to eat immediately, but improves with keeping.

☆ **Degree of difficulty**
Easy

🍲 **Cooking time**
1½–2 hours

🔪 **Special equipment**
Preserving pan; sterilized jars and sealants (see pages 42–43)

🫙 **Yield**
About 1.5kg (3lb)

🫙 **Shelf life**
2 years

Plum Jam

You can use any type of plum to make this delicious jam. Choose Mirabelle plums for a golden jam, Victoria or River's Czar for a red jam, and greengage for a greenish-yellow one.

— TIP —
• Red Plum Jam can be enlivened by the addition of 75g (2½oz) finely shredded fresh ginger root, which should be stirred in with the sugar.

INGREDIENTS

1.25kg (2½lb) plums, stoned and halved or quartered if large

350ml (12fl oz) water

1kg (2lb) preserving or granulated sugar

1 Put the plums and water in the preserving pan. Bring to the boil, then reduce the heat and simmer for about 25 minutes, stirring occasionally, or until the plums are soft.

2 Add the sugar, stirring until it has dissolved. Return to the boil and boil for 25–30 minutes, or until the setting point is reached (see page 76).

3 Remove the pan from the heat and leave the jam to settle for a few minutes. Ladle the jam into the hot sterilized jars, then seal.

— VARIATIONS —

✦ **Greengage Jam**
Replace the plums with greengages. Crack open 10 stones and tie the kernels in muslin. Place the fruit and kernels in the pan with the juice of 1 lemon and 250ml (8fl oz) water. Complete as for the main recipe.

✦ **Damson Jam**
Replace the plums with whole damsons. Simmer with 750ml (1¼ pints) water until mushy, then sieve out the stones. Measure the pulp and add 625g (1¼lb) sugar for every 500ml (17fl oz) pulp. Boil for 10–15 minutes, or until the setting point is reached.

☆ **Degree of difficulty**
Easy

🍲 **Cooking time**
About 1 hour

🔪 **Special equipment**
Preserving pan; sugar thermometer; sterilized jars and sealants (see pages 42–43)

🫙 **Yield**
About 1.75kg (3½lb)

🫙 **Shelf life**
2 years

✎ **Serving suggestions**
Substitute for raspberry jam in Linzer Torte or use to make a quick and easy plum crumble

Greengage Jam

Damson Jam

Plum Jam

Raspberry Jam

(see page 33 for illustration)

This is made without water to give an intensely flavoured, perfumed jam.

INGREDIENTS

1kg (2lb) raspberries

1kg (2lb) preserving or granulated sugar

juice of 1 lemon

1 Layer the raspberries and sugar in the preserving pan. Cover with a cloth and leave overnight.

2 The next day, add the lemon juice to the pan. Bring slowly to the boil, stirring frequently until the sugar has dissolved.

3 Increase the heat and boil rapidly for 20–25 minutes, or until the setting point is reached (see page 76). Stir constantly towards the end of cooking to prevent it from sticking. If wished, pass half the jam through a sieve to reduce the seed content, then return to the boil for 5 minutes.

4 Remove the pan from the heat and leave the jam to settle for a few minutes. Ladle into the hot sterilized jars, then seal.

☆ **Degree of difficulty**
Easy

Cooking time
About 45 minutes

Special equipment
Preserving pan; sugar thermometer; sterilized jars and sealants (see pages 42–43)

Yield
About 1.5kg (3lb)

Shelf life
2 years

Blueberry Jam

(see page 33 for illustration)

Blueberries make a soft set jam. Use as a topping for cheesecakes or fold into whipped cream as a filling for sponge cakes.

INGREDIENTS

1kg (2lb) blueberries

1kg (2lb) preserving or granulated sugar

4 tbsp water

juice of 1 lemon

1 Put the blueberries, sugar, water and lemon juice in the preserving pan. Bring slowly to the boil, stirring occasionally until the sugar has dissolved.

Reduce the heat and simmer for about 10 minutes.

2 Increase the heat and boil rapidly for 15–20 minutes, or until the setting point is reached (see page 76).

3 Remove the pan from the heat and leave the jam to settle for a few minutes. Ladle into the hot sterilized jars, then seal.

☆ **Degree of difficulty**
Easy

Cooking time
About 45 minutes

Special equipment
Preserving pan; sugar thermometer; sterilized jars and sealants (see pages 42–43)

Yield
About 1.5kg (3lb)

Shelf life
2 years

Blackcurrant Jam

Blackcurrants are high in pectin, which makes them ideal for jams and jellies.

INGREDIENTS

1kg (2lb) blackcurrants

750ml (1¼ pints) water

750g (1½ lb) preserving or granulated sugar

a little brandy, to seal

1 Put the blackcurrants and water in the preserving pan. Bring slowly to the boil, then reduce the heat and simmer gently for 20–25 minutes, stirring occasionally, until the mixture has reduced by a third.

2 Add the sugar to the pan. Slowly return to the boil, stirring until the sugar has dissolved, then boil rapidly for

15–20 minutes, or until the setting point is reached (see page 76).

3 Remove the pan from the heat and leave to stand until the jam is completely cold.

4 Ladle the cold jam into the sterilized jars. Cover each jar with a waxed paper disc dipped in a little brandy, then seal.

——— VARIATION ———

✦ *If you prefer a smooth, seedless jam, press the fruit pulp through a sieve at the end of step 1. Return the mixture to the cleaned pan and proceed as for the main recipe.*

☆ **Degree of difficulty**
Easy

Cooking time
About 1 hour

Special equipment
Preserving pan; sugar thermometer; sterilized jars and sealants (see pages 42–43)

Yield
About 1.5kg (3lb)

Shelf life
2 years

Serving suggestion
Serve with thick natural yogurt as a simple dessert

Apricot Jam

Fragrant and mellow with a beautiful golden hue, apricot jam captures the essence of summer. It is a very versatile jam: use as it is to fill pastries and cakes; or warm and sieve it to make a wonderful yellow glaze. Be sure to choose ripe but firm apricots for this recipe.

INGREDIENTS

1.25kg (2½ lb) apricots

juice of 1 lemon

1kg (2lb) preserving or granulated sugar

300ml (½ pint) water

1 Halve the apricots, then remove and reserve the stones. Put the apricots in a glass bowl and sprinkle with the lemon juice. Mix well and cover until needed.

2 Crack open 10 of the apricot stones with a hammer or nutcracker and extract the kernels. Taste one – if it is very bitter use only half of them. Blanch the kernels for 1 minute in boiling water and either split into two segments or chop finely.

3 Put the sugar and water in the preserving pan. Bring slowly to the boil, stirring until the sugar has dissolved, then boil rapidly for 3–4 minutes. Add the apricots, return to the boil, then simmer for 5 minutes.

4 Return to the boil and boil rapidly, stirring frequently, for 20–25 minutes, or until the setting point is reached (see page 76). About 5 minutes before the jam is ready, stir in the split or chopped apricot kernels.

5 Remove the pan from the heat and leave the jam to settle for a few minutes. Skim well. Ladle the jam into the hot sterilized jars, then seal.

VARIATION

♦ *To make a smooth apricot jam, follow the recipe to step 3. Leave the jam to cool slightly, then pass through a sieve or a food mill. Return to the cleaned pan and proceed as above. Do not add the apricot kernels if the jam is to be used as a glaze.*

 Degree of difficulty
Easy

 Cooking time
45–55 minutes

 Special equipment
Hammer or nutcracker; preserving pan; sugar thermometer; sterilized jars and sealants (see pages 42–43)

 Yield
About 1.5kg (3lb)

 Shelf life
2 years

 Serving suggestions
Use to glaze a leg of lamb before roasting or to glaze fruit tarts

Green Tomato and Orange Jam

The earthy flavour of tomatoes and the refreshing tang of oranges combine to make a delightfully fresh breakfast jam. Sweet oranges are available all year round so this jam can be made in summer when green tomatoes are in season.

INGREDIENTS

4 large sweet oranges

2 lemons

1kg (2lb) green tomatoes

750ml (1¼ pints) water

1kg (2lb) preserving or granulated sugar

1½ tbsp coriander seeds, roughly crushed

1 Cut the oranges into slices and remove the pips. Squeeze the juice from the lemons and reserve the pips. Tie all the pips into a piece of muslin.

2 Put the tomatoes and oranges through the mincer or process them in the food processor until they are finely chopped.

3 Place the chopped tomato and orange in the preserving pan with the water and muslin bag. Bring to the boil, then reduce the heat and simmer for about 45 minutes, or until the orange peel is soft.

4 Add the sugar and the lemon juice to the pan, stirring until the sugar has dissolved.

5 Bring to the boil and boil over a medium heat, stirring occasionally, for 30–35 minutes, or until it is thick enough for a wooden spoon drawn through the centre to leave a clear channel.

6 Remove the pan from the heat and leave the jam to settle for a few minutes. Skim if necessary, then remove the muslin bag and stir in the crushed coriander seeds. Ladle the jam into the hot sterilized jars, then seal.

 Degree of difficulty
Easy

 Cooking time
1½–1¾ hours

 Special equipment
Mincer or food processor; preserving pan; sterilized jars and sealants (see pages 42–43)

 Yield
About 2kg (4lb)

 Shelf life
1 year

 Serving suggestion
Superb on hot buttered toast

Carrot Jam
(see page 23 for illustration)

Root vegetable jams used to be made during the winter, when fresh fruit was not available. Try this as a filling for Swiss rolls, tarts and sponge cakes.

TIP

• Almost any root vegetable can be used, but beetroot, parsnips, turnips or kohlrabi need blanching several times first to mellow their strong flavour.

INGREDIENTS

1kg (2lb) carrots, finely grated
250g (8oz) sultanas
500ml (17fl oz) water
750g (1½lb) preserving or granulated sugar
rind of 2 lemons
juice of 3 lemons
2 tsp ground ginger

1 Put the carrots, sultanas and water in the preserving pan. Bring to the boil, reduce the heat and simmer for 10–15 minutes, until the carrot is just soft.

2 Add the sugar, lemon rind and juice, stirring until the sugar has dissolved. Bring to the boil, then simmer, stirring frequently, for 1 hour or until very thick (there is no need to test for setting point).

3 Add the ginger and remove the pan from the heat. Ladle into the hot sterilized jars, then seal.

☆ **Degree of difficulty**
Easy

Cooking time
About 1¼ hours

Special equipment
Preserving pan; sterilized jars and sealants (see pages 42–43)

Yield
About 1.25 kg (2½ lb)

Shelf life
2 years

Exotic Fruit Jam
(see page 76 for technique)

Other types of fruit, like pawpaw, mango or fragrant melon, can be used in the same way, but always add the same quantity of apple.

INGREDIENTS

1 medium pineapple, about 1.25kg (2½lb)
1 kg (2lb) cooking apples, peeled, cored and coarsely chopped
300g (10oz) fresh lychees, peeled, pitted and halved, or 425g (14oz) can lychees, drained and halved
250ml (8fl oz) water
rind of 1 lemon
juice of 2 lemons
1.25kg (2½lb) preserving or granulated sugar

1 Peel, core and chop the pineapple (see steps below), then finely chop in the food processor with the apple.

2 Transfer to the preserving pan and add the lychees, water and lemon rind and juice. Bring to the boil, then reduce the heat and simmer for 20–25 minutes, or until the apples have disintegrated and the pineapple is soft.

3 Add the sugar to the pan, stirring until the sugar has dissolved. Return to the boil and boil, stirring frequently, for 20–25 minutes, or until the setting point is reached (see page 76).

4 Remove the pan from the heat and leave the jam to settle for a few minutes. Skim off any froth.

5 Ladle the mixture into the hot sterilized jars, then seal. The jam is ready immediately but improves with longer keeping.

☆ **Degree of difficulty**
Easy

Cooking time
About 1 hour

Special equipment
Food processor; preserving pan; sugar thermometer; sterilized jars and sealants (see pages 42–43)

Yield
About 1.5kg (3lb)

Shelf life
2 years

Serving suggestions
Serve with scones and clotted cream or as a filling for cream cakes

PREPARING PINEAPPLE

1 Cut the top and bottom off the pineapple with a sharp long-bladed knife.

2 To peel the pineapple, cut off the skin in sections, following the curve of the fruit.

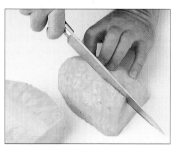

3 To cut out the hard central core of the pineapple, halve it lengthways, then cut into quarters.

4 Remove the hard central core of the pineapple, then cut the fruit into large chunks.

Fig Konfyt (Preserved Green Figs)

This recipe comes from South Africa, where making rich preserves has been developed into a fine art. The figs should be fully mature but not ripe, otherwise they will not withstand the cooking process.

INGREDIENTS

1kg (2lb) green, unripe figs

4 tbsp salt

1 tbsp bicarbonate of soda (optional)

1kg (2lb) preserving or granulated sugar

125ml (4fl oz) water

1 Trim the stalk end off each fig, then, with a small sharp knife, cut a deep cross into the top.

2 Place the figs in a large glass bowl. Cover with cold water and add the salt. Mix well until the salt has dissolved, then weight down with a plate (see page 46) and leave to stand overnight.

3 The next day, bring a large pan of water to the boil with the bicarbonate of soda, if using (it helps to preserve a good green colour). Drain the figs and add to the pan.

4 Return to the boil, then reduce the heat and simmer gently for 25–30 minutes, or until the figs are just tender. Have ready a large bowl of very cold water and immediately transfer the figs to it. Leave to cool, then drain the figs well. Place them in the preserving pan.

5 Put the sugar and water in a separate pan. Bring to the boil, stirring until the sugar has dissolved, then skim well. Boil for 5 minutes, then pour over the figs. Weight down and leave overnight.

6 The next day, bring slowly to the boil, then simmer very gently for 2–2½ hours, or until the figs look translucent. Lift them out of the syrup with a slotted spoon and arrange in the hot sterilized jars.

7 Return the syrup to the boil and boil for 10 minutes, until it has the consistency of runny honey. Pour into the jars, then seal.

VARIATIONS

✦ Add a 5cm (2in) piece fresh ginger root, finely shredded, to the sugar syrup in step 5.

✦ *Melon Konfyt*
Replace the figs with 1kg (2lb) melon, peeled and cut into 4cm (1½ in) chunks. Omit the bicarbonate of soda. Cook for 15–20 minutes in step 4.

 Degree of difficulty
Advanced

 Cooking time
Day 2, 40–45 minutes;
Day 3, 2¼–2¾ hours

 Special equipment
Preserving pan; sterilized jars and sealants (see pages 42–43)

 Yield
About 1kg (2lb)

 Shelf life
2 years

 Serving suggestions
Serve as a sweetmeat or with cream as a dessert; use instead of glacé fruit to decorate cakes

Black Cherry Confiture

Black cherry confiture is one of the greatest European preserves — sour-sweet cherries embedded in an intensely flavoured red jelly.

INGREDIENTS

1.25kg (2½ lb) black cherries, pitted

750g (1½ lb) preserving or granulated sugar

250ml (8fl oz) blackcurrant or redcurrant juice (see Hot Crab Apple Jelly for method, page 166)

4 tbsp kirsch or cherry brandy

1 Layer the cherries and sugar in the preserving pan. Add the blackcurrant or redcurrant juice, cover and leave for a few hours.

2 Bring the mixture slowly to the boil, occasionally shaking the pan gently. Skim well, then boil for 20–25 minutes, or until the setting point is reached (see page 76).

3 Remove the pan from the heat and leave the fruit to settle for a few minutes. Stir in the kirsch or brandy. Ladle into the hot sterilized jars, then seal.

TIPS

• The juice of 3 lemons could be used instead of the currant juice.
• Any type of sour black cherry can be used but Morello is the best.

 Degree of difficulty
Easy

 Cooking time
About 30 minutes

 Special equipment
Preserving pan; sugar thermometer; sterilized jars and sealants (see pages 42–43)

 Yield
About 1.5kg (3lb)

 Shelf life
2 years

 Serving suggestions
Superb for breakfast or as a filling for cakes

Wild Strawberry Confiture

Wild strawberries are highly aromatic and full of flavour. Marinating the fruit, followed by careful cooking, helps to maintain the texture and fragrance of this sublime confection. Use to fill tarts or serve with freshly made scones and clotted cream.

INGREDIENTS

750g (1½ lb) preserving or granulated sugar
1kg (2lb) wild strawberries
250ml (8fl oz) vodka (40% proof)

1 Layer the sugar and wild strawberries in a large glass bowl, starting and finishing with a layer of sugar. Pour over the vodka, cover with a clean cloth and leave to stand overnight.

2 The next day, drain the liquid into the preserving pan. Bring to the boil and boil rapidly for a few minutes, or until it reaches 116°C (240°F) on the sugar thermometer.

3 Add the wild strawberries. Return to the boil and boil for 5–7 minutes, or until the setting point is reached (see page 76). This recipe produces a soft set.

4 Remove from the heat and leave the fruit to settle for a few minutes. Skim well. Ladle into the hot sterilized jars, then seal.

☆☆ **Degree of difficulty**
Moderate

 Cooking time
25–30 minutes

 Special equipment
Preserving pan; sugar thermometer; sterilized jars and sealants (see pages 42–43)

 Yield
About 1.25kg (2½ lb)

 Shelf life
6 months

Shallot Confiture

(see page 19 for illustration)

This spicy, sour-sweet confiture is my adaptation of an ancient Middle Eastern recipe. Cooked in a spiced syrup, the caramelized shallots turn a beautiful, glistening golden brown. The slow, careful cooking is important, otherwise the shallots tend to lose their shape.

INGREDIENTS

1.3kg (2lb 10oz) shallots
150g (5oz) salt
1.5 litres (2½ pints) distilled white vinegar or white wine vinegar
1kg (2lb) preserving or granulated sugar
For the spice bag (see page 47)
4 cardamom pods
2 cinnamon sticks
3 strips lemon rind
1 tbsp caraway seeds
1 tbsp cloves
½ tsp bird's eye chillies

1 Peel the shallots by blanching in boiling water for a few minutes (see page 46). Make sure that the root end remains intact otherwise the shallots will disintegrate during cooking.

2 Place the peeled shallots in a large glass bowl. Cover with cold water and add the salt. Mix well until the salt has dissolved, then weight down (see page 46) and leave for 24 hours.

3 Put the vinegar, sugar and spice bag in the preserving pan. Bring to the boil and boil steadily for 10 minutes, stirring occasionally. Skim well.

4 Drain the shallots, rinse well, then drain again. Carefully add them to the boiling syrup. Return to the boil, then reduce the heat to minimum and simmer very gently for 15 minutes. Remove from the heat and leave to cool, then cover and leave to stand overnight.

5 The next day, bring the mixture slowly to the boil, then reduce the heat and simmer very gently for 15 minutes. Cool and leave overnight as before.

6 The next day, bring the mixture slowly to the boil, then simmer very gently for 2–2½ hours, or until the shallots are translucent and golden brown.

7 Carefully lift the shallots out of the syrup with a slotted spoon and pack them loosely into the hot sterilized jars. Return the syrup to the boil and boil rapidly for about 5 minutes. Pour into the jars, then seal. The shallots are ready to eat immediately, but improve with keeping.

☆ ☆☆ **Degree of difficulty**
Advanced

Cooking time
Day 2, 30–35 minutes;
Day 3, about 20 minutes;
Day 4, 2¼–2¾ hours

Special equipment
Non-corrosive preserving pan; sterilized jars and vinegar-proof sealants (see pages 42–43)

Yield
About 1.25kg (2½ lb)

Shelf life
2 years

Serving suggestions
Especially good with venison and lamb

Aubergine Preserve

This unusual recipe comes from Morocco and makes a surprisingly fragrant sweet preserve. Traditionally, it is eaten by the spoonful and served with steaming hot tea or coffee and a glass of water.

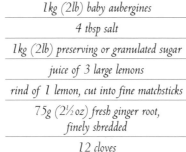

INGREDIENTS

1kg (2lb) baby aubergines
4 tbsp salt
1kg (2lb) preserving or granulated sugar
juice of 3 large lemons
rind of 1 lemon, cut into fine matchsticks
75g (2½oz) fresh ginger root, finely shredded
12 cloves
2 cinnamon sticks

1 Remove the green crown from around the stalk of each aubergine but leave the stalk attached. Prick each aubergine in a few places with a wooden cocktail stick.

2 Put the aubergines in a large glass bowl and sprinkle with the salt. Mix well, then cover and leave to stand for a few hours. Rinse thoroughly under cold running water.

3 Bring a large pan of water to the boil and add the rinsed aubergines. Return to the boil, then reduce the heat and simmer for 5 minutes. Lift out the aubergines and drain well.

4 Put the sugar and lemon juice in the preserving pan. Bring to the boil, stirring until the sugar has dissolved, then skim well. Add the lemon rind, ginger, cloves and cinnamon sticks and boil for 5 minutes.

5 Gently slide the aubergines into the boiling syrup. Reduce the heat and simmer very gently, stirring occasionally, for 1½–2 hours, or until the aubergines have absorbed about half the syrup and look translucent.

6 Gently lift the aubergines out one at a time with a slotted spoon. Transfer to the hot sterilized jars. Return the syrup to the boil, pour it into the jars, then seal. The preserve is ready to eat immediately, but improves with keeping.

 Degree of difficulty
Moderate

 Cooking time
1¾–2¼ hours

 Special equipment
Preserving pan; sterilized jars and sealants (see pages 42–43)

 Yield
About 1.5kg (3lb)

 Shelf life
2 years (the preserve may crystallize in this time but it will still be fine to eat)

 Serving suggestion
Serve as a sweetmeat, Moroccan-style

TIPS

• Select very small, unblemished aubergines. Both black and light purple varieties are suitable.
• If you do not like whole spices in your preserve, tie them in a piece of muslin (see spice bags, page 47), which can be lifted out at the end of cooking.

Marrow and Ginger Preserve

This recipe is a perfect example of the magic of preserving: it transforms humble ingredients into a delicious and versatile product.

VARIATION

♦ *Turnip Preserve*
Replace the marrow with 1.5kg (3lb) peeled and cubed turnip. Cook following the main method.

INGREDIENTS

1.5kg (3lb) marrow, peeled, cored and cut into 4cm (1½in) cubes
1kg (2lb) preserving or granulated sugar
500ml (17fl oz) water
juice of 1 lemon
5cm (2in) piece fresh ginger root, finely shredded
3–4 strips of lemon rind
1 tbsp orange-flower water (optional)

1 Put the cubed marrow in a large pan and add enough cold water to cover. Bring to the boil, then reduce the heat and simmer for 10–15 minutes, or until the marrow just starts to soften. Drain thoroughly.

2 Put all the remaining ingredients in the preserving pan. Bring to the boil, stirring until the sugar has dissolved. Boil for a few minutes, then add the marrow. Return to the boil, reduce the heat to minimum and simmer very gently for 2–2½ hours, or until the marrow is translucent.

3 Lift the marrow out of the pan with a slotted spoon. Transfer to the hot sterilized jars. Bring the syrup to a rapid boil and boil for about 5 minutes.

4 Pour the syrup into the hot sterilized jars, then seal. The preserve is ready immediately, but improves with keeping.

 Degree of difficulty
Easy

 Cooking time
2½–2¾ hours

 Special equipment
Preserving pan; sterilized jars and sealants (see pages 42–43)

 Yield
About 1.5kg (3lb)

 Shelf life
2 years

 Serving suggestions
Chop finely and add to fruit cakes, or serve as a topping for ice cream

Yellow Tomato Preserve

(see page 15 for illustration)

Yellow tomatoes make a wonderfully golden jam. Select sound, slightly underripe tomatoes with a good yellow colour. Soft, overripe fruit will make a watery preserve.

INGREDIENTS

1kg (2lb) yellow tomatoes

2 lemons, thinly sliced into semi-circles

1 lemongrass stalk, finely chopped (optional)

75ml (3fl oz) water

750g (1½lb) preserving or granulated sugar

250g (8oz) soft light brown sugar

1 Put all the ingredients in the preserving pan (there is no need to chop the tomatoes).

Bring slowly to the boil, then simmer gently for 15 minutes.

2 Return to the boil and boil steadily, stirring frequently, for 25 minutes, or until the setting point is reached (see page 76).

3 Remove the pan from the heat and leave the tomatoes to settle for a few minutes. Ladle the preserve into the hot sterilized jars, then seal.

 Degree of difficulty
Easy

 Cooking time
About 1 hour

Special equipment
Preserving pan; sugar thermometer; sterilized jars and sealants (see pages 42–43)

 Yield
About 1.5kg (3lb)

 Shelf life
2 years

Orange Marmalade with Coriander

(see page 29 for illustration)

There are literally hundreds of recipes for orange marmalade. This one is unusual since it is flavoured with coriander seeds and orange liqueur. Although sweet oranges can be used, for best results try to obtain bitter Seville oranges. They have a very short season and are available only in midwinter.

INGREDIENTS

1kg (2lb) Seville oranges

2 lemons

2 litres (3½ pints) water

1.5kg (3lb) preserving or granulated sugar

3 tbsp coriander seeds, crushed

75ml (3fl oz) dry orange liqueur such as Triple Sec

1 Cut all the citrus fruit in half. Remove and reserve the pips. Slice the fruit thinly (see step 1, below). Tie the pips in muslin (see step 2, below). Put the fruit and muslin bag in a large glass bowl with the water. Cover and leave overnight (see step 3, below).

2 The next day, transfer the citrus fruit and water to the

preserving pan. Bring to the boil, then reduce the heat and simmer for 45 minutes –1 hour, or until the orange rind is just soft and the mixture has reduced by half.

3 Add the sugar to the pan. Slowly return to the boil, stirring until the sugar has dissolved. Skim well, then stir in the crushed coriander seeds.

4 Boil the mixture rapidly for 10–15 minutes, or until the setting point is reached (see page 76). Remove the pan from the heat and leave the fruit to settle for a few minutes. Add the liqueur and stir in thoroughly. Ladle the marmalade into the hot sterilized jars, then seal.

 Degree of difficulty
Easy

 Cooking time
1–1½ hours

Special equipment
Preserving pan; sugar thermometer; sterilized jars and sealants (see pages 42–43)

 Yield
About 2kg (4lb)

 Shelf life
2 years

 Serving suggestion
Serve on toast for breakfast

PREPARING THE FRUIT

1 Scrub the oranges and lemons well to remove the wax coating. Halve them, reserving all the pips, then slice crossways into thin semi-circles.

2 Place all the pips in a small square of clean muslin. Gather up the ends of the cloth and secure with string to form a small bag.

3 Place the fruit and cold water in a large glass bowl. Weight down with a plate (see page 46) to keep the oranges submerged.

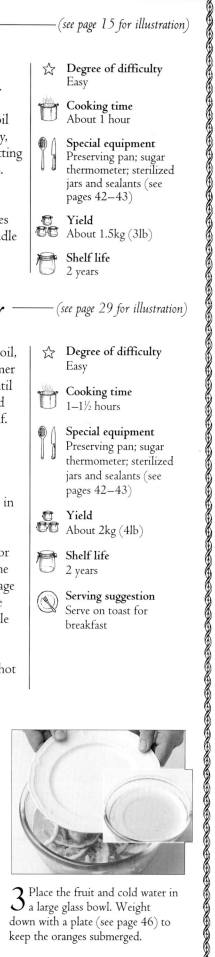

Pumpkin Marmalade

(see page 21 for illustration)

During autumn pumpkins appear on the market in all sizes, shapes and hues. Pumpkin is particularly good for making jams and marmalades as it absorbs sugar beautifully.

INGREDIENTS

1.5kg (3lb) pumpkin

1 litre (1¾ pints) water

2 oranges, sliced into thin semi-circles

3 lemons, sliced into thin semi-circles

100g (3½ oz) fresh ginger root, finely shredded

1kg (2lb) preserving or granulated sugar

1 Peel the pumpkin and remove all the seeds and fibres. Slice the flesh into pieces and grate coarsely lengthways so the strands are as long as possible.

2 Put the grated pumpkin in the preserving pan with the water, oranges, lemons and ginger. Bring to the boil, then simmer for 25–30 minutes, or until the citrus peel is just soft.

3 Add the sugar, stirring until it has dissolved. Return to the boil, then cook over a medium heat for 25–30 minutes, or until the mixture is thick enough for a wooden spoon drawn through the centre to leave a clear channel.

4 Remove the pan from the heat and leave the fruit to settle for a few minutes. Ladle the marmalade into the hot sterilized jars, then seal.

 Degree of difficulty
Easy

 Cooking time
About 1¼ hours

 Special equipment
Preserving pan; sterilized jars and sealants (see pages 42–43)

 Yield
About 1.75kg (3½ lb)

 Shelf life
2 years

Serving suggestions
Serve for breakfast or with scones and cream, or use as a flan filling

Onion Marmalade

(see page 19 for illustration)

This unusual, sweet preserve is exceptionally good and, remarkably, does not taste of onions. It has a sharp, refreshing flavour and a rich colour. I sometimes add dried mint to it. Serve with lamb, mutton or game.

INGREDIENTS

1.25kg (2½ lb) onions, sliced into thin rings

3 tbsp salt

1kg (2lb) preserving or granulated sugar

500ml (17fl oz) vinegar

1½ tsp cloves tied in a piece of muslin

2 tsp caraway seeds

1 Sprinkle the onions with the salt. Mix well and leave to stand for 1 hour. Rinse and dry.

2 Put the sugar, vinegar and muslin bag in the preserving pan. Bring to the boil, then simmer for 5 minutes. Add the onions and caraway seeds. Return to the boil, skim, reduce the heat to minimum and cook for 2–2½ hours, or until the syrup is thick and the onion is translucent and golden brown.

3 Remove the pan from the heat and leave the onion to settle for a few minutes. Ladle the mixture into the hot sterilized jars, then seal. The marmalade is ready to eat immediately, but improves with keeping.

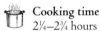 **Degree of difficulty**
Easy

Cooking time
2¼–2¾ hours

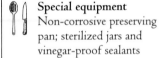 **Special equipment**
Non-corrosive preserving pan; sterilized jars and vinegar-proof sealants (see pages 42–43)

 Yield
About 1.5kg (3lb)

Shelf life
2 years

Red Tomato Marmalade

(see page 15 for illustration)

Tomatoes make an extraordinarily tasty marmalade, with an elusive flavour that will intrigue and surprise you.

INGREDIENTS

1kg (2lb) firm, ripe tomatoes, skinned, deseeded and coarsely chopped

1kg (2lb) preserving or granulated sugar

finely sliced rind and juice of 2 lemons

1½ tbsp coriander seeds, coarsely crushed (optional)

1 Put the tomatoes in the preserving pan with the sugar and lemon rind and juice. Bring slowly to the boil, then simmer for 5 minutes. Skim and add the coriander seeds, if using.

2 Return the mixture to the boil, and boil, stirring frequently, for 30 minutes, until the setting point is reached (see page 76). Remove the pan from the heat and leave the fruit to settle for a few minutes. Ladle the marmalade into the hot sterilized jars, then seal.

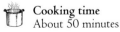 **Degree of difficulty**
Easy

Cooking time
About 50 minutes

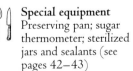 **Special equipment**
Preserving pan; sugar thermometer; sterilized jars and sealants (see pages 42–43)

Yield
About 1.5kg (3lb)

 Shelf life
2 years

Vanilla-flavoured Peach Marmalade

Although this fragrant conserve is rather fiddly to make, the results justify all the work. Select firm, unblemished, almost ripe peaches and handle them gently as they bruise easily.

INGREDIENTS

1.25kg (2½ lb) firm, just ripe, white or yellow peaches

1kg (2lb) preserving or granulated sugar

juice of 2 lemons

4 tbsp good-quality cognac

1–2 vanilla pods, cut into 7cm (3in) lengths

1 Skin the peaches by blanching in boiling water (see page 46). Halve them, remove the stones and cut the flesh into thick slices.

2 Place the peach slices in the preserving pan with the sugar and lemon juice. Cover and leave to stand for a few hours.

3 Bring the mixture to the boil, then reduce the heat and simmer gently for 20 minutes, or until the peaches are just soft.

4 Return to the boil and boil rapidly, stirring frequently, for 20–25 minutes, or until the setting point is reached (see page 76). The peaches produce a soft set marmalade.

5 Remove the pan from the heat, skim well and leave to cool for about 10 minutes. Stir in the cognac.

6 Ladle the preserve into the hot sterilized jars, inserting a piece of vanilla pod into each, then seal. The marmalade will be ready to eat in about 1 month, but improves with longer keeping.

TIP
• Skim the marmalade thoroughly at all stages of cooking as peaches tend to produce a large amount of froth.

☆ **Degree of difficulty**
Easy

Cooking time
50–55 minutes

Special equipment
Preserving pan; sugar thermometer; sterilized jars and sealants (see pages 42–43)

Yield
About 1kg (2lb)

Shelf life
1 year

Serving suggestions
Heavenly with scones and cream or with croissants for breakfast

Old-fashioned Blackcurrant Jelly

Although it is fairly lengthy, this method produces an intensely flavoured and highly coloured jelly.

INGREDIENTS

1kg (2lb) blackcurrants

preserving or granulated sugar

1 Put the blackcurrants in the casserole. Cover and bake in the oven at 140°C/ 275°F/gas 1 for 1 hour, or until they are mushy and juicy. Alternatively, put the stone jar in a pan of water and simmer for 1 hour.

2 Pour the fruit and liquid into the sterilized jelly bag (see page 80). Leave to drain until it stops dripping.

3 Remove the pulp from the jelly bag and put it into the preserving pan, adding enough cold water to cover. Bring to the boil, then reduce the heat and simmer for 20 minutes. Drain through the jelly bag as before.

4 Combine the two batches of juice and measure it. Allow 500g (1lb) sugar for every 500ml (17fl oz) juice.

5 Put the fruit juice and sugar in the preserving pan. Heat slowly, stirring until the sugar has dissolved, then increase the heat and bring to the boil.

6 Skim well and boil rapidly for 10 minutes, or until the setting point is reached (see page 76). Pour the liquid into the hot sterilized jars, then seal.

☆☆ **Degree of difficulty**
Moderate

Cooking time
About 1¾ hours

Special equipment
Casserole or stone jar; sterilized jelly bag; preserving pan; sugar thermometer; sterilized jars and sealants (see pages 42–43)

Yield
About 1.5kg (3lb)

Shelf life
2 years

Serving suggestions
Fold into whipped cream to make a simple fruit fool, or use to glaze a joint of lamb before roasting

Raspberry Jelly

(see page 80 for technique)

This clear, red jelly has a geranium leaf in the centre of each jar. The jelly is left to cool in the jar until semi-set, then a leaf is gently inserted into it. Be careful not to create any air bubbles as these will spoil the appearance.

INGREDIENTS

500g (1lb) cooking apples

1kg (2lb) raspberries

500ml (17fl oz) water

preserving or granulated sugar

juice of 1 lemon

scented geranium leaves (optional)

a little brandy, to seal

1 Remove the cores from the apples and set aside. Chop the apples coarsely, then put in the food processor with the raspberries and process until finely chopped.

2 Put the chopped fruit in the preserving pan with the apple cores and water. Bring to the boil, then reduce the heat and simmer for 20–30 minutes, or until the fruit is soft and pulpy.

3 Pour the fruit and liquid into the sterilized jelly bag (see

page 80). Leave to drain for 2–3 hours, or until it stops dripping. Measure the juice and allow 500g (1lb) sugar for every 500ml (17fl oz) juice.

4 Put the fruit juice, sugar and lemon juice in the cleaned pan. Heat gently, stirring until the sugar has dissolved. Bring to the boil, then reduce the heat and skim well. Return to a rapid boil for 10 minutes, or until the setting point is reached (see page 76).

5 Pour the liquid jelly into the hot sterilized jars, then seal if not adding the geranium leaves.

6 To add the geranium leaves, allow the jelly to cool until semi-set. Gently insert a leaf into the centre of each jar. Pierce any air pockets that form by prodding with a wooden skewer. Cover each jar with a waxed paper disc dipped in a little brandy, then seal.

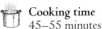

Degree of difficulty
Moderate

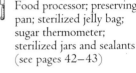

Cooking time
45–55 minutes

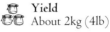

Special equipment
Food processor; preserving pan; sterilized jelly bag; sugar thermometer; sterilized jars and sealants (see pages 42–43)

Yield
About 2kg (4lb)

Shelf life
2 years

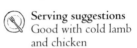

Serving suggestions
Good with cold lamb and chicken

VARIATION

♦ *Redcurrant Jelly*

Replace the raspberries with redcurrants and omit the apples. Cook with 600ml (1 pint) water, crushing the fruit against the pan. Complete following the main recipe. Omit the geranium leaves.

Hot Crab Apple Jelly

Crab apples make a firm jelly that can be flavoured in many ways. Here, red chillies are used to give a piquant, sweet-hot jelly.

INGREDIENTS

1kg (2lb) crab apples, cut in half

4–5 fresh or dried red chillies, coarsely chopped, plus 1 fresh chilli for each jar

preserving or granulated sugar

a little brandy, to seal

1 Put the crab apples and the chopped chillies in the preserving pan and add enough cold water to cover. Bring to the boil, then simmer for 25 minutes, or until the fruit is pulpy.

2 Pour the fruit and liquid into the sterilized jelly bag (see page 80). Drain for 2–3 hours, or until it stops dripping.

3 Measure the juice and allow 500g (1lb) sugar for every

500ml (17fl oz) juice. Put the juice and sugar in the cleaned pan. Bring slowly to the boil, stirring until the sugar has dissolved. Reduce the heat and skim well. Return to the boil for 15 minutes, or until the setting point is reached (see page 76).

4 Remove the pan from the heat and leave to settle for a few minutes. Skim well. Pour the liquid jelly into the hot sterilized jars.

5 Slit the chillies lengthways and trim off the stalks. When the jelly is semi-set, carefully insert a chilli into each jar. Pierce any air pockets that form by prodding with a long, thin wooden skewer. Cover each jar with a waxed paper disc dipped in brandy, then seal.

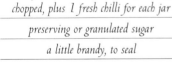

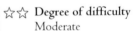

Degree of difficulty
Moderate

Cooking time
50–55 minutes

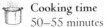

Special equipment
Preserving pan; sterilized jelly bag; sugar thermometer; sterilized jars and sealants (see pages 42–43)

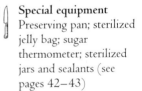

Yield
About 1.25kg (2½ lb)

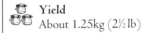

Shelf life
2 years

Serving suggestions
Serve with meat, add to sandwiches, or stir a tablespoonful into game casseroles just before serving

Minted Apple Jelly

Apples are nature's gift to jelly-makers, since they contain just the right balance of acidity and pectin to give a good set. Pure apple jelly is rather insipid, so enliven the flavour with other ingredients such as fragrant tea leaves or herbs. Some of my favourites are mint, thyme, tarragon and lavender flowers.

INGREDIENTS

small bunch of mint

a few strips of lemon rind

1kg (2lb) apples, coarsely chopped

1.75 litres (3 pints) water or dry cider

preserving or granulated sugar

juice of 1 lemon

3–4 tbsp finely chopped mint

a little brandy, to seal

1 Tie the mint and lemon rind together with string. Put in the preserving pan with the apples and 1.25 litres (2 pints) of the water or cider.

2 Bring to the boil, then simmer, stirring occasionally, for about 25 minutes, or until the apples are pulpy. Pour into the sterilized jelly bag (see page 80). Leave for 2–3 hours, until it stops dripping.

3 Remove the pulp from the jelly bag and return it to the cleaned pan. Add the remaining water or cider. Bring to the boil, then simmer for 20 minutes. Drain through the jelly bag as before.

4 Combine the two batches of juice and measure it. Allow 500g (1lb) sugar for every 500ml (17fl oz) juice. Pour the juice into the cleaned preserving pan and add the lemon juice.

5 Bring to the boil and boil for about 10 minutes. Add the sugar, stirring until it has dissolved, and boil rapidly for 8–10 minutes, or until the setting point is reached (see page 76).

6 Remove the pan from the heat, and allow to cool for about 10 minutes. Stir in the chopped mint, then pour into the hot sterilized jars and leave to cool completely. Cover each jar with a waxed paper disc dipped in a little brandy, then seal.

 Degree of difficulty
Easy

 Cooking time
About 1¼ hours

 Special equipment
Preserving pan; sterilized jelly bag; sugar thermometer; sterilized jars and sealants (see pages 42–43)

 Yield
About 1.25kg (2½lb)

 Shelf life
2 years

 Serving suggestion
Wonderful with lamb

TIP

• There is no need to core the apples if you chop them by hand; if you are using a food processor, remove the cores first as broken pips can impart a bitter flavour to the jelly. Remember to put the cores in the pan with the apples, as they contain a large amount of pectin.

Red Plum Jelly

This jelly has an interesting hint of bitter almonds. Use a dark red variety of plums such as River's Czar, Monarch or Early River.

INGREDIENTS

1kg (2lb) red plums

15 bitter almonds, coarsely pounded, or 1 tsp bitter almond extract

preserving or granulated sugar

4 tbsp slivovitz (or other plum brandy)

a few blanched bitter almonds for each jar (optional)

1 Put the whole plums in the preserving pan with the bitter almonds or almond extract and add enough cold water to cover. Bring to the boil, then reduce the heat and simmer for 20–25 minutes, or until pulpy.

2 Pour the fruit and liquid into the sterilized jelly bag (see page 80). Leave to drain for 2–3 hours, until it stops dripping. Measure the juice and allow 500g (1lb) sugar for every 500ml (17fl oz) juice.

3 Put the juice and sugar in the cleaned pan. Bring to the boil, stirring until the sugar has dissolved. Boil for a few minutes, then reduce the heat and skim well. Boil rapidly for 10 minutes, or until the setting point is reached (see page 76).

4 Leave to cool for 5 minutes. Skim well and stir in the slivovitz. Pour into the jars, then seal if not adding the almonds. If adding almonds, allow the jelly to semi-set, then insert a few into each jar. Cover each jar with a waxed paper disc dipped in a little slivovitz, then seal.

 Degree of difficulty
Easy

 Cooking time
40–50 minutes

 Special equipment
Preserving pan; sterilized jelly bag; sugar thermometer; sterilized jars and sealants (see pages 42–43)

 Yield
About 1.25kg (2½lb)

 Shelf life
2 years

 Serving suggestions
Serve with roast lamb, venison or cold chicken

Pineapple and Orange Jelly

A clear, bright-yellow jelly with a hint of orange and a concentrated pineapple flavour. There is no need to peel and core the fruit for this recipe. If wished, you can add 1½ tablespoons of coriander seeds to the jelly in step 1.

INGREDIENTS

1 small pineapple, about 500g (1lb), sliced
500g (1lb) apples, sliced
2 oranges, sliced
1.5 litres (2½ pints) water
preserving or granulated sugar

1 Put all the ingredients, except the sugar, in the preserving pan. Bring slowly to the boil, then reduce the heat and simmer for 30 minutes, or until the fruit is soft and pulpy.

2 Pour the fruit and liquid into the sterilized jelly bag (see page 80). Drain for 2–3 hours, or until it stops dripping.

3 Remove the fruit pulp from the jelly bag, return it to the pan and add enough cold water to cover. Bring to the boil, then simmer for 30 minutes.

4 Drain through the jelly bag as before. Combine the two batches of juice and measure it. Allow 500g (1lb) sugar for every 500ml (17fl oz) juice.

5 Put the juice and sugar in the cleaned pan. Bring slowly to the boil, stirring until the sugar has dissolved. Boil for a few minutes, then reduce the heat and skim well. Return to the boil, and boil rapidly for 10–12 minutes, or until the setting point is reached (see page 76).

6 Remove the pan from the heat, leave the jelly to settle for a few minutes and skim very well. Pour the liquid jelly into the hot sterilized jars, then seal.

VARIATION

✦ *Quince Jelly*
Put 1kg (2lb) quinces and 1.25 litres (2 pints) water in the preserving pan. Bring to the boil then simmer gently for 1–1½ hours. Top up with boiling water if necessary to keep the fruit covered. Strain through the jelly bag and return the pulp to the pan as for the main recipe. In step 5 add the juice of 2 lemons to the quince juice and sugar. Bring to the boil and boil rapidly for 1–2 minutes, skim well, then return to a rapid boil for 10–15 minutes, or until the setting point is reached. Pot as above. Serve with game and other dark meat.

 Degree of difficulty
Moderate

 Cooking time
About 1½ hours

 Special equipment
Preserving pan; sterilized jelly bag; sugar thermometer; sterilized jars and sealants (see pages 42–43)

 Yield
About 1.25kg (2½lb)

 Shelf life
2 years

 Serving suggestion
Use as a yellow glaze for cooked hams or fresh fruit tarts

Guava Jelly

Guavas are a subtropical fruit with a haunting, exotic perfume. They are delicious eaten raw and also make a very elegant, rust-red jelly. Do not use white guavas as the colour is too insipid.

TIP

• Do not worry if the jelly seems too soft. Leave for a day or two and then check again. If still too soft, reboil until the setting point is reached.

INGREDIENTS

1kg (2lb) firm guavas, coarsely chopped
1 lime, coarsely chopped
preserving or granulated sugar

1 Put the guavas and lime in the preserving pan, and add cold water to cover. Bring slowly to the boil, then reduce the heat and simmer for about 30 minutes or until the fruit is soft and pulpy.

2 Pour the fruit and liquid into the sterilized jelly bag (see page 80). Leave to drain for 2–3 hours, or until it stops

dripping. Measure the juice and allow 325g (11oz) sugar for every 500ml (17fl oz) juice.

3 Put the fruit juice and sugar in the cleaned pan. Bring slowly to the boil, stirring until the sugar has dissolved, then reduce the heat and skim well.

4 Return to the boil and boil rapidly for 10–12 minutes, or until the setting point is reached (see page 76).

5 Pour the liquid jelly into the hot sterilized jars, then seal.

 Degree of difficulty
Easy

 Cooking time
45–55 minutes

 Special equipment
Preserving pan; sterilized jelly bag; sugar thermometer; sterilized jars and sealants (see pages 42–43)

 Yield
About 1kg (2lb)

 Shelf life
2 years

 Serving suggestions
Spread on bread or serve with cold meat and cheese

Spicy Prickly Pear Jelly

(see page 35 for illustration)

The recipe for this soft-set jelly was given to me by Ya'akove Lishansky, who lives in Haifa, Israel. Now over 80 years old, he still produces some of the most delicious preserves I have ever tasted. Prickly pears are available throughout the summer from many ethnic food shops and some large supermarkets. Purple ones are especially good for this recipe.

INGREDIENTS

1kg (2lb) purple, red or orange prickly pears
300g (10oz) cooking apples, chopped
750ml (1¼ pints) water
500ml (17fl oz) cider vinegar or white wine vinegar
125ml (4fl oz) lemon juice
preserving or granulated sugar
1 tbsp arrack, ouzo or Pernod
For the spice bag (see page 47)
1 tsp allspice berries, lightly crushed
4–6 dried bird's eye chillies, including the seeds, crushed
3 dried bay leaves, crumbled

1 Wearing protective gloves, top and tail the prickly pears. Run a sharp knife the length of the fruit and cut through the thick skin. Remove the skin and wash the fruit thoroughly. Place the fruit in a bowl and crush to a pulp with a potato masher.

2 Put the pulp in the preserving pan with the apples and water. Bring slowly to the boil, then simmer for 25 minutes, or until the fruit is soft and pulpy.

3 Pour the fruit and liquid into the sterilized jelly bag (see page 80). Leave for 2–3 hours, or until it stops dripping. Add the vinegar and lemon juice to the prickly pear juice and measure the liquid. Allow 500g (1lb) sugar for every 500ml (17fl oz) liquid.

4 Put the liquid, sugar and spice bag in the cleaned pan. Bring slowly to the boil, stirring until the sugar has dissolved. Boil for 25 minutes, or until the setting point is reached (see page 76).

5 Remove the pan from the heat and discard the spice bag. Stir in the arrack, ouzo or Pernod. Pour the liquid jelly into the hot sterilized jars, then seal.

 Degree of difficulty
Moderate

 Cooking time
About 1 hour

 Special equipment
Non-corrosive preserving pan; sterilized jelly bag; sugar thermometer; sterilized jars with vinegar-proof sealants (see pages 42–43)

 Yield
About 1.5kg (3lb)

Shelf life
2 years

Serving suggestions
Delicious with cold meats or stirred into steamed vegetables

Rich Mincemeat

Mincemeat is one of the most glorious inventions of the British medieval kitchen. In the past, it contained fatty mutton, and suet is still considered indispensable for providing moisture and texture. I make my mincemeat once every two years and add either grated chilled butter or vegetarian suet – about 125g (4oz) per 1kg (2lb) – just before use.

INGREDIENTS

300g (10oz) cooking apples, coarsely grated
200g (7oz) carrots, finely grated
125g (4oz) dried apricots, coarsely chopped
125g (4oz) prunes, coarsely chopped
125g (4oz) glacé cherries, coarsely chopped
125g (4oz) fresh ginger root, finely grated
250g (8oz) raisins
250g (8oz) sultanas
250g (8oz) currants
175g (6oz) mixed peel
grated rind and juice of 2 lemons
grated rind and juice of 2 oranges
125g (4oz) honey or molasses sugar
2–3 tbsp Sweet Masala (see page 117) or your favourite sweet spice mix
250ml (8fl oz) brandy, plus extra for the jars

1 Put all the ingredients in a large bowl and mix very well. Cover with a clean cloth and leave to stand in a warm kitchen for 2–3 days.

2 Pack the mincemeat tightly into the sterilized jars and cover with waxed paper discs. Pour 1–2 tablespoons of brandy into each jar, then seal.

3 Every 6 months or so, open the jars, pour a little brandy over the top and reseal.

TIP

• If possible, use whole candied citrus peel rather than ready-chopped peel, and cut it yourself. Of course you could always make your own candied peel (see page 181).

 Degree of difficulty
Easy

Special equipment
Sterilized jars and sealants (see pages 42–43)

Yield
About 2.5kg (5lb)

Shelf life
2 years

Serving suggestions
Use to make mince pies or tarts, or to fill baked apples; for sheer indulgence, serve topped with thick cream

VARIATION

◆ For a milder mincemeat, add a quarter of its weight in grated apples or quince or ground almonds, or a mixture of these, before use.

FRUIT BUTTERS, CURDS & CHEESES

THESE ARE CLOSELY related to jams and jellies, in which a fruit pulp is cooked, together with sugar, to a thick consistency. Cheeses have the firmest texture and are usually moulded and served in chunks. With butters, the concentration of sugar is lower, they are cooked for less time, and consequently are softer and have a shorter shelf life. Curds are softer still, and are made from fruit juice thickened with eggs and butter. Traditionally, fruit cheeses and butters were served as sweet spreads as well as accompaniments to roasted and cold meats. All these products are essential for the larder. They are delicious spread thickly on bread and butter, make instant fillings for cakes and flans, or can be mixed with cream or curd cheese for quick and simple dessert toppings.

Orchard Fruit Butter

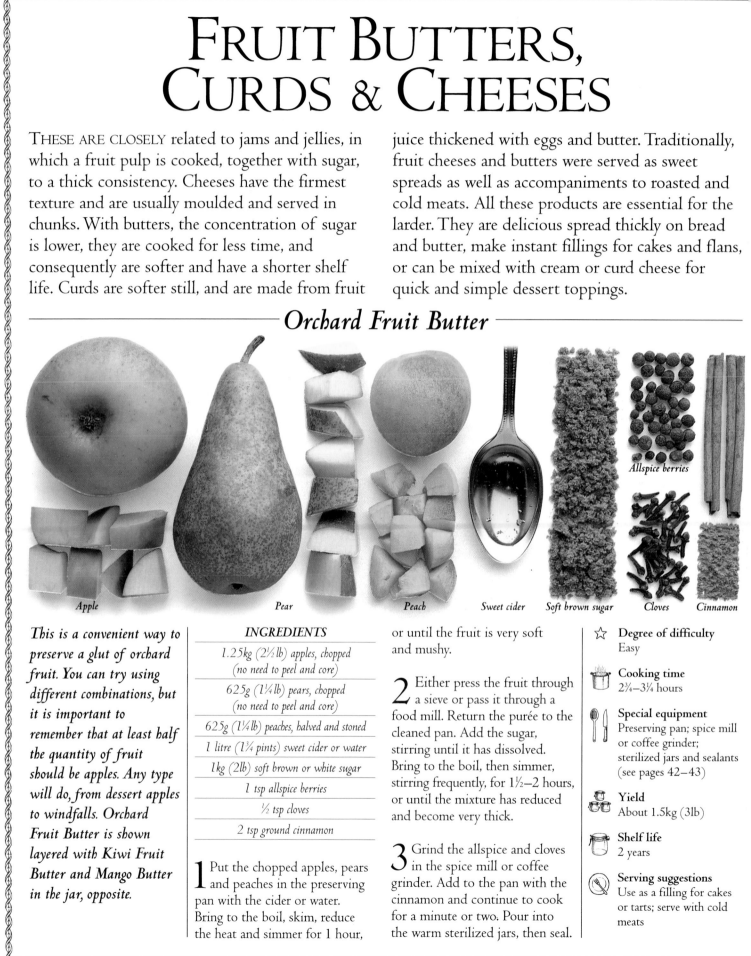

Apple   Pear   Peach   Sweet cider   Soft brown sugar   Allspice berries   Cloves   Cinnamon

This is a convenient way to preserve a glut of orchard fruit. You can try using different combinations, but it is important to remember that at least half the quantity of fruit should be apples. Any type will do, from dessert apples to windfalls. Orchard Fruit Butter is shown layered with Kiwi Fruit Butter and Mango Butter in the jar, opposite.

INGREDIENTS

1.25kg (2½ lb) apples, chopped (no need to peel and core)
625g (1¼ lb) pears, chopped (no need to peel and core)
625g (1¼ lb) peaches, halved and stoned
1 litre (1¾ pints) sweet cider or water
1kg (2lb) soft brown or white sugar
1 tsp allspice berries
½ tsp cloves
2 tsp ground cinnamon

1 Put the chopped apples, pears and peaches in the preserving pan with the cider or water. Bring to the boil, skim, reduce the heat and simmer for 1 hour, or until the fruit is very soft and mushy.

2 Either press the fruit through a sieve or pass it through a food mill. Return the purée to the cleaned pan. Add the sugar, stirring until it has dissolved. Bring to the boil, then simmer, stirring frequently, for 1½–2 hours, or until the mixture has reduced and become very thick.

3 Grind the allspice and cloves in the spice mill or coffee grinder. Add to the pan with the cinnamon and continue to cook for a minute or two. Pour into the warm sterilized jars, then seal.

☆ **Degree of difficulty**
Easy

Cooking time
2¾–3¾ hours

Special equipment
Preserving pan; spice mill or coffee grinder; sterilized jars and sealants (see pages 42–43)

Yield
About 1.5kg (3lb)

Shelf life
2 years

Serving suggestions
Use as a filling for cakes or tarts; serve with cold meats

MANGO BUTTER can be
flavoured with orange,
vanilla or cinnamon

ORCHARD FRUIT
BUTTER is lightly spiced
with a warming hint of
allspice, cloves and
cinnamon

TIP

• To make this attractive layered preserve,
place about 300g (12oz) Kiwi Fruit Butter
(see page 172 for recipe) in a small pan
and heat gently until it comes to the
boil. To prevent it from burning, add
1–2 tablespoons water. Pour into a warm
sterilized jar and leave to cool. Repeat with
the Orchard Fruit Butter and the Mango
Butter (see page 172 for recipe). Cover the
surface with a waxed paper disc dipped in
a little brandy, then seal (see page 43).

ORCHARD FRUIT BUTTER *makes*
an unusual filling for a Swiss roll.

KIWI FRUIT BUTTER
has a slightly sharp taste

Mango Butter
(see page 34 for illustration)

Wonderfully golden and fragrant, this simple butter is an ideal way to use up very ripe mangoes. Try adding different flavourings, such as grated orange rind, vanilla or cinnamon.

INGREDIENTS

2kg (4lb) ripe mangoes
300ml (½ pint) sweet cider or water
1kg (2lb) preserving or granulated sugar
grated rind and juice of 2 lemons

1 Prepare the mango flesh (see page 175) and cut into large chunks. Put the mango and cider or water in the preserving pan. Bring to the boil, then simmer for 15–20 minutes, until the fruit is soft and pulpy. Either press the mixture through a sieve or pass it through a food mill. Return the purée to the cleaned pan.

2 Add the sugar and lemon rind and juice, stirring until the sugar has dissolved. Bring to the boil, then simmer, stirring frequently, for 35–40 minutes or until reduced and thickened. Pour into the warm sterilized jars, then seal.

 Degree of difficulty
Easy

 Cooking time
About 1 hour

 Special equipment
Preserving pan; sterilized jars and sealants (see pages 42–43)

 Yield
About 1.5kg (3lb)

Shelf life
2 years

Melon Butter
(see page 21 for illustration)

Melon makes a very pleasant butter with a subtle, fruity scent. Use fragrant varieties such as Ananas or Galia, or ripe Charentais for a beautiful deep orange colour.

INGREDIENTS

2kg (4lb) ripe melons, peeled, deseeded and chopped
500ml (17fl oz) sweet cider or water
1kg (2lb) preserving or granulated sugar
juice of 2 lemons
2 lemongrass stalks, finely chopped (optional)
1 tbsp orange-flower water

1 Put the melon in the preserving pan with the cider or water. Bring to the boil, skim, then simmer for 40 minutes, or until the fruit is soft.

2 Either press the mixture through a sieve or pass it through a food mill. Return the purée to the cleaned pan.

3 Add the sugar, lemon juice and lemongrass, if using, stirring until the sugar has dissolved. Bring to the boil, then simmer, stirring frequently, for 1 hour or until reduced and thickened.

4 Remove from the heat and stir in the flower water. Pour into the warm sterilized jars, then seal.

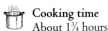 **Degree of difficulty**
Easy

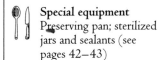 **Cooking time**
About 1¼ hours

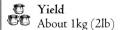 **Special equipment**
Preserving pan; sterilized jars and sealants (see pages 42–43)

 Yield
About 1kg (2lb)

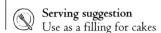 **Shelf life**
2 years

Serving suggestion
Use as a filling for cakes

Kiwi Fruit Butter
(see page 34 for illustration)

Don't worry if this delightful butter doesn't thicken much in the pan; it will thicken considerably once it has cooled.

INGREDIENTS

1kg (2lb) ripe kiwi fruit, chopped (no need to peel)
750ml (1¼ pints) dry cider or water
grated rind and juice of 1 lemon
75g (2½ oz) fresh ginger root, finely shredded
preserving or granulated sugar
1 tsp freshly ground black pepper (optional)

1 Put the kiwi fruit, cider or water and lemon juice in the preserving pan. Bring to the boil, skim, reduce the heat and simmer for 15–20 minutes, until the fruit is soft and mushy.

2 Either press the mixture through a sieve or pass it through a food mill. Measure the purée and allow 400g (13oz) sugar for every 500ml (17fl oz) of purée. Return the purée to the cleaned pan.

3 Add the lemon rind, ginger, sugar and pepper, if using, stirring until the sugar has dissolved. Bring to the boil, then simmer, stirring frequently, for 30–35 minutes, or until the butter has reached the consistency of a soft-set jam. Pour into the warm sterilized jars, then seal.

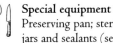 **Degree of difficulty**
Easy

Cooking time
About 1 hour

Special equipment
Preserving pan; sterilized jars and sealants (see pages 42–43)

 Yield
About 1kg (2lb)

Shelf life
2 years

Serving suggestions
Use as a filling for flans or spread on bread

Passion Fruit Curd

The passion fruit seeds add a surprisingly crunchy texture to this curd, which for me is part of its attraction. However, if you prefer a smooth curd, use 1kg (2lb) of fruit and sieve it before adding the eggs.

———— TIP ————
• Choose wrinkled passion fruit as they are riper and contain more juice.

INGREDIENTS
750g (1½lb) passion fruit

juice of 1 lemon

300g (10oz) preserving or granulated sugar

150g (5oz) butter, softened

4 eggs (size 2), beaten

1 Slice the passion fruit in half and scoop out the seeds and pulp; there should be about 500ml (17fl oz).

2 Put in a small pan, add the lemon juice and sugar and heat gently, stirring until the sugar has dissolved. Add the softened butter and stir until melted.

3 Transfer the mixture to the double boiler or a bowl placed over a pan of barely simmering water. Seive in the eggs and cook very gently, stirring frequently, for 25–40 minutes, until the mixture coats the back of a spoon. Do not allow it to boil or it will curdle.

4 Pour the curd into the warm sterilized jars and seal. Allow to cool, then keep refrigerated.

☆☆ **Degree of difficulty**
Moderate

Cooking time
30–45 minutes

Special equipment
Double boiler; sterilized jars and sealants (see pages 42–43)

Yield
About 1kg (2lb)

Shelf life
3 months, refrigerated

Serving suggestion
Use to fill tarts

Lemon Curd
(see page 29 for illustration)

Lemon curd can be used to create a wide range of sweet delicacies, such as meringue pies, pavlovas and trifles. This recipe uses less sugar than usual; if you prefer a sweeter curd, increase the quantity by up to a third.

INGREDIENTS
grated rind and juice of 6 lemons

400g (13oz) preserving or granulated sugar

150g (5oz) butter, softened

5 eggs (size 3), beaten

1 Put the lemon rind and juice in a small pan with the sugar. Heat gently, stirring until the sugar has dissolved. Add the butter and stir until melted.

2 Transfer the mixture to the double boiler or a bowl placed over a pan of barely simmering water. Seive in the eggs and cook very gently, stirring frequently, for 25–40 minutes, until the mixture coats the back of a spoon. Do not allow it to boil or it will curdle.

3 Pour the curd into the warm sterilized jars and seal. Allow to cool, then keep refrigerated.

☆☆ **Degree of difficulty**
Moderate

Cooking time
30–45 minutes

Special equipment
Double boiler; sterilized jars and sealants (see pages 42–43)

Yield
About 750g (1½lb)

Shelf life
3 months, refrigerated

Pink Grapefruit Curd
(see page 78 for technique)

A delicious, delightfully pink curd with an interesting texture. Try to find ruby red grapefruit, which have an intense colour; the ordinary pink grapefruit make an anaemically pale product. This curd takes time to thicken so be patient – the results are well worth it.

INGREDIENTS
grated rind and juice of 1 ruby red or pink grapefruit

segmented flesh of 1 ruby red or pink grapefruit (see steps 2 and 3, page 78)

juice of 2 lemons

400g (13oz) preserving or granulated sugar

100g (3½oz) butter, softened

4 eggs and 2 egg yolks (size 3), beaten

3 tbsp orange-flower water

1 Put the grapefruit rind, juice and flesh, the lemon juice and sugar in a small pan. Heat gently, stirring until the sugar has dissolved. Add the softened butter and stir until melted.

2 Transfer the mixture to the double boiler or a bowl placed over a pan of barely simmering water. Sieve in the eggs and cook very gently, stirring frequently, for 25–40 minutes, until the mixture coats the back of a spoon. Do not allow it to boil or it will curdle.

3 Remove from the heat and stir in the orange-flower water. Pour the curd into the warm sterilized jars and seal. Allow to cool, then keep refrigerated.

☆☆ **Degree of difficulty**
Moderate

Cooking time
30–45 minutes

Special equipment
Double boiler; sterilized jars and sealants (see pages 42–43)

Yield
About 1kg (2lb)

Shelf life
3 months, refrigerated

Serving suggestion
Use to fill pavlovas

Quince Cheese

(see page 82 for technique)

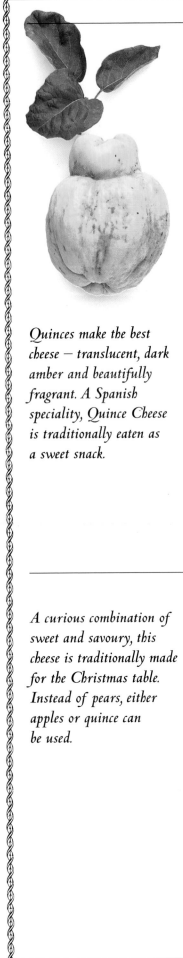

Quinces make the best cheese — translucent, dark amber and beautifully fragrant. A Spanish speciality, Quince Cheese is traditionally eaten as a sweet snack.

INGREDIENTS

1.5kg (3lb) ripe quinces
about 2 litres (3½ pints) water or dry cider
2–3 strips of lemon rind
juice of ½ lemon
preserving or granulated sugar
mild oil, such as almond or groundnut, for brushing
caster sugar for dusting

1 Wash the quinces well to remove any fluff, then chop coarsely. Put in the preserving pan with enough water or cider to cover and add the lemon rind and juice. Bring to the boil, then simmer for 30–45 minutes, until the fruit is soft and mushy.

2 Press the mixture through a sieve or pass it through a food mill. Measure the purée and allow 400g (13oz) sugar for every 500ml (17fl oz) purée.

3 Return the purée to the cleaned pan and add the sugar.

Bring slowly to the boil, stirring until the sugar has dissolved. Reduce the heat and simmer, stirring frequently, for 2½–3 hours, until the mixture "plops" and becomes very thick. Remove from the heat and leave to cool slightly.

4 Brush a baking tray or roasting tin with plenty of oil. Pour the cooled cheese into the tray and smooth to an even layer about 2.5–4cm (1–1½ in) thick. Allow to cool completely, then cover loosely with a clean cloth and leave in a warm, dry place for 24 hours.

5 Loosen the cheese with a palette knife, then turn out on to greaseproof paper. Cut into squares or diamonds and dust with caster sugar. Arrange on a baking tray and leave to dry, loosely covered with baking parchment.

6 To store, arrange the cheese in layers between sheets of waxed paper in an airtight container.

 Degree of difficulty
Moderate

 Cooking time
3–3¾ hours

 Special equipment
Preserving pan; airtight container

 Yield
About 2.25kg (4½ lb)

 Shelf life
2 years

Serving suggestion
Serve as a sweetmeat

Pear and Tomato Cheese

A curious combination of sweet and savoury, this cheese is traditionally made for the Christmas table. Instead of pears, either apples or quince can be used.

INGREDIENTS

1kg (2lb) plum tomatoes, coarsely chopped
750g (1½ lb) ripe pears, cored and coarsely chopped
250g (8oz) apples, cored and coarsely chopped
1 lemon, coarsely chopped
500ml (17fl oz) water
preserving or granulated sugar
1 tsp freshly ground black pepper
1 tsp ground coriander
½ tsp ground cinnamon
¼ tsp ground cloves

1 Put the tomatoes, pears, apples, lemon and water in the preserving pan. Bring to the boil, then reduce the heat and simmer

for about 30 minutes, until the fruit is soft and mushy.

2 Press the mixture through a sieve or pass it through a food mill. Measure the resulting purée and allow 400g (13oz) sugar for every 500ml (17fl oz) purée.

3 Return the purée to the cleaned pan and add the sugar and spices. Bring to the boil, then simmer, stirring frequently, for 1–1½ hours, until the mixture has reduced and become very thick.

4 Pour into the warm sterilized jars, then seal, or pack into the oiled moulds, leave to cool, then cover with clingfilm.

 Degree of difficulty
Easy

Cooking time
2–2½ hours

Special equipment
Preserving pan; sterilized jars and sealants (see pages 42–43) or individual jelly moulds, oiled

 Yield
About 1.25kg (2½ lb)

 Shelf life
2 years in sealed jars

 Serving suggestions
Good with cold roast meats, especially turkey, or spread on bread

Fruit Leathers

Sun-dried fruit pulp (leather) was probably the predecessor to jam-making. This recipe is for mango leather, but almost any ripe fruit can be used – apricots, lychees and peaches are especially good, as are tomatoes.

---TIP---

• If the leather is too brittle, add more sugar the next time you make it.

INGREDIENTS

1kg (2lb) fully ripe fruit, e.g. mangoes, peeled, cored and coarsely chopped

1 tbsp lemon juice

2–3 tbsp sugar, or more to taste

1 Purée the prepared fruit (see steps 1 and 2, below) in the food processor or food mill. Add the lemon juice and sugar, stirring until the sugar has dissolved.

2 Line a large, dampened baking tray with clingfilm or foil, allowing about 2.5cm (1in) to hang over the edge. Pour the purée on to the tray.

3 Spread the purée out (see step 3, below). Put in an oven preheated to 110°C/225°F/gas ¼ for 12–14 hours, leaving the door slightly ajar, or until it is dry but pliable (see step 4, below).

4 Allow the leather to cool, peel off the clingfilm, then roll the leather up in waxed paper. Store in an airtight container.

5 Alternatively, dry the fruit in the sun for 1–2 days, until it is dry to the touch and pulls away easily from the baking tray. Invert the leather directly on to the tray and dry for a further day.

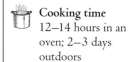 **Degree of difficulty**
Easy

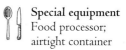 **Cooking time**
12–14 hours in an oven; 2–3 days outdoors

 **Special equipment**
Food processor; airtight container

 Yield
About 150g (5oz)

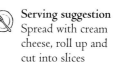 **Shelf life**
2 years

Serving suggestion
Spread with cream cheese, roll up and cut into slices

MANGO LEATHER

1 Cut the mango flesh from either side of the large central stone and score into squares.

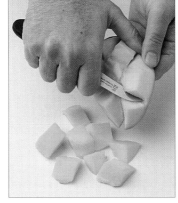

2 Turn the mango halves inside out and cut off the cubes of flesh. Purée the flesh.

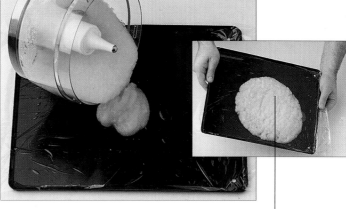

3 Pour the purée into the centre of the lined tray. Tilt to spread it out in an even layer.

SPREAD THE PURÉE in an even layer about 5mm (¼in) thick by tilting the tray; the purée should almost reach the edge

4 Dry the purée as directed above. It should be dry yet pliable. Peel off the clingfilm when cool.

FORM THE FRUIT leather into a horn-of-plenty and fill with dried and candied fruit as a centrepiece for the dessert table

PRESERVED FRUIT & FRUIT SYRUPS

STEEPING IN ALCOHOL is probably the easiest way to preserve different types of ripe fruit. The result is an appetizing concoction that yields the most delicious combination of intoxicating flavours. Candied and crystallized fruit add colour, flavour and texture to fruit cakes and make succulent sweetmeats, especially for Christmas. Fruit syrups can be diluted with water to make refreshing, thirst-quenching drinks or used "neat" to add sweetness to a wide variety of desserts and puddings.

Clementines in Brandy

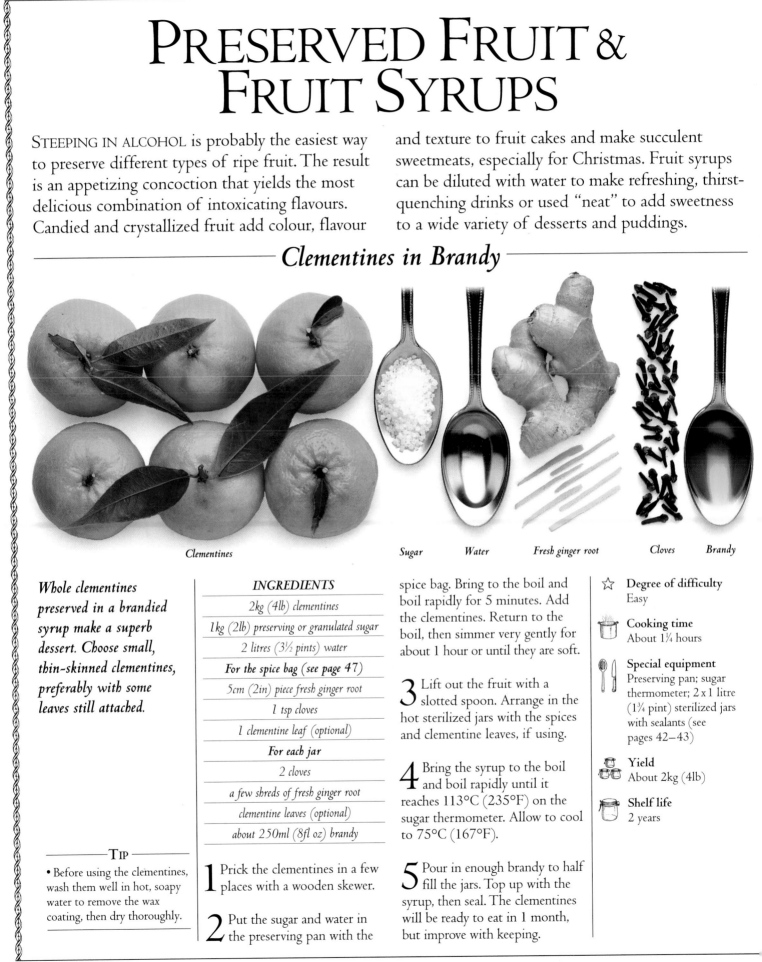

Clementines Sugar Water *Fresh ginger root* *Cloves* *Brandy*

Whole clementines preserved in a brandied syrup make a superb dessert. Choose small, thin-skinned clementines, preferably with some leaves still attached.

INGREDIENTS

2kg (4lb) clementines
1kg (2lb) preserving or granulated sugar
2 litres (3½ pints) water
For the spice bag (see page 47)
5cm (2in) piece fresh ginger root
1 tsp cloves
1 clementine leaf (optional)
For each jar
2 cloves
a few shreds of fresh ginger root
clementine leaves (optional)
about 250ml (8fl oz) brandy

TIP
• Before using the clementines, wash them well in hot, soapy water to remove the wax coating, then dry thoroughly.

1 Prick the clementines in a few places with a wooden skewer.

2 Put the sugar and water in the preserving pan with the spice bag. Bring to the boil and boil rapidly for 5 minutes. Add the clementines. Return to the boil, then simmer very gently for about 1 hour or until they are soft.

3 Lift out the fruit with a slotted spoon. Arrange in the hot sterilized jars with the spices and clementine leaves, if using.

4 Bring the syrup to the boil and boil rapidly until it reaches 113°C (235°F) on the sugar thermometer. Allow to cool to 75°C (167°F).

5 Pour in enough brandy to half fill the jars. Top up with the syrup, then seal. The clementines will be ready to eat in 1 month, but improve with keeping.

☆ **Degree of difficulty**
Easy

Cooking time
About 1¼ hours

Special equipment
Preserving pan; sugar thermometer; 2 x 1 litre (1¾ pint) sterilized jars with sealants (see pages 42–43)

Yield
About 2kg (4lb)

Shelf life
2 years

VARIATIONS

✦ **Kumquats in Brandy**
Use the same quantity of washed and pricked
kumquats and cook for about 25 minutes, or until
the fruit is just soft. Continue as for the main recipe.
✦ Other alcohol, such as vodka, rum or eau de vie,
can be used instead of brandy.

CLEMENTINES IN BRANDY

make a delicious dessert, served in their
own syrup, for special and festive occasions.
Accompany with clotted or extra-thick
double cream for an indulgent treat.

A FEW FRESH
clementine leaves
and spices add
decoration as well
as flavour

THE FRUIT
may have a
wrinkled
appearance once
they have matured

Peaches in Brandy

(see page 84 for technique)

A perfect match of alcohol and fruit – sweet, succulent peaches with fragrant brandy. Although cheap cooking brandy will suffice, the finer the brandy, the tastier the end product. Many other fruit, such as pitted apricots, whole plums, peeled and pitted nectarines and peeled and cored pears, can be used.

INGREDIENTS

1.5kg (3lb) firm peaches
1 litre (1¾ pints) water
1.5kg (3lb) preserving or granulated sugar
300ml (½ pint) good-quality brandy
100g (3½oz) glacé cherries, halved (optional)

For the spice bag (see page 47)

1 vanilla pod
small piece of cinnamon stick
3–4 cardamom pods
4 cloves

1 Blanch the peaches (see page 46), then cut them in half and remove the stones.

2 Put the water and 500g (1lb) of the sugar in a pan. Bring to the boil, skim off any froth, then reduce the heat and simmer for 5 minutes to make a syrup.

3 Gently slide the peaches into the syrup. Return to the boil, then simmer gently for 5 minutes. Remove the peaches with a slotted spoon and leave to cool.

4 Place 600ml (1 pint) of the syrup in a small pan with the remaining sugar and the spice bag. Bring to the boil, stirring until the sugar has dissolved. Skim, then boil rapidly until the mixture reaches 104°C (219°F) on the sugar thermometer. Cool slightly, then add the brandy.

5 Secure a cherry half in the cavity of each peach, if liked, using a wooden cocktail stick. Pack the peaches loosely into the hot sterilized jar.

6 Remove the spice bag from the pan and pour the syrup into the jar, making sure that the peaches are completely covered. Shake the jar gently to ensure there are no air pockets, then seal. The peaches will be ready in 2 weeks, but improve with keeping.

 Degree of difficulty
Moderate

 Cooking time
About 15 minutes

 Special equipment
Sugar thermometer; sterilized, wide-necked jar and sealant (see pages 42–43)

 Yield
About 1kg (2lb)

Shelf life
2 years

 Serving suggestions
Use to make a superb open flan; serve with cream or ice cream with plenty of the brandied syrup

---

Rumtopf

This ingenious Christmas dish is made by layering fresh fruit with alcohol and sugar in an earthenware pot. It is topped up with more fruit as different varieties come into season. In Germany, where this dish originated, special rumtopf pots are available, but you could use a large earthenware casserole or a glass jar.

INGREDIENTS

selection of fresh, ripe fruit (see Tips, below)

For every 1kg (2lb) prepared fruit

250g (8oz) preserving or granulated sugar
about 1 litre (1¾ pints) light rum

1 To prepare the fruit, remove any stems and bruised parts. Quarter large fruit, such as pears. Peaches should be blanched and peeled (see page 46).

2 Mix the prepared fruit with the sugar in a large bowl. Cover and leave to stand for about 30 minutes.

3 Spoon into the rumtopf pot and pour over the rum. Cover with clingfilm and the lid.

4 Every week or so, mix the contents by shaking the pot.

5 As more fruit come into season, prepare as above and add to the pot, together with the appropriate amount of sugar and rum. It will be ready 3 months after the last fruit has been added.

TIPS

• Any ripe, perfect juicy fruit can be used, such as strawberries and other berries, black, red, and white currants, peaches, pears, plums, and cherries.
• The amount of sugar given makes a slightly sharp rumtopf; for a sweeter version use up to 400g (13oz) sugar for every 2lb (1kg) fruit.
• If using a glass pot or jar, keep it in a dark place as light affects the colour of the fruit.

 Degree of difficulty
Easy

 Special equipment
Rumtopf pot or large jar or casserole with lid

 Yield
As the size of pot or jar

 Shelf life
Keeps indefinitely

 Serving suggestions
Serve as a topping on ice cream and other desserts, or eat the fruit with a spoon, washing it down with the liquor

Pears in Eau de Vie
(see page 31 for illustration)

In France, pear buds are inserted into slim-necked bottles and allowed to grow in their individual hothouse. The bottles are then filled with alcohol and left to mature. The result is a heady, flavoured liqueur and a fragrant, alcoholic pear. This is my homage to that tradition.

INGREDIENTS

3–4 ripe pears

300–400g (10–13oz) preserving or granulated sugar

1 vanilla pod

about 1 litre (1¾ pints) eau de vie

1 Wash the pears, dry, and prick in a few places with a silver needle or a sharp wooden skewer.

2 Arrange the pears in the sterilized jar. Add the sugar and vanilla pod and pour in enough eau de vie to cover the pears, then seal.

3 Keep in a cool, dark place for 3–4 months. For the first few weeks, shake the jar every few days to help dissolve the sugar.

TIPS
• Pear brandy or vodka can be substituted for eau de vie.
• For a sweeter result, add up to 500g (1lb) sugar.

 Degree of difficulty
Easy

 Special equipment
2 litre (3½ pint) sterilized, wide-necked jar and sealant (see pages 42–43)

 Yield
About 1kg (2lb)

 Shelf life
2 years

Serving suggestion
Serve as a dessert to cheer up a cold winter night

Pineapple in Kirsch
(see page 35 for illustration)

When this luscious fruit is stored in alcohol, its delicate fragrance is preserved – and so, too, is the enzyme it contains that aids digestion. Vodka, eau de vie or white rum are also suitable. Serve with cream as the ultimate dessert.

INGREDIENTS

4–5 baby pineapples (queens), peeled, cored and cut into rings 1cm (½ in) thick

3–4 cinnamon sticks

3–4 strips of orange peel

300–500g (10oz–1lb) preserving sugar

5–6 bitter almonds, blanched (optional)

about 1¾ pints (1 litre) kirsch

1 Arrange the pineapple with the cinnamon and orange peel in the sterilized jar. Add the sugar and almonds, if using. I find 300g (10oz) sugar is sufficient, but if you prefer the pineapple sweeter, add the larger amount.

2 Pour enough kirsch into the jar to cover the pineapple, then seal. Keep in a cool, dark place for 2–3 months. For the first few weeks, shake the jar every few days to help dissolve the sugar.

 Degree of difficulty
Easy

 Special equipment
2 litre (3 pint) sterilized, wide-necked jar with sealant (see pages 42–43)

 Yield
About 1kg (2lb)

Shelf life
2 years

Cassis

This traditional French blackcurrant liqueur is extremely delicious and very easy to make.

TIPS
• Make sure the fruit is ripe and discard any damaged or mouldy berries.
• Do not throw away the pulp left in the jelly bag after straining the fruit. If you cook it with an equal quantity of sugar and a little water it makes a delightfully boozy jam.
• Other berries, such as strawberries, redcurrants, blueberries, and raspberries, can be treated in the same way.

INGREDIENTS

1kg (2lb) blackcurrants, washed

500ml (17fl oz) brandy

350–500g (11½ oz–1lb) preserving or granulated sugar

1 Place the blackcurrants in the sterilized jar and crush them well with a potato masher.

2 Pour over the brandy, then cover the jar tightly. Leave in a cool, dark place for about 2 months, shaking the jar from time to time.

3 Pour the fruit and liquid into the sterilized jelly bag (see page 80). Leave for a few hours, or until it stops dripping. Squeeze the bag to extract as much liquid as possible. Filter the juice through a double layer of muslin (see page 47), then return it to the jar.

4 Add the sugar to taste (I prefer the smaller amount), then seal. Leave in a cool, dark place for 2 weeks, shaking the jar every few days, until all the sugar has dissolved and the liquid is clear.

5 Filter the liquid again if necessary. Pour into sterilized bottles, then seal. The liqueur can be used immediately, but improves with keeping.

Degree of difficulty
Easy

Special equipment
1.5 litre (2½ pint) sterilized, wide-necked jar; sterilized jelly bag and muslin; sterilized bottles and sealants (see pages 42–43)

Yield
About 1 litre (1¾ pints)

Shelf life
Keeps indefinitely; once opened, consume within 3 months

Serving suggestion
Add 1–2 teaspoons to a glass of dry white wine

Raspberry Syrup

Making syrup is a good way to use up soft fruit that are too ripe for jams or jellies. The hot method used here is easier than the cold method (see *Blackcurrant Syrup, opposite*) but does not produce the same intensity of flavour. Any ripe, juicy berries can be prepared in the same way, but discard any that are bruised or mouldy.

INGREDIENTS

1kg (2lb) raspberries
75ml (3fl oz) water
preserving or granulated sugar

1 Put the raspberries and water in a bowl and mash well. Set over a pan of simmering water for 1 hour, mashing occasionally.

2 Pour into the sterilized jelly bag (see page 80). Leave for a few hours, or until it stops dripping. Squeeze the bag to extract as much liquid as possible.

Filter the juice through a double layer of muslin (see page 47).

3 Measure the juice and allow 400g (13oz) sugar for every 500ml (17fl oz) juice. Put in a pan and bring slowly to the boil, stirring occasionally until the sugar has dissolved. Skim off the froth and boil for 4–5 minutes. Do not overcook or the mixture will start to set.

4 Pour into the hot sterilized bottle and cork. Leave to cool, then seal with wax (see page 43).

 Degree of difficulty
Easy

 Cooking time
About 1¼ hours

 Special equipment
Sterilized jelly bag and muslin; 750ml (1¼ pint) sterilized bottles and corks (see pages 42–43)

 Yield
About 750ml (1¼ pints)

Shelf life
2 years

Cassis

Blackcurrant Syrup

Pomegranate Syrup

Raspberry Syrup

Serving suggestions
Dilute with water to make a drink; pour over desserts and ice cream; the syrup makes a pleasant treat when frozen

Pomegranate Syrup — *(see page 35 for illustration)*

A wonderful ruby-red syrup. Sour pomegranates are preferable (available from Indian or Middle Eastern grocers), but if sweet ones are all you can find, add the juice of 3 lemons or 1 teaspoon of citric acid.

INGREDIENTS

2kg (4lb) very red pomegranates

400g (13oz) preserving or granulated sugar

1 tsp orange-flower water (optional)

1 Cut the pomegranates in half, horizontally, and use a lemon squeezer to extract all the juice; you should end up with about 500ml (17fl oz) juice.

2 Filter the juice through a double layer of muslin (see page 47) into a pan. Add the sugar and bring slowly to the boil, stirring until it has dissolved.

3 Boil for 10 minutes, then remove from the heat, skim well and stir in the orange-flower water, if using. Pour the syrup into the hot sterilized bottle, then seal.

 Degree of difficulty
Easy

 Cooking time
About 15 minutes

 Special equipment
Sterilized muslin; sterilized bottle and sealant (see pages 42–43)

 Yield
About 500ml (17fl oz)

Shelf life
2 years

Blackcurrant Syrup

Blackcurrants make the best syrup — perfumed and refreshing. This recipe extracts the juice when cold, which produces a very fresh flavour. The slight fermentation period before draining the fruit is necessary to destroy as much of the pectin as possible, otherwise the syrup will start to set.

INGREDIENTS

1kg (2lb) ripe blackcurrants

preserving or granulated sugar

1 Purée the blackcurrants in the food processor. Transfer to a bowl, cover, and leave for 24 hours.

2 Pour the fruit purée into the sterilized jelly bag (see page 80). Leave for a few hours, or until it stops dripping. Squeeze the bag to extract as much liquid as possible. Filter the juice through a double layer of muslin (see page 47).

3 Measure the juice and add 400g (13oz) sugar for every 500ml (17fl oz) juice. Stir well until the sugar has dissolved.

4 Pour the syrup into the sterilized bottles, filling them to within 5cm (2in) of the top. Cork, heat process, then seal with wax (see pages 43–45).

 Degree of difficulty
Easy

 Cooking time
About 20 minutes

 Special equipment
Food processor; sterilized jelly bag and muslin; sterilized bottles and corks (see pages 42–43)

 Yield
About 750ml (1¼ pints)

 Shelf life
2 years

Candied Citrus Peel

This recipe is a wonderful way to use citrus peel. Traditionally, some of the outer skin is removed to make the peel less bitter but I find it unnecessary. Any thick-skinned citrus fruit can be used, such as orange, grapefruit, citron and pomelo. The last two are especially good.

INGREDIENTS

1kg (2lb) citrus peel, cut into 5cm (2in) strips

1kg (2lb) preserving or granulated sugar

350ml (12fl oz) water

1 Put the peel in a non-corrosive pan with enough water to cover. Bring to the boil, then simmer for 10 minutes. Drain, discard the cooking liquid and cover with fresh water. Return to the boil, then reduce the heat and simmer for 20 minutes. Drain again.

2 Put the cooked peel in a large bowl, cover with cold water and leave for 24 hours.

3 Drain the peel. Put the sugar and water in a pan. Bring to the boil, stirring until the sugar has dissolved. Add the peel, then reduce the heat and simmer very gently for 2–3 hours, or until the peel is translucent and most of the syrup has been absorbed. Stir frequently to prevent sticking.

4 To preserve the peel in syrup, spoon the mixture into the jar, then seal. Alternatively, lift the peel out of the syrup, arrange on wire racks and dry in the oven (see Candied Pineapple, page 182). Dust with caster sugar and store in an airtight container, between layers of waxed paper.

 Degree of difficulty
Easy

 Cooking time
2¾–3¾ hours

Special equipment
Airtight container or 1 litre (1¾ pint) sterilized jar and sealant (see pages 42–43)

 Yield
About 1.5kg (3lb)

 Shelf life
2 years in syrup; 1 year with a crystallized finish

 Serving suggestions
Cover with chocolate or use for decoration

Candied Pineapple Rings

(see page 86 for technique)

Technically, candying is an easy process, but it takes a long time to complete. The results, however, are really worth the trouble — sweet fruit that last for a long time. Select slightly underripe, unblemished fruit that will withstand the long preparation. Plums, peaches, apricots, figs, kiwi fruit, cherries, kumquats, clementines, pears and angelica also candy well.

INGREDIENTS

1 large pineapple, peeled, cut into slices 1.5cm (⅝in) thick and cored

1kg (2lb) preserving or granulated sugar

juice of 1 lemon

caster sugar for dusting

1 Put the pineapple in a pan with enough water to cover. Bring to the boil, reduce the heat and simmer for 15–20 minutes, or until the pineapple has started to soften. Lift the rings out, drain well and place in a glass bowl.

2 Measure 1 litre (1¾ pints) of the cooking liquid. Strain it through a muslin-lined sieve into the preserving pan. Add 250g (8oz) of the sugar and the lemon juice. Bring to the boil, stirring until the sugar has dissolved. Skim and boil rapidly for 2–3 minutes.

3 Pour the sugar syrup over the pineapple and weight down with a plate (see page 46). Leave for 24 hours at room temperature.

4 Drain the rings. Return the syrup to the pan and add 100g (3½oz) of the sugar. Bring to the boil, stirring until the sugar has dissolved, and boil for 1–2 minutes. Skim well and pour over the pineapple again. Weight down and leave for 24 hours.

5 Repeat step 4.

6 Drain the rings. Return the syrup to the pan and add 150g (5oz) of the sugar. Bring to the boil, stirring until the sugar has dissolved. Boil for 1–2 minutes, skim well and pour back over the pineapple. Weight down and leave to stand for 24 hours.

7 Repeat step 6.

8 Drain the pineapple. Return the syrup to the pan and add the remaining sugar. Bring to the boil, stirring until the sugar has dissolved. Boil for 1–2 minutes, skim well and pour over the rings. Weight down and leave to stand for 48 hours.

9 Put the fruit and syrup in the preserving pan. Simmer for about 5 minutes, then remove from the heat. Lift out the pineapple rings with a slotted spoon and arrange on a wire rack placed over a foil-lined baking tray. Leave to drain and cool.

10 Place the rack and tray in an oven preheated to 120°C/250°F/gas ½, leaving the door slightly ajar. Dry for 12–24 hours, or until the pineapple rings are dry but just sticky to the touch.

11 Remove the pineapple rings from the oven and leave to cool completely. Dust with caster sugar. Store between sheets of waxed paper in an airtight container. Instead of dusting the pineapple rings with the sugar, you could preserve them in their syrup (see Candied Apricots, step 8, opposite).

 ☆☆ **Degree of difficulty**
Moderate

 Cooking time
Day 1, about 30 minutes;
Days 2–6, 5 minutes each day; Day 8, 5 minutes plus 12–24 hours drying

 Special equipment
Sterilized muslin; preserving pan; airtight container

 Yield
About 1kg (2lb)

 Shelf life
1 year with a crystallized finish; 2 years in syrup

 **Serving suggestions**
Dip into, or drizzle over, melted chocolate

Candied Apricots

This is a simplified method for candying. The fruit does not keep so well, lasting only a few months. To prevent deterioration, store it in the heavy syrup or crystallize just before use. The fruit should be slightly underripe with a good colour. Keep soft fruit like apricots whole, to maintain their shape. Firmer fruit, like pears or peaches, can be halved or stoned.

TIP

• To hasten the sugar absorption process, first steep the pricked fruit in a strong salt solution (75g/2½oz salt per 500ml/ 17fl oz water) for 24–48 hours.

INGREDIENTS

1kg (2lb) apricots
1.5kg (3lb) sugar
250ml (8fl oz) water
juice of 1 lemon or 1 tsp citric acid

1 Prick each apricot a few times with a sharp wooden skewer.

2 Put 1kg (2lb) of the sugar in the preserving pan with the water and lemon juice or citric acid. Bring to the boil, stirring until the sugar has dissolved, then skim well and boil until it reaches 110°C (230°F) on the sugar thermometer.

3 Slide the apricots into the pan and simmer for 3 minutes. Remove with a slotted spoon and place in a large glass bowl. Return the syrup to the boil and boil for 5 minutes. Pour over the apricots, weight down with a plate (see page 46) and leave for 24 hours.

4 Drain the apricots. Return the syrup to the pan, adding 250g (8oz) of the sugar. Bring slowly to the boil, stirring until the sugar has dissolved. Skim well and boil for about 5 minutes.

5 Add the apricots to the pan. Return to the boil, then reduce the heat and simmer very gently for about 5 minutes. Remove the apricots with a slotted spoon and place in the bowl. Bring the syrup back to the boil and boil for 5 minutes. Pour over the apricots, weight down and leave for 24 hours.

6 Drain the apricots. Return the syrup to the pan and add the rest of the sugar. Bring to the boil, stirring until it has dissolved. Skim, then boil for 2–3 minutes.

7 Add the apricots to the pan. Return to the boil, then reduce the heat to minimum and simmer very gently (the syrup should only bubble occasionally) for 3–4 hours, or until the fruit looks clear and candied.

8 Arrange the fruit in the hot sterilized jar, top up with the hot syrup, then seal. Alternatively, lift the fruit out of the syrup on to wire racks. Leave for 24 hours or until dry to the touch. Sprinkle with caster sugar, then dry in the oven for 12–24 hours (see Candied Pineapple, opposite).

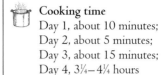

☆☆ **Degree of difficulty**
Moderate

Cooking time
Day 1, about 10 minutes;
Day 2, about 5 minutes;
Day 3, about 15 minutes;
Day 4, 3¼–4¼ hours

Special equipment
Preserving pan; sugar thermometer; 1.5 litre (2½ pint) sterilized, wide-necked jar and sealant (see pages 42–43) or airtight container

Yield
About 1.5kg (3lb)

Shelf life
2 years in syrup;
3–4 months with crystallized finish

Serving suggestions
Use to decorate cakes, sweets and desserts; or serve as a sweetmeat

Crystallized Flowers

The most suitable flowers for crystallizing are strongly perfumed roses, violets, pansies, orange blossom and the blossom of orchard fruit such as apples and pears. Edible leaves can also be crystallized in the same way. Vary the quantity of egg white and sugar to match the number of flowers being covered.

INGREDIENTS

egg white, to coat
pinch of salt
a few drops of rose- or orange-flower water
perfect flowers (see left)
caster sugar

1 Beat the egg white with the salt and rose- or orange-flower water until frothy. Leave to stand for a few minutes.

2 With a small, soft brush, paint the flower petals evenly

inside and out with the egg white. Generously sprinkle them with sugar, making sure that all the surfaces are evenly covered.

3 Fill a baking tray with a layer of sugar about 1cm (½in) deep. Gently lay the sugared flowers on top and generously sprinkle with sugar. Leave to dry in a warm, well-ventilated place for 1–2 days or until the flowers are hard and dry to the touch. Store in an airtight container, between layers of waxed paper.

☆ **Degree of difficulty**
Easy

Special equipment
Artist's small paint brush; airtight container

Shelf life
3 months

Serving suggestion
Use to decorate cakes and desserts

PRESERVING & DRYING GUIDE

MAKE THE MOST of seasonal fresh produce by referring to the chart below to find out which methods of preserving are best suited to individual fruit and vegetables. The chart also indicates the pectin content and acidity levels of fruit used to make jams, jellies and other sweet preserves, as these factors directly affect the setting ability of the finished product. If there is too little pectin and acid, a set will not be achieved without the addition of commercially prepared pectin or a homemade pectin stock (see page 47 for recipe). Alternatively, you can mix pectin-rich fruit with fruit that has a low concentration, and then test the pectin level (see page 47) to ensure that it is high enough to achieve a set.

OVEN-DRYING FRUIT AND HERBS

To dry fruit and herbs, preheat an oven to 110°C/225°F/gas ¼. Select unblemished fruit or herbs and prepare as described in the chart, right. Most fruit are dipped in acidulated or sweetened water (see page 61 for recipe) to help retain their colour and prevent them from browning. Place on wire racks and dry for the time specified.

Preserving Fruit and Vegetables

KEY
H . . . . High content
M . . . . . . Medium content
L . . . . Low content
X . . . . . Recipe given in book
X* . . No recipe given, but can be preserved by this method

	Apples	Apricots	Artichokes (Globe)	Aubergines	Beans	Beetroot	Blackberries	Blackcurrants	Blueberries	Cabbages	Carrots	Cauliflower	Celeriac	Celery	Cherries	Chillies	Clementines/Mandarins	Courgettes	Crab Apples	Cranberries	Cucumbers/Gherkins	Damsons	Figs	Garlic	Gooseberries	Grapefruit	Grapes	Greengages	Guavas
Pectin content	H	M	–	–	–	–	M	H	M	–	–	–	–	–	L	–	H	–	H	H	–	H	L	–	H	H	M	H	H
Acidity level	M	M	–	–	–	–	M	H	M	–	–	–	–	–	M	–	H	–	M	M	–	H	L	–	H	H	M	M	M
Pickling and spicing	X*	X*	X*	X	X	X	X*	–	X*	X	X	X	X	X	X*	X	X*	X	X*	X*	X	X*	X*	X	X	–	X	X*	–
Jams/jellies/marmalades	X	X	–	X	–	X*	X	X	X	–	X	–	–	–	X	X*	X*	–	X	X*	–	X*	X	X*	X*	X*	X	X	X
Curds/butters/cheeses	X	X*	–	–	–	–	X*	X*	X*	–	–	–	–	–	X*	–	–	–	–	X*	–	X*	X*	–	X*	X	–	X*	X*
Chutneys/relishes/sauces	X	X*	–	X	X*	–	X*	X*	–	X	X	X*	–	X*	X*	X	–	X*	X*	X	X	X	X	X	X*	–	X*	–	–
Preserving in oil	–	–	X	X	X*	–	–	–	–	–	–	–	–	–	–	X	–	–	–	–	–	–	X*	–	–	–	–	–	–
Syrups/alcohol/vinegar	–	X*	–	–	–	–	X	X	X	–	–	–	–	–	X*	X*	X*	X	–	–	X*	X*	X*	–	X*	X*	X	X*	X*

Oven-drying Fruit and Herbs

	PREPARATION	DIP	DRYING TIME
APPLES	Peeled, if desired, cut into 5mm (¼ in) rings	Acidulated water	6–8 hours, until no trace of moisture when cut
APRICOTS	Halved and stoned	Acidulated water	36–48 hours, until dry and leathery
BANANAS	Peeled and halved lengthways	Acidulated water	10–16 hours
BERRIES	Left whole	Dip in boiling water for a few seconds	12–18 hours
CHERRIES	Stoned, if desired	Dip in boiling water for a few seconds	18–24 hours
CITRUS PEEL	Cut into long strips, all white pith removed	–	10–12 hours
HERBS	Tied in bunches or laid on racks	–	12–16 hours in the oven; 2–3 days in the sun
PEACHES	Peeled, halved, stoned; sliced, if desired	Acidulated water	Halved: 36–48 hours; sliced: 12–16 hours
PEARS	Peeled, if desired, halved and cored	Acidulated water	36–48 hours
PINEAPPLE	Peeled, if desired, cored and sliced into 5mm (¼ in) rings	Honey	36–48 hours
PLUMS	Whole or halved and stoned	Dip in boiling water for a few seconds or prick all over	Whole: 36–48 hours; halved: 18–24 hours
STRAWBERRIES	Halved	Honey	12–18 hours, until dry and brittle

Jerusalem Artichokes	Kiwi Fruit	Kohlrabi	Kumquats	Lemons	Limes	Lychees	Mangoes	Marrow	Melon	Mushrooms	Okra	Onions	Oranges	Parsnips	Passion Fruit	Peaches	Pears	Peppers	Pineapples	Plums	Pomegranates	Pomelos	Prickly Pears	Quinces	Radishes	Raspberries	Redcurrants	Shallots	Squash & Pumpkins	Strawberries	Sweetcorn	Tomatoes	Turnips	White Currants
–	L	–	H	H	H	L	L	–	L	–	–	–	H	–	L	L	L	–	L	H	L	H	M	H	–	M	H	–	–	L	–	M	–	H
–	L	–	H	H	H	L	L	–	L	–	–	–	H	–	L/M	L	L	–	L	H	M/H	H	L	M	–	M	H	–	–	L	–	L/M	–	H
X*	X	X*	X*	X	X	–	–	X*	X	X*	X	X	X	X*	–	X*	X	X	X*	X	–	–	–	X*	X*	–	–	X	X*	–	X*	X	X	–
–	X*	X*	X*	X*	X*	X	X*	X	X	–	–	X	X	X*	X*	X	X*	–	X	X	–	X*	X	X	–	X	X	X	X	X	–	X	X	X*
–	X	–	–	X	X*	X*	X	–	X	–	–	–	X*	–	X	X	X	–	X*	X*	–	X*	X*	X	–	X*	X*	–	X*	X*	–	X	–	X*
–	–	–	X	X*	X*	–	X	X	–	X	–	X	X	–	–	X	–	X	X	X	–	–	–	X	–	–	–	–	X	–	X	X	–	–
–	–	–	–	X*	X*	–	X	X	–	X	–	–	–	–	–	–	–	–	–	X	–	–	–	–	–	–	–	–	X	–	X	X	–	–
–	–	–	X	X*	–	–	X*	–	–	–	X*	–	–	X*	X	X	X*	–	X	X	X*	–	X*	–	X	X	X*	–	X	–	–	–	–	X*

TROUBLE-FREE PRESERVING

AS SO MANY FACTORS affect the preserving process, it is possible that the end-product may not look, smell or taste as you expected. If this is so, you need to know what went wrong and, more importantly, whether the food is safe to eat. The most common problems that are encountered during preserving are listed below with clear guidelines on when a product should not be eaten.

Pickles

The pickles are not crunchy
• The vegetables were not salted for long enough beforehand.
• The vinegar or salt solution was not strong enough.

The pickles are hollow
• The raw ingredients were too mature or kept for too long before use.

The pickles are dark
• Iodized (table) salt was used.
• Too many spices were added.
• Iron or copper utensils were used.
• A dark vinegar was added.
• The brine was made with hard water – try filtered or bottled water.

The pickles look pale or bleached
• The jar must have been exposed to light during storage.

The pickles are soft and slippery
• The salt or vinegar solution was not strong enough.
• The jar had a poor seal.
Discard the product immediately.

Garlic looks green
• Fresh garlic may turn a harmless but unappetizing shade of green when steeped in vinegar: blanch in boiling water before using.

Jams & Sweet Preserves

The jam or jelly is not setting
• There is too little pectin. Add pectin stock or commercial pectin and re-boil until the setting point is reached (see page 47). Note: frozen fruit contains less pectin than fresh fruit.
• There was an incorrect balance between pectin and acid. Add lemon juice and re-boil (see page 47).

The fruit looks too dark
• The preserve was cooked for too long and the sugar started to caramelize. (The traditional advice is to warm the sugar before adding it to shorten the cooking time, but this makes little difference.)

Fruit has risen to the top of jam
• The jam was not allowed to settle. Leave it until cold, fold in the fruit evenly, then pot. Cover with waxed paper discs dipped in brandy and seal.
• The syrup is too thin, drain it off and return to the pan with more sugar. Boil rapidly until the setting point is reached (see page 47).

The jam has crystallized
• Too much sugar was added.
• The storage temperature was too cold. This is harmless and does not affect the flavour of the product.

Sweet & Savoury Preserves

There is mould on the surface
• A result of a fungus contamination. *Discard the product. Moulds send out a network of invisible threads and produce spores that may be harmful.*

The preserve has fermented
• If a sweet preserve ferments, too little sugar was added.
• For a pickle or chutney, the brine or vinegar solution was too weak.
• Storage conditions were too warm.
• Equipment or containers were not sterilized thoroughly.
• Cooking time was too short.
Discard the product immediately; this fermentation may produce harmful toxins. Note: some pickles are fermented as part of a recipe.

Unpleasant odours have developed
• *Any product that develops an off-putting smell should be discarded immediately.*

Salami & Cured Meat

There is a white powdery mould on salamis or cured meat
• This naturally occurring mould is encouraged by the right storage conditions. It is harmless and adds to the flavour of the product.

There is green or black mould on salamis or cured meat
• The salt solution was too weak.
• The meat was not cured properly.
• The storage atmosphere was too damp and warm.
Discard the product immediately.

White salt burns appear on drying cured meat
• The salt solution was too strong.

The dried cured meat has a powdery texture
• Too much vinegar in the cure.

The curing liquid turns syrupy
• Not enough salt was added.
• Storage temperature was too high.
Discard the curing liquid and make up a new batch. Resterilize the container. Wash the meat well with cold running water, then rub with vinegar. Dry the meat thoroughly with paper towels and immerse in the new cure.

INDEX

Page numbers in **bold** refer to the pages with illustrations.

ACKNOWLEDGMENTS

Author's Appreciation

This book is the fulfilment of a life-long obsession with preserving, and would not have been possible without the help of hundreds of passionate picklers, recipe writers, recorders, housewives, grocers, farmers and taxi drivers, who shared with me their culinary secrets. Without good-quality raw ingredients pickling is impossible, and I would like to thank my local suppliers, especially Graham and David at Graham Butchers, Pedro at Pedro Fisheries, Green Health Food Store (Finchley), and Gary at Ellinghams, for their help and advice.

As always I would also like to thank Saul Radomsky for his patience and support, and the many friends who have helped, schlepped, tasted and commented:

Trudy Barnham, Jon, Ann and Marjorie Bryent, the Blacher family, Iris and John Cole, the Hersch family, Jill Jago, Dalia Lamdani, Joy Peacock, Bob and Ann Tilley, Eric Treuille, Jo Wightman; and a special thanks to Rosie Kindersley who made this book possible.

Finally, many thanks to my assistant Alison Austin; photographer Ian O'Leary and his assistant Emma Brogi; Jane Bull, Jane Middleton, Kate Scott, and all at Dorling Kindersley, whose enthusiasm, help and expert eye made the writing of this book such a happy experience.

Dorling Kindersley would like to

thank Carole Ash for initial design work; Lorna Damms for editorial work; Paul Wood and Harvey de Roemer for DTP design; Cynthia Hole for picture research; Tables Laid for props; Tate and Lyle for the supply of preserving sugar; Graham Brown at Meridian Foods for the supply of fruit concentrate; Cecil Gysin at the Natural Casing Co. Ltd for the supply of sausage casings.

Special thanks to Ian Taylor at Taylor Foodservice for the supply of a smoker; Barry Chevalier from Aspall Cyder for the supply of cider vinegar; and Maureen Smith at SIS Marketing Ltd for the supply of a food dehydrator.

Picture Credits: key to pictures: t= top; b= bottom
Ann Ronan, Image Select 9t; E.T. Archive 9b, 10t; Corbis-Bettmann 11t

USEFUL ADDRESSES

In large towns and cities, supermarkets and chain-stores carry a wide range of equipment and specialist ingredients; while local markets and ethnic shops are the perfect places to find exotic spices and herbs.

If you have any problems finding certain ingredients or equipment, most of the following companies offer a mail order service:

General kitchen equipment:
Andrew Nisbets,
1,110b Aztec West, Bristol
BS12 4HR
Tel: 01454 855555
Fax: 01454 855565

Speciality chillies:
Cool Chile Co.,
P.O. Box 5702, London
W10 6WE
Tel/Fax: 0171 229 9360

Exotic spices and herbs from all over the world:
Fox's Spices,
Masons Road,
Stratford-upon-Avon,
Warwickshire
CV37 9NF
Tel: 01789 266420
Fax: 01789 267737

Free-range meat:
Richard Guy's Real Meat Co.,
51 Market Place,
Warminster, Somerset
BA12 9AZ
Tel: 01985 219020
Fax: 01985 218950

Sausage-making equipment and ingredients:
Natural Casing Company Ltd.,
P.O. Box 133,
Farnham, Surrey
GU10 5HT
Tel: 01252 850454
Fax: 01252 851284

Preserving equipment and sausage makers:
Lakeland Plastics Ltd,
Alexandra Building,
Windermere,
Cumbria
LA23 1BQ
Tel: 015394 88100
Fax: 015394 88300

Food dehydrator:
SIS Marketing Ltd.,
9 The Square,
Vicarage Farm Road,
Peterborough
PE1 5TS
Tel: 01733 358666

Food smoker:
Taylor Foodservice,
22 The Knolls, Beeston,
Sandy,
Bedfordshire
SG19 1PL
Tel: 01767 680083
Fax: 01767 692237

INFORMATION

Organic food information:
Soil Association/British Organic Farmers,
86 Colston Street,
Bristol
BS1 5BB
Tel: 0117 9299666
Fax: 0117 9252504

Herbs:
The Herb Society,
134 Buckingham Palace Road,
London
SW1W 9SA
Tel: 0171 823 5583

Information on food-related matters:
MAFF Helpline
Tel: 0645 335577